Copyright © 2015 by Heather Grossman

All rights reserved

Dedication

To my children Lauren, Joseph and Ronnie. I love you and am very proud of you.

To my parents who have sacrificed so much to keep me alive.

To my friend Khalaf Ahmad Al Habtoor.

To all my nurses who cared for me and have made my life better.

Without the people mentioned above, I would not be here today, mentally strong and with faith in God.

Acknowledgments

Arizona Voice for Crime Victims. Thank you for your support.

Ellen Wesson and Greg Tobin, my editors. Thank you for your kindness and wisdom.

Steve Twist, my friend. Thank you for everything.

Rebecca Nittle, Thank you for your time and effort.

Table of Contents

Introduction i
Chapter 1 1
Chapter 2 3
Chapter 3 9
Chapter 4 17
Chapter 5 19
Chapter 6 23
Chapter 7 27
Chapter 8 31
Chapter 9 33
Chapter 10 37
Chapter 11 41
Chapter 12 45
Chapter 13 55
Chapter 14 59
Chapter 15 63
Chapter 16 67
Chapter 17 71
Chapter 18 73
Chapter 19 79

Chapter 20	83
Chapter 21	87
Chapter 22	91
Chapter 23	99
Chapter 24	105
Chapter 26	107
Chapter 27	117
Chapter 28	121
Chapter 29	127
Chapter 30	133
Chapter 31	137
Chapter 32	149
Chapter 33	153
Chapter 34	159
Chapter 35	161
Chapter 36	165
Chapter 37	171
Chapter 38	181
Chapter 39	187
Chapter 40	193
Chapter 41	199
Chapter 42	207
Chapter 43	211
Chapter 44	215
Chapter 45	219

Chapter 46 223
Chapter 47 225
Chapter 48 233
Chapter 49 241
Chapter 50 247
Chapter 51 257
Chapter 52 265
Chapter 53 275
Chapter 54 283
Chapter 55 293
Chapter 56 303
Chapter 57 307
Chapter 58 325
Chapter 59 329
Chapter 60 339
Chapter 61 345
Chapter 62 351
Chapter 63 357
Chapter 64 361
Chapter 65 365
Chapter 66 369
Chapter 67 375
Chapter 68 381
Chapter 69 387
Chapter 70 395

Chapter 71 401
Chapter 72 407
Chapter 73 409
Chapter 74 417
Chapter 75 421
Chapter 76 427
Chapter 77 429
Chapter 78 433
Chapter 79 435
Chapter 80 437
Chapter 81 439
Chapter 82 447
Chapter 83 449
Chapter 84 451
Chapter 85 457
Epilogue 459

Introduction

Domestic violence has reached epic proportions in the United States. One in four women has been, or can expect to be, a victim of abuse at some time in her life. There are nearly five hundred women raped or sexually assaulted every day by someone who supposedly loves them. More than seven million children live in homes where severe abuse occurs. And every day, one woman is killed by her abusive partner.

I was almost one of those women.

My name is Heather Grossman and this is my story.

Chapter 1

I was born in Anoka, Minnesota, a suburb of Minneapolis, on April 19, 1966. I grew up enjoying a simple family life with my parents, Ralph and Florence Stephens, and my sister, Tiffany, who was younger than me by four years. I did well in school and was always involved in activities, from softball and track to gymnastics and cheerleading. I never missed a day of school because I enjoyed it so much. My sister and I were always close except, of course, for our occasional sisterly fights. When I was in elementary my family moved to the Middle East. This was an adjustment for all of us. The food seemed strange and we had to get used to a dramatic change in our schooling.

My father worked for a large Middle Eastern business man. He helped build the airport and many hotels in the Dubai area. We traveled around the world extensively as a family, visiting Thailand, Switzerland, India, Pakistan, and Europe. Traveling taught me things you can never learn inside a classroom. After my father finished his work there, my family returned to Minnesota. I finished high school at Anoka Senior High and then went to college to pursue a business degree.

Concordia College was not what I expected. After all, I had traveled around the world. Concordia is in Moorhead, Minnesota, by North Dakota. Farmland did not excite me. I found myself driving back to Minneapolis every weekend so I could have some sense of life. I went to college there for two years. When I came home the summer of 1986, between my sophomore and junior years, my girlfriend Katie was applying to Eastern Airlines as a flight attendant and asked if I would like to go with her. In two weeks' time I was on my way to flight school in Miami, Florida.

The airline business was simple and enjoyable. I was young and excited to travel anywhere for a mere twelve dollars roundtrip. I was first stationed in Newark, New Jersey. I hated it the moment I got there. I lived in Woodbridge, New Jersey, with Robin and Ann, flight attendants from my graduating class in Miami. The town was twenty minutes from the airport, but we had few options because of the cost. I always felt unsafe in the area. After six months I moved to Marietta, Georgia, near Atlanta.

Atlanta is a beautiful Southern city. The people were friendly and I enjoyed my time going to Atlanta Braves games, attending outdoor concerts, and running by the lakeshore. I developed many friendships and when I wasn't flying I'd go out to eat and enjoy the nightlife. I felt comfortable in the area and loved living there. I was assigned to work on international routes and flew to San Juan, Puerto Rico, Europe, and South America. This was exciting and fulfilled my desire for adventure. I had missed traveling around the world as I'd done with my family.

I worked half the month and had the other half off and enjoyed benefits such as free flights and reduced hotel and rental car prices. My girlfriend and I could fly from Atlanta to New York City for the weekend, catch a Broadway show, have dinner, shop, and go out dancing. When I was young we did some crazy things. I had a dream job and was getting paid to travel around the world. I had no idea how much my life was about to change.

Chapter 2

I met Ron Samuels on February 12, 1986. I was leaving Utah and meeting my crew at the hotel to catch the shuttle to the airport. Ron and his girlfriend had been at the same hotel, and he came up to me and started a conversation. My first impression of him was that he was charismatic, polite, and loved to joke. He was a well-dressed man in a tailored, navy-blue suit, six-foot-five and handsome with dark hair. Much to my surprise, we were all taking the same shuttle to the airport. His girlfriend turned out to be another flight attendant who was working on the flight with me back to Atlanta. I was working first class, where Ron was sitting, while his girlfriend worked in coach.

Because he was a passenger he kept asking me for different things during the flight, trying to be funny and charming. While I had to be nice to all the passengers, I kept my distance and tried to ignore his flirting with me until the flight was over. When the plane touched down, Ron said, "Thank you so much for a great flight." I thought I would never see him again. I turned in my paperwork, hopped in my car, and went home.

A week later I got a call from Ron. I was shocked because I hadn't given him my name or number. He said, "Oh, this is Ron here, remember me? I was on the flight from Utah, Salt Lake City." And I said, "Oh, yes, how is your girlfriend, Tammy?" I did not understand how he had gotten my number. When I asked him, he told me he'd had a friend at Eastern Airlines pull my employee information from the computer. I was leaving on a three-day trip out of town; we talked for a little while, but I had to finish packing. Ron had caught me by surprise, and I didn't know what to think of his call. He was persistent, however, and called back again within a week.

On our first date Ron flew into Atlanta from Daytona Beach, Florida, and took me to a ball game and dinner. Ron was a real gentleman—he opened the car door for me, pulled out my chair at the table, and listened intently to every word I said. That night we laughed and had a great time together. He flew home the next day, and I received two dozen roses the day after that with a card stating, "I had a wonderful time and I'll see you next week."

We never had a boring or a normal date. Ron liked expensive things, which was obvious from the clothes he wore, his Rolex watch, and the cars he drove (a Mercedes and a Porsche). But, in spite of all his possessions, he was down to earth.

He told me about his childhood. He'd grown up in Brooklyn, New York, where he'd played football and worked as a lifeguard on the beach in Long Island. His mother, Francis, was a police officer and his father, Sam, a judge. He had a brother named Mark. He'd been a happy child and came from a good family.

When I met him, Ron owned radio stations with his partners, Carl Tuterra and Norman Drubner. His first station was in Daytona Beach, Florida. The first time I flew down to Florida I had a wonderful time with Ron and his friends. He was like a little kid—one moment he'd say, "Let's go to Six Flags," and the next, "Let's charter a plane and fly to the Bahamas." And we did.

We went to the Bahamas with one of Ron's good friends, Dr. John Hall, and his girlfriend, Candy Johnson. We were there for three days. I wasn't prepared to go, but Ron insisted on buying me a whole vacation wardrobe when we got there. We lay in the sun, paraglided, ate great food, and danced away the nights. We went to the casino in one of the hotels and Ron won $38,000. He was good at blackjack, and I was amazed at the bets he was making. We had a great time, but I had to fly back to Atlanta for work. The next day Ron sent me two dozen roses with a card saying, "I miss you and love you."

Ron was incredibly romantic. After four months I found myself falling for him. He was unlike anyone I had ever dated before. I had only had a couple of relationships in the past, and he knocked my socks off.

My job, and the fact that we were living in and traveling to different cities, made dating difficult. Ron had to travel to his different radio stations to oversee the daily operations and productivity. We tried to plan around my scheduled days off to see each other, but sometimes Ron would just call up and say, "Let's go to Paris for a week." He couldn't understand why I couldn't just take off with him. Even though I wanted to go, I valued my job and had to schedule time off.

Ron was a self-made multimillionaire and used to doing whatever he wanted. He owned his own company and could take off whenever he chose. Don't get me wrong: Ron always worked very hard. His work ethic was one of the things that impressed me most.

One time I flew from Atlanta to Daytona, expecting to see Ron for only two days. John and Candy met us at his favorite Italian restaurant in Daytona. After a great meal and crazy conversation, Ron decided we all should go to Jamaica. So he called up and chartered a plane to take us there. I had to change all my plans and call Eastern Airlines to get off work.

We left the next morning on a small plane with two pilots. I was nervous because on the news I had seen a lot of small planes go down. They assured me the flight would be fine and the weather was perfect. Everybody was laughing and ready for fun.

When we arrived, the hotel was beautiful. We spent time on the beach, in the casino, and shopping in the local stores. I had to be back at work in three days; Ron wanted to stay longer. He repeatedly told me he never wanted me to leave him. I felt bad, but I had to go back to Atlanta.

The next big step in our relationship came when Ron asked me to move to Daytona and live with him. I knew I could not commute and keep my job, so this was a big decision for me. We were in love and excited to start our life together. So I moved.

I liked Daytona Beach. Ron had a beautiful home there with a pool, and there was an inlet at the back of the house where you could launch a boat into the ocean. I met more of Ron's friends. They were all successful: John Hall, whom I had met before, was a doctor with his own practice. Terry Taylor owned car dealerships. They had various girlfriends who worked hard but enjoyed having fun just like Ron and I did. We would all go out in Daytona for dinner, dancing, and private parties.

Terry and Ron bought three racehorses, so we ventured to races at the Belmont and Aqueduct racetracks in New York. We'd spend the day at the track, catch a Broadway show at night, and then have dinner after. I loved shopping and sightseeing, shuttling around the city in limos, relaxing in our room at the Plaza Hotel or Helmsley Palace.

One time, after dinner, Terry and Ron wanted to go to Atlantic City, so the casino sent a helicopter to the pier to pick us up. I was excited because Ron had invited his family to come along. This was the first time I met Francis, Sam, and Mark. Francis and Sam were both older than my parents, by about fifteen years. They seemed excited to meet me and they were both kind. Mark was nothing like Ron; in fact, they were total opposites. Mark was shy, kind of nerdy, and lived an uneventful, modest life doing things with his parents.

The three days we spent in Atlantic City were amazing. Again, Ron was successful at cards; by the time he finished playing Baccarat, he had won over $150,000. I was nervous because he was gambling $10,000 at a time, and I had never seen anybody do that before. Terry, also lucky, won even more.

We stayed in the suites at the casino, and Ron got rooms for his family that were adjacent to ours. We had our own butler and all the fabulous food you could ask for. We shopped, saw shows, and had a great time. Terry and Ron always made life exciting.

My parents had not met Ron yet, and they flew to Florida with my sister, Tiffany, for Christmas that year. It was 1987. Everybody loved Florida because they missed the beaches in Dubai. The weather was warm and they were not trapped in a snowstorm or freezing like they would be back home. We had fun planning our holiday dinner and buying gifts for everybody.

My first gift from Ron was a pair of beautiful diamond earrings. My father thought they were too big. They were six carats, three carats for each ear. I cried when I opened the gift but Ron hugged me gently and gave me a kiss. "They're beautiful!" I told him.

On Christmas Day we celebrated with Terry, his girlfriend, Liz, and their families at Terry's home. After dinner, we all exchanged gifts. Liz was upset over my gift from Ron, because Terry had given her one-carat diamond earrings. I knew Ron's gift was extravagant. But if there was one thing I'd learned about Ron it was this: he did everything in big ways.

Chapter 3

After the holidays, Ron had to fly to South Padre Island to check on a radio station in Brownsville, Texas. My family and I spent the rest of their visit at Disney World. My parents were impressed with Ron and could see how much he cared for me.

Ron loved the Brownsville area. On the flight there, he sat next to a man named Fausto Yturria. They hit it off right away, and Fausto showed Ron all the different areas and businesses, trying to entice him to move there. South Padre Island was a perfect spring break destination; radio promotion would be attractive to beer companies and other advertisers. Ron called his friend, Pat Link, and they spent time looking at the financials of the radio station.

While they were down there, I enrolled myself in school. I flew down on the weekend and saw the radio station, met some of the employees, and enjoyed the weather and beach in South Padre. During the day, while Ron worked, I drove around, shopped, and prepared dinner for those nights we didn't eat out. The grocery stores carried traditionally Hispanic foods. I'd never experienced so many fresh tortillas and peppers!

I flew back again the next weekend because Ron was thinking about purchasing the radio station from Norman Drubner, his partner at the time. Fausto believed Ron could bring new business ideas to Brownsville. He and his wife, Saundra, threw a large party to welcome us to their community. They owned a two-hundred-acre ranch in town. Fausto's family was one of the oldest in Brownsville and had been granted land by the King of Spain hundreds of years ago. Saundra's family owned Banco De México.

When we arrived at the party, there were already more than thirty people there. Most of the couples owned different businesses in the community and were welcoming to us. Fausto and Saundra were kind and made me feel special. Ron, of course, impressed everybody. This was also the first time I shot a gun. Everybody was skeet shooting. I missed every disc but Ron hit every one like a pro. After all, he had been in Vietnam, a subject he never talked about with me.

After the skeet shooting, the men went in jeeps and hunted wild boar, while the women sat by the pool. We then joined the guys for cocktails at sunset on the ranch, before heading back to the house for dinner. Saundra gave me a gift of a beautiful silk Hermès scarf. When we left, we thanked Fausto and Saundra for their generous hospitality.

After we awoke the next morning, Ron and I went for a walk on the beach holding hands and talking about the possibilities of life in Brownsville. Ron planned to build up the radio station and then sell it. As I flew back to Florida, I felt confident about the move to Texas and called my parents to tell them the news.

Ron started negotiating with Norman and Carl to purchase the Brownsville radio station and leave the partnership. Norman wasn't happy about this: Ron's stations were number one in the market and his expertise was invaluable. He wanted to keep Ron in the partnership. Ron, however, wanted to stop traveling back and forth and work for himself. He wasn't used to answering to someone.

Ron couldn't wait to tell Terry about South Padre, and he and Liz flew down to investigate. We had fun showing them the area and going out to dinner. The next day, after many cocktails, we went to a real estate party. Terry and Ron bought a condo on the water and Ron purchased a penthouse in the tallest building on the beach. I think Terry and Ron were too impulsive; they had too much fun and too much money. The next morning, Ron rolled over in bed and said he hoped they would sell him the radio station.

Terry and Liz flew back and forth every other week and we all had a great time furnishing our places. Unfortunately, the sale of the radio station did not go through because Norman asked for an outrageous price.

We were both upset and there was tension between Norman, Carl, and Ron. There wasn't anything Fausto or Ron could do to salvage the deal.

Saundra and Fausto continued to be close friends of ours and we attended their daughter's wedding, where they filled a whole pool with Dom Perignon champagne.

My life was exciting at that time, but I needed to get serious about a career. I went back to college in Daytona and started taking more business classes. Ron was unhappy because I wasn't able to do everything he wanted to, as I had to devote time to studying.

At this time, Ron sold his portion of the radio stations. He decided to retire at age thirty-six. It took him only six months to realize he was bored out of his mind. He became focused on my life—he interfered with my studying and questioned me often about my whereabouts. I had to reassure him on a daily basis that I was just going to school and he was the love of my life. I wasn't interested in anybody else.

Ron had always loved the Miami Dolphins, and so he and Terry decided to buy a suite at Joe Robbie Stadium in 1986. During football season, we flew in Terry's Learjet to all the home games. We'd go with a group of couples and enjoy the Fort Lauderdale and Miami Beach restaurants and nightlife. At this time, Terry and Ron were spending a lot of time together. Liz, Terry, Ron, and I traveled out of town or socialized in Daytona Beach every weekend.

Terry's father, Warren Taylor, was in the process of selling his car dealership. Terry thought he and Ron should purchase it. Ron had a lot of experience in advertising and sales, and they thought it would be a profitable purchase. They flew to Pensacola, Florida, to meet with Warren and the "big wigs" at Southeast Toyota. Jim Moran, owner of Southeast Toyota Distributors—a multibillion-dollar company that distributed Toyotas to most of the dealerships in the south—and the board of directors had to approve the sale of the dealership. Mr. Moran was impressed with Ron's work ethic and enthusiasm, and Terry and Ron bought the dealership. I was surprised that our lives had changed again within two months' time—that I was helping Ron pack up and move to Pensacola, Florida.

Terry and Ron were busy hiring new employees for the dealership, which they decided to name Ron Samuels' Toyota. I wasn't thrilled about having Ron's name on the dealership, because I wanted to protect our privacy. I was busy looking at homes to buy in Gulf Breeze and Pensacola Beach.

Pensacola and the beach area were divided by a three-mile bridge and even though the dealership would be far away, we chose to look for a place on the water. Everyone we met in Pensacola seemed inviting and had down-home Southern charm. Even though we were in Florida, Pensacola bordered Mobile, Alabama. I just loved all the southern foods and hospitality. However, I was shocked to see men driving around in pick-up trucks with Confederate flags. They were country and proud of it.

After two weeks I began helping out at the dealership. My first task was to get rid of the animal preserve in back of the dealership. Crazy Warren loved animals and the first day Ron and I drove up there was a peacock walking across the parking lot. We had ostriches, emus, parrots, geese, and a pair of peacocks. The geese would jump on the roof of the cars and the emus would chase people. I donated all the animals to the zoo.

My favorite employee was Ben Bentfield, who inventoried new and used cars. I became close friends with his wife, Helen. She loved to cook, just as I did, and we would exchange recipes. Ron worked on promoting sales through the *Pensacola News Journal* and a couple of top television stations. While he was busy at work, I would go to the gym, shower, and come back so that we could have dinner.

The dealership was doing well because of Ron's diligence, advertising knowledge, and work ethic. I tried to help out at work while getting everything situated at the house. Life was different than we had envisioned when planning our move to South Padre, but we were comfortable, busy, and happy together.

Heather in her 20s.

Heather and Ron shortly after meeting.

Heather and her stewardess class. Heather is in front row, second from the right.

15

Chapter 4

    The first time I remember Ron being cross with me was in October 1987, when I washed a pair of his slacks and shrunk them by mistake. He went berserk. He lost his temper so quickly it scared me. I couldn't understand why he was so angry. He made me cry and I felt it was uncalled for. It only took Ron about an hour to apologize and say he was sorry.

    I missed my family, so Ron and I decided to go to Minnesota for Thanksgiving. While sitting on the plane in first class, Ron became irritated because he realized he wasn't wearing a bracelet his mother had given him in high school. He made it seem like it was my fault he had lost it. I told him to calm down because people were listening. I pulled out my cell phone—which looked like a heavy brick with large, black antennae—and called Helen Bentfield to see if she could drive to our home and look for Ron's bracelet. Obviously, it had a lot of sentimental value. By the time we landed, Helen had called to say she'd found the bracelet. I was proud of myself for putting out the fire, but I questioned Ron's behavior. I was afraid he would blow up again and ruin our trip.

    When we arrived at my parents' home, we immediately called everyone and planned to go to dinner at Murray's Steakhouse in Minneapolis. Ron impressed all my friends with his generosity and humor. Thanksgiving Day was the next day, and I woke up and started helping my mom with the meal. Ron wanted me to drive with him to White Castle for lunch in a blizzard. He wouldn't take no for an answer.

    My aunts, uncles, and cousins all joined us for Thanksgiving dinner. We watched football and played cards, and everyone thought Ron was a perfect gentleman. When we woke up the next morning there was so much snow it was hard to get out of the driveway. Ron had already read the paper and wanted to go shopping downtown.

After having lunch at Dayton's department store, Ron took us upstairs and told my mother and me to pick out any mink coats we liked, because he was buying us each a pre-Christmas gift. Ron said every lady needs a mink. I'd never had a mink coat before, but I absolutely loved it because I'm always cold. I think Ron enjoyed surprising us almost as much as we enjoyed the coats. He was like a kid in a candy store; he wouldn't stop trying to buy me things. I appreciated it but felt like it was a little too much.

The next day, our plane was delayed because they were de-icing the aircraft. So we sat on the runway for an hour. As we talked in first class, Ron was in a good mood. He said he'd had a great time, and his holidays were usually not enjoyable.

The next week we were back to work. Ron was hiring a few new managers and I started working in the office, doing all the payroll for the employees. I flew to Jacksonville, Florida, with our office manager to train at Southeast Toyota's headquarters. The program focused on payroll, financial expenditures, and managerial business skills. I left with a firm grasp of the overall business operation of the dealership. I felt like I could contribute something to our relationship. Sales at Ron Samuels' Toyota were going well. Everything was coming together.

Chapter 5

In 1987, Ron and I hopped on a plane to New York because Sam, Ron's father, was not feeling well. Francis and Sam lived in Long Island and while visiting with them we stayed with Mark, Ron's brother. Mark took care of his parents' every need, but it was clear that Ron was their shining star. Our being there created problems between Ron and Mark. We took a trip into Manhattan to see *The Phantom of the Opera*. Mark refused to join us and I didn't understand why.

The next day, we had lunch in Little Italy. Ron and Mark fought the entire way home, until Ron pulled over to the side of the road and told Mark to "get out, you piece of shit." Mark got out and Ron drove away. I told him it was ridiculous for them to fight, to turn around and pick up his brother. I was upset with their behavior—after all, they were grown men. I didn't like confrontation between the two of them and I felt uncomfortable because we were staying with Mark. I tried to reason with Ron, but he wouldn't listen.

The next day Ron rented a limo and we had lunch with a high school friend of his and his wife. Ron had gone to New York Military Academy, a prestigious high school in upstate New York, and had stayed close to a few friends with whom he had graduated. After lunch, we hopped in the limo and went to a New York Giants football game. I was freezing, even in my mink coat. We sat in the stands and passed around flasks of brandy. Phil Simms was the quarterback and the Giants won. After the game we went for dessert and then dropped off Ron's friends.

After the confrontation between Ron and Mark, Ron wanted to leave. We changed our flight and returned to Florida. Two weeks later Terry flew into Pensacola, and next thing I knew, we were flying back to New York City in the Lear. We stayed at the Plaza Hotel and were introduced to Terry's new girlfriend, Madeline. Madeline was beautiful and had Terry totally smitten. Ron and Terry went suit shopping at Bijan while Madeline and I went to Henri Bendel. At night we saw *Les Miserables* and then capped off our evening with frozen hot chocolate at Serendipity. The trip was quick. Terry dropped us off in Pensacola and then continued to Daytona Beach, where he still lived.

Ron met Ted Ciano while at a business meeting in Pensacola. He was the owner of the Key Ford dealership. They hit it off right away. I met Natalie, Ted's wife, when we went out to dinner at the Executive Club. We also hit it off right away, even though there was a fifteen-year difference in our ages. They had two daughters: Debbie worked at her father's dealership, and Kim was in college. Natalie was a wonderful mother. The two of us loved to cook, exchange recipes, and shop. Once a week we'd meet at the movies and then go out to dinner.

About a month later, in July of 1987, Ron said, "Let's fly to New York for the weekend. It's my mother's birthday and we can take my parents to dinner." We went to the diamond district, where Ron picked out a bracelet for Francis's birthday, and then to Saks Fifth Avenue to pick up more gifts. Dinner was at a lobster restaurant right on the water. Ron's friend Pauline and her husband, Tom, joined us. Pauline was a ticket distributor Ron had met while purchasing show and sporting event tickets.

During dinner, Ron suddenly began tapping his champagne glass with a spoon. He then got down on his knees and asked me to marry him, in front of the entire restaurant. I was shocked. It was a wonderful moment, and I said yes. His mom cried and everyone in the restaurant clapped. I asked Ron if he would mind if I called my mom, and he told me to go ahead. My parents were both happy to hear the news.

My ring was five carats and absolutely beautiful. Ron then gave his mother her gift, and she loved it. Frances was beaming. She said she was happy because she got to see Ron on her birthday and she was going to have a daughter-in-law. Ron got his parents a room at the hotel so they wouldn't have to drive back at night. When we returned to Florida, Ron called Terry to tell him the news—and to our surprise, Terry was engaged to Madeline.

It took a while to plan the wedding. My mother and my sister, Tiffany, helped me. A couple of friends from the office went cake-tasting with me and helped me pick out flowers. The dealership was selling cars like crazy at the time and was in first place in the district. We won a trip to Mauna Kea resort in Hawaii. Toyota paid for the entire trip and sent the top dealers to the resort as a perk. I wanted to go on the trip but was so busy planning the wedding I had reservations. Then Ron told me he couldn't go because he needed to stay in town for a huge tent sale. I wanted to take my mom, but Ron insisted I bring Mark, because he was trying to patch things up with his brother before the wedding. I was disappointed; it felt strange to take Mark on the trip.

I met Mark in Los Angeles, where we boarded the plane with all the other dealers and their wives. Mauna Kea is a luxury resort on the Big Island and absolutely beautiful. They believed in total relaxation: the rooms had no televisions or distractions from everyday life. Mark and I started out every morning with breakfast downstairs, after which I would run on the beach or play tennis at the courts. I asked Mark to join me, but he was not athletic and had no interest in coming along. Toyota had set up different sightseeing opportunities for us to enjoy. We went to Honolulu on an excursion and to Maui with different couples.

I became upset because, on the second day of the trip, Terry and Madeline showed up at the hotel. Terry had also purchased a Toyota store in Charlotte, North Carolina, and they too had won first place. I called Ron and told him if Terry could be there with Madeline, then he should be there with me. I did not win the argument. Many couples invited us to dinner on the resort property. I was shocked, however, not to receive a single invitation from Terry. I knew Madeline had something to do with it. Terry was a decent person and had always included me.

Jim Moran, the owner of Southeast Toyota, gave a large presentation to all the dealers and their wives at dinner that night. Then, by dealership ranking, each wife was able to choose a piece of jewelry to take home. I picked a beautiful diamond tennis bracelet. Even though the trip was wonderful and I was able to lie on the beach and have fresh piña coladas, I missed having Ron there with me.

Once I was back in Pensacola, I stayed busy working at the dealership and finishing the wedding plans. Ron let me plan everything while he worked at the dealership. He insisted I go to Kleinfeld Bridal in Brooklyn for my wedding dress, and said money was no object. Ron went to lunch while I chose my dress so that he wouldn't get a glimpse of it before the wedding.

My sister, parents, and aunts flew in early to help me with the wedding plans. Tiffany was my maid of honor and Terry was Ron's best man. All our friends from Daytona Beach were there as well. The night before the wedding, Terry hosted a dinner at Scotto's, an Italian restaurant in downtown Pensacola. We had a wonderful dinner and our party lasted for hours.

We were married at St. Anne's Catholic Church and our reception was at the Pensacola Executive Club right after. It was filled with beautiful chandeliers, flowers, and flowing champagne. Sixty-five of our friends and family were able to attend, including Saundra and Fausto Yturria from Texas, Ted and Natalie Ciano, and Ben and Helen Bentfield. Ron's parents were there, but not Mark, which really hurt Ron's feelings. I thought the size of the group was perfect, because we were able to visit with every guest who attended.

The next day, I packed our clothes for our honeymoon in Hawaii. I was exhausted but happy. We spent ten days in Honolulu, where we took long walks along the beach and went parasailing, hiking, and snorkeling. At night we enjoyed fabulous food and dancing. We flew to Maui, rented a car, and drove all over the island sightseeing. Back at the hotel, we enjoyed lying by the pool and soaking up the sun. I couldn't imagine life getting any better.

Chapter 6

I hated returning home. However, I knew it was time to get back to everyday life and work. Ron was focusing on advertising and sales at the dealership. He would occasionally travel to car auctions to purchase used cars. Usually the used car manager would do this, but Ron insisted on micromanaging the business. Sometimes he would work thirteen-hour days, getting home at nine thirty at night. I continued doing payroll at the dealership. After work, I would stop at the gym before going home to prepare dinner for us. I was an excellent cook and Ron enjoyed eating everything I made.

One day in the spring of 1988, Helen and I made plans to meet for lunch and go shopping. After a nice day out, I returned home and found two police cars in front of my house. I immediately ran in to see what was going on. Ron was talking to the police and crying.

When he saw me, he grabbed me in his arms and said, "Oh my God, I thought you had been kidnapped!"

"Kidnapped?" I said. "Why would you think that?"

"I called you numerous times and you didn't answer your cell phone, and I needed you to bring something to the dealership," Ron said. "I drove home and saw your purse scattered on the bed with things pulled out of it. Why didn't you answer your phone? I had to call the police."

After the officers left, he started screaming at me about my phone. I explained to him that I'd changed purses and accidently left my phone in the car. He said, "Always keep your phone with you so I can reach you at all times." After talking to him for a while, I was finally able to calm him down.

The next week, I was feeling sick to my stomach and weak. Ron made me go to the doctor, who did a blood test. Together we found out I was pregnant. I couldn't believe it. I always knew I wanted to have children, but this seemed fast. Ron was overjoyed. Immediately we drove back to the office and Ron called friends and told them. He announced it all over the dealership.

I had morning sickness right away and every smell from coffee to perfume bothered me. Ron was diligent about attending all my OB/GYN appointments with me. He was a doting husband, happy and upbeat about the baby coming. He watched my every move and would not let me carry anything. Every week he would bring me flowers and buy me gifts. It was a happy time in our lives. I was a little scared about being a mother and didn't know what to expect. Every week I did baby aerobics and baby yoga.

Around this time, I met Dawn Loftness. Ron had hired her husband, Andy, to run the dealership's finance department, and from our first dinner I knew we would become close friends. Dawn had a bubbly personality and a strong southern accent. She also liked working out. Dawn helped me put the nursery together and we shopped for a stroller, car seat, crib, clothing, and many other things. My pregnancy went by quickly and soon my friends were throwing my baby shower. Helen had it at her house and twenty-five people came. Everyone was kind and I was grateful for every gift I received.

Francis and Sam couldn't wait for me to have the baby, and my parents felt the same way. Art Weiss, a friend of Terry and Ron's, was in town running a tent sale for five dealerships. The morning of the sale, we got up early and I worked with the finance guys filling out papers. It was hot, so Dawn and I left a little early. On the way home, I went into labor. Dawn grabbed my suitcase and took me to the hospital. I called Ron immediately and had him meet me there. After nine hours of labor, I had a baby boy. We named him Ronald Samuels II. I called him Ronnie. There were about fifteen people waiting to see us after the nurses brought me to the room. Both employees and friends hung around, talking and laughing with us. Ron, a huge grin on his face, said, "Good job, baby. I have a gift for you." It was a Rolex President watch with diamonds and rubies. I had always wanted one. I kissed Ron and said, "You're too good to me. I love you so much."

Ronnie was a quiet and happy baby. I could take him anywhere and he wouldn't fuss. When I went back to work, if Helen couldn't babysit, I would bring him to the dealership and he would play while I finished my work. Ron still continued to work long hours and wasn't the hands-on dad I wanted. He certainly didn't change diapers and never got up to feed Ronnie at night. I couldn't complain, though; he was always happy to spend time playing with his son.

We asked Terry Taylor and Betty Bancroft to be Ronnie's godparents. The morning of the baptism, Terry, Betty, and Madeline flew in and met us at St. Anne's Church. Father Kelly baptized Ronnie, and Ben and Helen took pictures of the occasion. Afterward, we all went to the house for lunch. I wished my parents and Ron's could have been there, but they couldn't make the trip.

Francis and Sam finally visited us after Ronnie turned five months old. Ron was at work, so I picked them up at the airport with Ronnie. They were excited to meet their first grandchild and hugged and kissed him all over. They brought gifts for Ronnie, and Nova Scotia salmon and fresh New York bagels for me. I took Francis to the salon and Sam to the barber for a cut and shave. They were older and I wanted to help them in any way I could. They enjoyed sightseeing and going to the dealership to see Ron at work. I made Ron promise to take off three days so that he could spend time with his parents and Ronnie.

Ted and Natalie invited all of us to dinner in Destin at the Marina Café. Francis and Sam were having a good time but seemed to irritate Ron because they would not stop talking. After two hours of dining, Ron graciously paid the bill and we all drove home. I could tell that Ron's parents were starting to get on his nerves, and he was becoming short with them.

The next day I was making breakfast, when all of a sudden there was screaming and yelling coming from the patio where I had set the table. Ron and Francis were going at it full force—I could not believe how loud it became. He called her a "bigmouth" and a "pushy idiot," and accused her of embarrassing him and driving him crazy. She kept saying he was an ungrateful son and she couldn't stand him. I don't know how the fight started, but before I could get out there, Francis and Sam said they were leaving. Ron yelled, "I don't ever want you to see Ronnie again." I couldn't believe Ron's behavior.

    The following day, when Ron went to work, Ronnie and I went to see Francis and Sam. I assured them that they would always be able to see Ronnie, and that Ron would eventually come to his senses and apologize. They left two days later—without an apology from Ron.

Chapter 7

A couple of months later, the dealership won another trip. This time we headed for the Mediterranean and Istanbul. It was a wonderful, beautiful experience and therefore all the more difficult to return to reality—being a mom, working full time, cooking, and keeping it all together. I came back exhausted from the trip and felt like I needed another vacation.

Ronnie was so excited to see us that I couldn't remove him from my hip. Ron jumped into work full-time almost immediately, and I started meeting with realtors to find a home in the Gulf Breeze area. Since we moved to Pensacola, we had been renting and it was time to find a place of our own. We ended up in Tiger Point Country Club with a home on the waterfront. I was eager to move in before Christmas.

The week we moved, Pensacola experienced some of its coldest weather ever. Our pipes froze and we had snowflakes on the front lawn. I panicked because Ron had invited a few friends and employees over for Christmas dinner, and I wasn't ready. Fortunately, friends dropped by turkey, ham, and gift baskets, so putting together the dinner ended up being easy. Ronnie's first Christmas, in 1989, turned out to be special, but I wished my family could have spent the holiday with us.

Father Lacari invited the Cianos and us to a dinner at St. Anne's Christmas celebration, the church's big annual fund-raiser. The church was decorated like a winter wonderland, with more than a million lights intertwined between the branches of the trees. Afterward, we picked up Ronnie from Ben and Helen's. While driving home, a car followed us close, intentionally riding our bumper. Ron became enraged. The car started honking but Ron would not move over into the other lane. The driver pulled in front of us and intentionally started driving slow, braking, flashing his lights, and giving us the finger. This upset Ron even more and when the car made a right turn, Ron proceeded to follow him.

"What are you doing?" I asked.

"That son of a bitch is not getting away with this!" he said.

Ron started chasing him down the road and both cars were speeding. The man stopped and jumped out of the car, and Ron tried to run him over. Ron had him pinned between his car and our car. He was out of control. I was crying and I screamed, "Stop, stop, please stop!"

Ronnie woke up in his car seat with all the commotion and started crying too. I was terrified that Ron was going to kill this man and the rage and adrenaline flowing inside him made it impossible to get him to listen to me. Ron got out of the car, grabbed the man, and started punching him. I got out of the car and pleaded, "Ron, please, please don't do this." I was yelling, "You're scaring me! You're scaring Ronnie!" Suddenly Ron stopped and the man began running. I was relieved and asked him, "Are you crazy? I know he made you mad, but it's not worth losing everything and going to jail. Please, I want to go home." Ron had a glare over his eyes and was still mad. I knew enough about his temper that I shouldn't say any more.

When we arrived home I put Ronnie to bed and went back to look at the Land Cruiser. Leftover lasagna completely covered the back seat. The smell of it made me sick. The next morning Ron said, "Give me your keys. I'm getting your car detailed and I will have one of the guys drive it back after." He never said one word about his road rage, but the whole situation still made me upset inside.

One of the things I loved about Pensacola was the proximity to New Orleans. Every month and half Natalie and I would drive up to Saks Fifth Avenue and get our hair done. We would spend the night at the Westin, have dinner, and shop. It was our time away to relax. I wanted to tell Natalie what had happened, but I was embarrassed and I thought she might say something to Ted. Ron's behavior was changing. Sometimes he even seemed jealous of Ronnie because he took time away from him. I knew that I spoiled my husband and did everything I could to make him happy, but I thought that was the right thing to do. Ronnie was just an innocent baby and he too deserved my attention. I felt torn between my duties as a wife and a mother, but I was confident I could work it out.

About three months later I got pregnant again. I didn't say anything to Ron right away. My doctor, a good friend of mine, performed the ultrasound.

"Guess what?" he said, "I hear two heartbeats."

"Knock it off, Al," I replied. "That's really funny."

"Heather, I'm not kidding. You're having twins!"

This was a surprise to me! Ron and I hadn't discussed having more kids. Ronnie had just turned one a few months ago, and I wasn't sure how Ron would react. I decided to mail him a baby bottle at work with a message wrapped inside saying, "Guess what? It's twins!" We were both at the dealership when it arrived. When he opened the box, I expected him to pass out, but to my surprise he came running toward me saying, "Oh baby, I'm so happy! I love you so much!" Ron was absolutely ecstatic. He called Ted and Natalie and our parents to tell them. That night we took a group of employees to McGuire's Irish Pub and celebrated. Later that night, we made passionate love.

Even though Ron was happy, I could see that he was under a lot of pressure at work. He always wanted to have the top dealership in his region and meet all his sale quotas for the month. He was driven and wanted to succeed on his own. Ron decided to buy Terry's portion of the dealership so that he owned it outright. This wasn't a problem for Terry, who already owned other dealerships. Around this time, Terry and Madeline were married and Terry wanted to start a family.

At this time, Ron told me we were going to Australia on a Toyota trip. Natalie and I took our regular trip to New Orleans so I could pick up a few dresses and outfits for the trip. I had to pack not only my suitcases but also Ron's. I gathered his clothes and took them to the dry cleaner, but I forgot to take his black Armani suit. When Ron realized that I hadn't packed his suit, he started screaming at the top of his lungs: "What's wrong with you? Can't you get anything right?" Then he picked up a wooden hanger sitting on the bed and threw it at my head.

"What's wrong with you?" I said. "I'm sorry."

The look in his eyes terrified me. I hardly spoke to him and didn't know if I wanted to go on the trip. Ron apologized and said, "I'm sorry, please come to bed." The next morning we left on our trip.

Chapter 8

Cairns is on the southern side of Australia and is one of the most beautiful places I've been to. Our resort was right on the beach and our suite overlooked the ocean. When we arrived, right away there was a problem. One of my Louis Vuitton garment bags had been dropped in water. When I opened it up, my clothes were wet and one of my blue dresses had stained my suede dress from Cache. The bellman must have dropped the bag in water because it had been dry at the airport. Ron was livid because the dress was expensive. Everything had to be dry cleaned. I told him to calm down and assured him the hotel management would take care of it, which they did.

In the morning, we left for the Great Barrier Reef with the other dealers and their wives. Over the next few days, we enjoyed scuba diving, snorkeling, and touring the tropical rainforest by Jeep. Ron seemed a little bored at this point, but I enjoyed taking in the beauty of the area.

We flew to Sydney and went to a classical concert at Sydney's famous Opera House. We decided to extend our trip and visit Christchurch and Queenstown, New Zealand. When we got there, Ron suggested we interview nannies at some of their professional schools. I wasn't too keen on this idea because I was a hands-on mom, but I didn't want to fight over it; after all, Ron was in a good mood. We interviewed two women, both named Susan. We told the school we'd be in touch.

Queenstown was the second stop for us, and because it was winter there we were unable to enjoy a lot of outdoor activities. We did, however, enjoy spa treatments at the hotel. At night we indulged in food and fine wine. All this relaxation was a perfect ending to our trip.

We met up with Ted and Natalie a couple nights later and had dinner. Ron enjoyed telling them about our trip. They shared Ron's opinion on getting a nanny to help us out. Ron said if he wanted to do things with me or travel, we would need the help—the two of us needed to enjoy life, and we could afford this luxury. So we hired Susan Foster and flew her out a month before my twins were born.

Chapter 9

Over the next few months things were back to normal, except for the fact that Ron seemed to be working more. By the time he came home at night Ronnie was already tucked in bed. I convinced Ron to have Francis, Sam, and my parents come for the holidays. Dawn and I went to pick out a Christmas tree and I couldn't wait to have it delivered. The fresh pine smell reminded me of Christmas in Minnesota. Ronnie couldn't wait to see Grandma and Grandpa Stephens, so I brought him to the airport to pick them up. The next day, I picked up Francis and Sam.

Evenings we went out to dinner or I cooked at the house. Ron spent his days at the dealership. I could tell he needed to get out of the house. There were too many people around and his anxiety level was high. Christmas Eve we had Ted and Natalie join us for dinner, and we opened all the family gifts together before going to midnight mass. Christmas morning we watched Ronnie open all of Santa's gifts, lounged around, and ate breakfast together.

Two days later Dad, Mom, and I were sitting in the family room having coffee and Ronnie was playing with his toys. Ron came out of the bedroom and made himself a bowl of cereal. He was on the phone with the dealership again and seemed frustrated.

I got up and went to the kitchen to find out what was going on. The dog started scratching at the door to come in, but nobody heard him over the TV. Ron screamed, "Let the damn dog in!" When my dad got up and let in the dog, Ron freaked out. I turned around and Ron had a switchblade aimed at my father. I immediately got between them and said, "What are you doing, Ron? It's just the dog; we didn't hear him." Ron continued to try to stab us and my mom yelled, "Watch out, Heather, you're pregnant!" I was screaming, "Please stop, please stop this! I'm going to call the police!" The minute Ron heard this, he ran to the bedroom, grabbed a gun, and put it in his briefcase. He left without saying a word. My parents and I stood in the middle of the kitchen, looking at each other, dazed. I said, "I can't believe this happened. I'm really afraid."

I called the Gulf Breeze police and an officer drove out to take our statements. I could hardly speak to the officer because I was shaking and crying. I told him I was terrified because Ron could have hurt one of us. The officer called the dealership and told Ron to come home.

When Ron got there the officer took him aside and they talked about what happened. Ron tried to smooth everything over. By that time, he had put the knife away and said there never was a knife. The officer didn't search him, but he could tell we were all upset and scared. Ron said we'd fought, and he didn't know what came over him. I told the officer I didn't feel safe having Ron in the house. The officer told him he would have to leave and sleep outside the house or at a hotel. Ron packed a few things and kept trying to talk to me, but the officer wouldn't let him.

I could not believe after all of that, Ron was acting like nothing had happened. My parents were both concerned. My father was scared and immediately wanted to leave, but my mother wanted to stay because she was worried about me.

I couldn't believe everything that had happened. I was glad that Francis and Sam had been out and hadn't seen the incident. Sam probably would have had a heart attack. Later that afternoon my father purchased a ticket and I drove him to the airport. Ron's parents returned and I honestly didn't know what to say to them. That night my mom stayed with me in my room, but I couldn't sleep. The next day Ron kept calling, saying, "I'm so sorry." He sent me flowers. I told him I didn't want to see him yet. Again he said, "I'm so sorry. I love you. I don't know what came over me." "I can't take your behavior," I replied. "It scares me."

I finally spoke to Ron after two days. Francis and Sam were pressuring me, and I couldn't put it off any longer. When Ron called, he said, "Well, can we have dinner? Let's go to Jubilee's on Pensacola

Beach. I know you love that restaurant." I agreed. He asked if he could pick me up and I said, "Of course."

I was nervous. When we arrived at Jubilee's, Ron had brought me roses and was on his best behavior. We ordered drinks and made small talk. Ron tried to kiss and hug me, but I was uncomfortable. We shared oysters Rockefeller and then ordered lobster for dinner. Everything was going fine until I approached the subject of what had happened. I told him his behavior scared me. "Are you okay?" I asked. "Is something going on? I don't know if I want to bring up my children in this type of life. I didn't grow up with knives or guns and it's terrifying me. I'm really struggling right now with whether I want to be married to you."

He immediately grabbed my hands hard and said, "I love you. I love you. Nothing else matters."

"Everything matters," I said.

"Well, let me tell you something, Heather. People don't cross me. And if you think you're going to break up our little family, you might just find one of your parents dead one day."

I got up and left the table. I walked out of the restaurant, but I had no car and didn't know what to do. My mother was watching Ronnie at the house. I was scared and confused. So I started walking. There I was, five months pregnant, in high heels, walking across the Pensacola Beach bridge, crying, trying to get home. I called my mother, but she didn't answer.

Ron drove up behind me and started yelling at me to get in the car. "Are you crazy? Heather, I'm sorry. Get in the car; you're going to hurt yourself." And I said, "No, you know you're scaring me." After more walking, and Ron begging me to get in the car, I was tired. I jumped in and told him to please take me home.

Everyone was awake when we drove up to the house. I felt beaten down and disturbed. I told Ron, "You're not coming in the house. I'm sorry, but you can't stay here." He kept grabbing me, but I asked him to please leave. "Don't you think you've done enough?" I asked.

I told my mom what happened at dinner. She said, "I'm shocked, Heather. What is wrong with him? I thought everything was going so well between the two of you." I proceeded to tell her about Ron's Dr. Jekyll and Mr. Hyde behavior, and a few other things I had seen and experienced with him. I told her I didn't know what to do, but something had to change. She was supportive and said that it would have to be my decision because it was my life. Meanwhile, every day Ron was calling and trying to patch things together, promising he would never do anything like that again, saying he loved me and Ronnie.

He started sending expensive jewelry, clothing, and flowers. I didn't care about these gifts. I just wanted everything to be back to normal. I had a beautiful life and I figured I could work this out. After all, I was raised Catholic and felt guilty even thinking about divorce. I have always thought the two hardest accomplishments are making your marriage work and raising your children successfully. I guess you could say Ron wormed his way back in by promising he wouldn't do anything like that again. He seemed to be attentive and on his best behavior.

Chapter 10

    The next few months flew by. I had to furnish Ronnie's new bedroom so that the twins could have their cribs together in the nursery. Dawn and Natalie helped me do all the shopping and preparing while Helen planned my baby shower. Our nanny, Susan, arrived a month before my due date. I was excited to pick her up at the airport and bring her to our home to meet Ronnie. I knew this would be a big adjustment for him because we were together every day. I wanted to introduce Susan slowly, to supervise and nurture their relationship.

    Susan was absolutely delightful and helped me with carrying, cleaning, and cooking during my tired pregnant state. Ronnie warmed up to her quickly. I couldn't believe I had argued with Ron about having extra help. Ron was acting like the perfect husband and was happy Susan was there to help. It gave us time alone. He was caring and made sure to leave the dealership early most nights so that we could spend time together as a family.

    It was getting close to the birth of my twins. I had to visit my doctor's office every two days to have an ultrasound to make sure everything was going well. My mother called and said that Grandma Ann had passed away. I sadly made arrangements for Ron and I to leave town and was upset when my doctor would not let me travel so close to the due date. I loved my grandmother, who had lived with us when my sister and I were growing up. Ron wanted to get Terry's Learjet to take us but I decided not to go. It's a good thing that I didn't.

    Lauren was breach, so I received daily ultrasounds to see if she would flip so the doctors could induce labor. One morning, on May 3, 1991, she turned. Al, my doctor, told me to call Ron and sent me to Sacred Heart Hospital. After five hours of labor, I had two beautiful six-pound babies. Joseph came out with blond hair and blue eyes, and Lauren had brown hair and hazel eyes. They couldn't be more different. After two days Ron drove us all home. My mother did not come out right away because of the altercation, and she knew Susan was there to help.

Lauren and Joe were precious and I kept them in the same room. I figured if they were together in my body for nine months I didn't want to separate them after birth. They were so much work that I was hardly getting any sleep, even with Susan there. I ended up getting strep throat and was down for two days. I had to make sure Ronnie was getting enough attention; I didn't want him to feel left out.

In October, I prepared for Grandma Doris to visit. I wanted to buy her a plane ticket, but she was afraid to fly because when she was younger her eardrum had burst. So she took the train and I drove to Mobile, Alabama, to pick her up. Both my grandmothers loved Ron. He was charming and kind to them. I think that's because he was so close to his grandmother, Blanche, and talked about her all the time.

I enjoyed showing my grandmother around Pensacola. She loved spending the afternoon at the beach with the twins and Ronnie, and then going to the fish market to purchase fresh shrimp that I brought home and grilled for dinner. Natalie, her daughter Debbie, Grandma Doris, and I all drove to New Orleans for a couple of days while Susan watched the kids. We shopped in antique stores and took Grandma to Café Du Monde for coffee and beignets. At night we listened to jazz and had an amazing Cajun meal at a restaurant owned by Emeril Lagasse, a friend of ours. Grandma had a wonderful time and I treasured our moments together.

When we arrived home, I wanted to tell Ron all about our trip. So we picked him up at the dealership and went to lunch. The kids were happy to see their dad, and Ronnie jumped on Ron's lap, hugging him and saying, "Dad, can I eat here?" Ron said, "No son, but you can sit next to me."

I thought everything was going great at lunch, but the twins started fussing. Grandma held Lauren to try to comfort her, and I grabbed Joe and gave him to Ron. Joe started to cry. "Just give me a minute," I said to Ron. "I have to cut Ronnie's food." Joe continued to cry and Ron started screaming at me. "Are you trying to drive me crazy? These kids are driving me crazy and I can't take it! Why did you even invite me to lunch? You've ruined it!" I was trying to fight back my tears because I didn't want Grandma to know I was upset. I said, "I'm sorry, Ron, I'm sure the kids are just tired. Please don't get upset!" I calmed Lauren and Joe down and didn't finish my lunch.

It was a disaster and a disappointment. Ronnie wanted to stay at the store with his dad, but Ron told him no and it really hurt Ronnie's feelings. I didn't know what to say to my grandmother. She asked me if I was okay, and I smiled and said yes.

The next day was Halloween. I put Ronnie in his lion costume and called Ron to see if he was able to go trick or treating with us. Susan was going to watch Lauren and Joe while I went with Ronnie. Ron could not come home, so my grandmother went with me. The next day I drove Grandma to the train station in Mobile but she wasn't excited about leaving because she was going home to a huge blizzard.

Ron was always advertising with local television and radio stations. As a perk we were given tickets to concerts and plays we would attend with our friends. One day Ron called and said, "I have a trip to Maui, all expenses paid, and I was thinking of giving it to your mom and dad. I just feel so bad about what happened. Do you think they'd like to go?" I said, "Call them." After all, their twenty-fifth wedding anniversary was coming up and it would be a nice time to celebrate. The following month Mom and Dad went to Maui and had a wonderful time.

Chapter 11

In 1991, we had Ted and Natalie, Ben and Helen, and Andy and Dawn over for Christmas dinner. Natalie and I had taken a trip to New Orleans to purchase fresh meats and Italian cheeses for the holiday dishes. There, I bought my family's gifts and sent them to Minneapolis so that they would be there for Christmas morning. It was hard to believe that my family was not coming this year. On New Year's Eve we went to a resort for dinner with Ted and Natalie and went dancing afterward. We put our arms around each other and sang "I'm Proud to Be an American" with everybody else on the dance floor. The Gulf War was going on at the time and it was a memorable moment.

The new car show that Toyota held for all its dealers each year was in Las Vegas, and Ron invited my parents and the Marchesis to join us. Don Marchesi was our office controller and he and his wife, Pat, had become friends. We checked into the Mirage Hotel and met everyone downstairs for lunch. Jim Moran hosted some of the festivities along with Toyota. I wanted to talk to Mr. Moran personally and thank he and his wife for all the baby gifts they had sent. I introduced my parents to Mr. Moran and his wife, Jan. Mr. Moran told Ron he was doing an excellent job with his dealership, which made Ron feel good.

We saw the upcoming Toyota models and viewed the new commercials. Barry Manilow performed, as did Wayne Newton. Toyota flew in chefs from Tokyo to prepare fresh sushi, and there were stations with caviar and Russian vodkas, fresh lobster, colossal shrimp, king crab legs, and fresh oysters from New Zealand. Kobe beef fillets were grilled to perfection. Everyone left so full that night, no one could even think about breakfast or lunch the next day.

I couldn't wait to get home because I missed the kids so much. It was nice to have a four-day break, but I was excited to take them to the zoo. Ron was back to work and left to have breakfast with Ted at the Village Inn. I stayed home cleaning and getting things in order. With three children there was always so much laundry to do, and it seemed like I was always straightening their rooms and picking up toys. I had Susan pack the diaper bag so that everything was ready for the zoo the next day. I had to run to the grocery store to pick up a few things for dinner, so Susan watched the kids and when I got back I made lasagna. I couldn't wait to have a home-cooked dinner after so many meals out in Las Vegas. I called Ron and told him dinner would be ready at six. I took the children outside to enjoy some fresh air and pushed Ronnie on his swing set while the twins played with their toys. There was a gentle breeze coming off the water and the temperature was seventy-eight degrees. It was a beautiful day.

It was six o'clock and the table was set but Ron wasn't home, so I called his cell phone to see if he was on his way. Ron picked up and said, "I can't make dinner. I'll eat later when I get home." I said, "That's fine. I'll feed the kids and wait to eat with you." During dinner Ronnie kept asking, "Where's Daddy?" I would tell him, "Honey, Daddy's at work, but you'll be able to see him in the morning." I gave the kids their baths and got them into their pajamas. I read a story to the twins and put them in their cribs. Ronnie couldn't wait for me to lie next to him and read him the story he picked out. This was a special routine we did before bedtime. Ronnie said his prayers and I tucked him into bed.

Ron came home around nine thirty and went to the bedroom to change out of his suit. I kissed him and asked him how his day was. He said it was hectic but okay. I put the lasagna on the table, and he said, "I don't want lasagna." I said, "You love lasagna. Are you kidding me?" Well, that was the wrong thing to say. Ron stood up and threw the whole pan of lasagna at me. It splattered all over my top, fell on the kitchen floor, and shattered the glass pan. I stood there scared and frozen. I didn't know what I had done wrong; after all, Ron was never picky about what I made. He loved my cooking. Ron screamed at me, telling me all the things I was doing wrong. I felt like I was walking on eggshells. I kept saying "I'm sorry" and "Next time I'll call and ask what you want for dinner." Ron stormed off and went to bed.

I sat sobbing on the floor while I cleaned up all the lasagna. I wondered what was going on with him again. I wanted to ask questions but was afraid to say anything. Ron came out later and said, "Please come to bed, Heather." I told him I had to get everything cleaned up before the kids woke up. I wanted him to be asleep before I came back to the room.

In the morning, Ron wrapped his arms tightly around me and wouldn't let me out of bed. I told him that I had to get up before the kids, but he said Susan could take care of them. He wouldn't let me go, and all I wanted was to get away from him.

After getting ready, Susan and I packed up Ronnie, Lauren, and Joe and headed to the zoo. The whole time I was driving I wondered if Susan had heard what happened the night before. She must have, because it was so loud, but she never asked me about it. We stayed at the zoo for about two hours. Susan pushed the twins in their large stroller, while I walked holding Ronnie's hand and carrying him when he was tired. The kids loved the different animals and had such a good time they didn't want to leave. I had a nice afternoon with them, but I was irritated because Ron kept calling my cell phone every fifteen minutes. He wanted to go out to dinner with Jim Franklin and his wife, Trudy, at the Tiger Point Country Club.

Jim Franklin was vice president at Barnett Bank, and Ron had to wine and dine our friends while talking business. Trudy and I caught up on our busy lives. I told her how our children were doing and she told me about theirs. The night was pleasant.

Coming home I kept hoping that Ron was still in a happy mood. I did not want a repeat of last night. I checked all the kids to make sure they were tucked into bed and then got ready myself. When I came to bed Ron was there with a big wrapped present. He said, "Heather, I love you so much! Open it, open it!" I was excited and ripped off the paper. In the box was a Mikimoto pearl necklace and diamond and pearl earrings to match. They were absolutely exquisite, and I turned to Ron and kissed and thanked him. Ron insisted that I try them on, and he helped me put the necklace around my neck. I knew that Ron felt bad about what had happened and—as usual—was trying to apologize in a big way.

Chapter 12

In the fall of 1992, Ron and I traveled to Hong Kong, China, and Japan for two weeks. Helen and Ben offered to stop by and help Susan take care of the children. Ron delegated all his work responsibilities to the managers, knowing that with the time change he would be unable to contact the dealership on a daily basis.

We arrived in Hong Kong at night and stayed at the Imperial Hotel, located by the premier shopping, cultural, and leisure district. Fashion is an important part of Hong Kong's culture. Just looking around the hotel, women were dressed stylishly in suits with matching purses and shoes. Ron and I immediately headed to the retail area, where some of our favorite designer shops were located—Escada, Giorgio Armani, Donna Karan. Ron had all the shops deliver our packages so we wouldn't have to worry about carrying them.

We strolled along the waterfront in Kowloon, went to the space museum, and then returned to the hotel. Later that night we had shark fin soup at a restaurant along the waterfront. We were having a great time with each other, and Ron was less stressed away from the business.

The next morning we went to Wong Tai Sin Temple for a tour. The temple was in a traditional Chinese style with huge red pillars in front and a pure gold roof. I saw many visitors come and light incense and kneel at the altar. The tour guide explained that they were in search of a spiritual answer.

We took a taxi to a traditional shopping area in Kowloon because Ron wanted to pick up a few things for the house. He found two beautiful Chinese painted vases and a large carved jade ship made by a local artist.

All these things had to be wrapped and shipped back to the United States because we intended to go to Tokyo.

When we arrived back at the hotel Ron was starved, so I asked the concierge to recommend a nearby restaurant that served Peking duck. The place was packed so we went to the bar to have a cocktail. Ron stepped away to go to the bathroom, and when he returned a man was hitting on me and would not leave me alone. Ron became infuriated and said, "Hey, that's my wife. Get your hands off her." I told the man to move away, but he wouldn't. This upset Ron even more, and he began to yell at him loudly. I told Ron, "Please calm down. The guy is obviously drunk. Let's check on our table." We ordered dinner, but I could hardly finish my meal. Ron could not stop talking about what had happened and how he wanted to beat the guy up. He kept asking me, "Why were you talking to him? What were you doing?" He made me feel like it was my fault. I was sick to my stomach, afraid of Ron's reaction. I knew to be quiet on the way back, but I could not understand Ron. He was confident and not the jealous type. I then remembered how crazy he would get when he couldn't locate me or I didn't answer my phone. In our room that night, I slithered into bed, trying not to make a sound, hoping not to wake Ron.

The next morning we flew to Beijing. When we arrived at the Great Wall I could not believe what a massive structure it was and how beautiful the countryside was around it. I asked a tour guide how long it took to build it; he said it was over several hundreds of years during the Ming Dynasty. On our way back we toured Tiananmen Square. We were exhausted and had an early dinner at the hotel. The following day, we went to the Forbidden City and the Ming Tombs.

It was Ron's idea to visit Tokyo, where he had set up meetings with executives at Toyota Motor Corporation. When we went through baggage check, the man looked at me and asked, "Are you traveling with your worldly belongings?" Ron just laughed and said, "You should see what she has at home!"

When we arrived at our five-star hotel, we could not believe the size of the room. It was small and double the price of our suite in Hong Kong. Our first meal there was at a tempura restaurant near the hotel.

Lunch for two people cost $150. I began to see that everything was going to be expensive.

 Ron was in business mode, so I was able to spend a little time relaxing. When he came back from his meetings, he was in a great mood. I told him about the Ginza area and we hopped in a taxi to check it out. We walked down the street looking at window displays of designer shops. Ron took me into a jewelry store known for top-quality pearl jewelry. He insisted I pick out a new necklace. I told him I already had a pearl necklace and didn't need a new one. But Ron wanted me to have one from Japan. Before turning in, we sat at the hotel bar and listened to music. It was such a wonderful evening, I was sorry it had to end. Yet as much as we were enjoying Japan, we could not wait to get home, see the kids, and sleep in our own bed.

 Every day was busy after we returned. Ron left early every morning and got home late at night. Just unpacking everything took two days and was constantly interrupted by Lauren or Joe grabbing onto my legs. I gave Susan a one-week vacation so she spent time with her friends. I couldn't wait to see Natalie and tell her about our trip, so I packed up the kids, diaper bags, and strollers and drove to her house. We spent the afternoon laughing, talking, and playing with the kids by the pool. Ron and Ted joined us after work and we all had dinner together.

 The following week, I had to go to the dealership to file some paperwork. My mother called and wanted to hear about our trip and how the kids were doing. I told her I was sorry I hadn't called her sooner, but I had been busy trying to catch up. I put her on hold, ran into Ron's office, and asked him if he minded my mom coming down to visit. He said, "No, not at all." I ended up buying tickets for my mother and my Aunt Donna. They arrived the next week.

 During their visit, I showed them the sites I enjoyed in the area. We spent a day at the beach and had fresh oysters for lunch. The next day, we went to the Naval Museum. On the way there, Ron called and needed me to bring his golf shoes to the dealership. I didn't want him to be upset, so I turned around, picked up the shoes, and brought them there. I had to fill the car with gas, so I pulled up to the pump at the dealership and asked one of the salesmen to fill it. All of a sudden, I saw Ron running up to the back of the car screaming and yelling at me in front of my mother and aunt about getting gas. I was confused because this was something I did on a regular basis. I was embarrassed and didn't know what was going on. When we drove off, I could tell my mom and aunt were upset. At the Naval Museum, we toured the flight deck and saw different naval aircrafts. While Aunt Donna went to the gift shop to purchase a few things to bring back with her, Ron called me and said, "Let's all go to McGuire's Irish Pub for dinner," like nothing had happened. McGuire's was busy as usual and we had to wait for a table. At dinner, Ron was his jovial self, shaking hands and talking to friends at the next table. Later that evening my mom thanked me and said they'd had a good time.

I was up early and made breakfast for everyone. Ron had already left for the office and I needed to run a few errands with Mom and Aunt Donna. While I was at the grocery store, Ron called and excitedly told me our packages had arrived from China. I was to drive to the US Customs building in Mobile, Alabama, to pick them up. When the customs agent brought out our boxes, he said there was a problem. One of them was damaged, and it happened to be Ron's favorite, the jade ship. Large pieces of jade were broken off the statue. I called Ron and told him about the accident. He asked to speak to the agent and yelled and screamed at the shipyard official so loudly we could hear him through the phone. I took the receiver and tried to calm him down. The gentleman was apologetic and helped us carry the boxes to the car, and we drove home.

Ron called my cell phone and was livid. He seemed to blame me.

"I'm sorry this happened," I said, "but it's not my fault."

"Well, maybe we should have brought it with us, and this never would have happened." Ron was furious and hung up on me.

I started to tear up. My mom looked at me and said, "Heather, I thought Ron's temper was under control and things were getting better."

"I thought so, Mom," I said. "Sometimes he is so good, and other times he really scares me. His mood can change so fast."

From the back of the car, Donna said, "I'm so sorry, Heather. He seemed to be so perfect and kind. It seems like you do everything to please him."

Both of them tried to be supportive. We talked about what we should make for dinner and the children, but somehow the conversation always came back to Ron. When Ron came home for dinner, all he talked about was the $8,000 ship and the jerk at customs. I sat there and listened, but really wanted to say, "get over it." Ron's behavior was getting more and more out of control, and I was getting scared.

Wedding to Ron Samuels 1988.

Heather with Ronnie Jr.

Right after the twins were born in1991.

Christmas 1994. Ronnie is 5, the twins, Lauren and Joe, are 3.

Chapter 13

"Come on, everybody," Ron said. "Let's go to Seaside for the day and I won't go into work."

I packed up the kids' swimsuits and our things and we drove south to Seaside, Florida. The trip was an hour and fifty minutes, but the sites along the way were breathtaking.

We passed through Destin, a town with white sand and almost turquoise-blue ocean. Aunt Donna, Mom, and I talked and the children chatted and made noise. Ron slept the whole way, despite Ronnie's repeated attempts to wake him up.

When we arrived, we had lunch and I could tell the children were irritating Ron. We all were having a great time laughing and eating, but Ron was in one of his moods, and was ignoring us. I asked him if he was feeling okay. "I'm tired," he replied.

I asked if we should go home, but he said, "No. You guys walk around while I stay in the car."

Seaside, Florida, is a quaint town with charming little cottages along the beach. Art galleries, farmers' markets, theater, music halls, and restaurants are just some of its attractions. My mother and Aunt Donna just loved it. When we arrived back at the car, Ron had woken up and was waiting for us.

"I wish you could have been with us," I said.

"I guess I'm exhausted from work," he said. "I'll feel better tomorrow."

The ride back was quiet, and the children slept most of the way. Ron ordered pizza for dinner and we sat outside on the patio talking about Seaside.

The next morning at breakfast, Aunt Donna and Mom wanted to know why Ron had suggested we go to Seaside, if he was going to ignore us and sleep the whole time. I felt bad; I didn't think Ron was in the right frame of mind for guests.

Ron came out of the bedroom and said, "Did you pick up my brown Armani suit from the dry cleaners? I'm meeting with two executives from World Omni, and I wanted to wear that suit."

"I had no idea," I said. "I didn't pick it up from the dry cleaners."

Ron started to scream and flail his arms, saying, "What is wrong with you? Can't you do anything right?" I could see the anger in his eyes and didn't know what he was going to do next.

All of a sudden, Ronnie, dressed in his Superman pajamas, said, "Don't yell at Mommy!" and Ron stopped. Everyone in the room was shocked. Ron picked up Ronnie and told him, "It's okay, son." After that, Ron got dressed for work and left in one of his other twenty suits.

I was beside myself and confused. I didn't understand why Ron was so crazy at times or how to make things better. I confided in my mother and aunt, looking for answers. We spent the afternoon lying by the pool with the kids and had a quiet, relaxing night. The next day, I was sad to see my family leave. I wished their stay could have been less stressful.

Ron and I went to lunch with Betty Bancroft, Ronnie's godmother. Ron was happy, and I was pleased that his spirits were up. After lunch, Betty and I sat in her office and talked. She noticed I seemed unhappy and asked if there was something wrong. I told her "Ron seems to be changing. He works all the time and seems jealous of the children when he's home, because I can't give him my full attention. I don't know what to do to make everything better."

"Heather," Betty replied, "I'm sure he's stressed from work. I think you should talk to him and tell him how you feel." I was reluctant to say anything that night because he was finally in a good mood and I didn't want to ruin it.

It took about a week for me to get the strength to talk to Ron. It was the opportune time because Susan was at the movies and the children were all in bed. I tried to explain my concerns and feelings, but Ron went absolutely crazy and thought I wanted to leave him. He picked me up and threw me against the wall, and while I was lying there on the floor crying, he grabbed a gun and held it to my head. He made me promise I would never leave him. He then made me promise that I loved him and told me if I did leave him, he would destroy me.

I was crying and shaking, terrified that my life might be over. Ron started crying, saying, "I love you. Why are you making me do this? Don't you love our little family?"

I tried to tell him that he misunderstood me and I would never leave him. He started kissing me all over and it made me feel sick. I just wanted him to stop. Finally, Ron calmed down, got up, and walked away. I sat there in shock. I thought to myself, "What the hell just happened?" That night Ron would not let me out of his sight, and I lay next to him in bed, terrified to go to sleep.

The next morning Ron left for work, confident that everything was fine between us. I made breakfast for Ronnie, Lauren, and Joe and dressed them for the day. I put on a long-sleeved blouse to cover the large, red mark on my arm where Ron had grabbed me.

Susan and I were taking the children to Natalie's for lunch. It was hard not telling Natalie what had happened, but I didn't want her to say anything to Ted and have it get back to Ron. That night Ron came home from work early. He brought me roses and a gift and kept saying he was sorry. I really felt he was upset about what had happened. Over the next two months, Ron seemed to be focused on being a good father and a doting husband. I could not believe the change in his attitude.

Chapter 14

Every summer, I took a trip to visit my family. It was the summer of 1992 and I was planning my trip to Minnesota for two weeks with Susan, Ronnie, Lauren, and Joe. I asked Ron if he was going to come meet us for the weekend, but he wasn't sure. It was a perfect time to get away and relax. The children loved playing with their cousins and enjoyed their outings with Grandma and Grandpa.

Even though I talked to Ron every day, he would call me five or six times a day. I was happy being home and there was no stress. I didn't have to worry about doing something wrong. Four days before we were supposed to go back I started packing and putting things together. Ronnie became upset and said, "I don't want to go back."

I asked why.

"It's so nice here," he replied. "I like it here."

"It's nice at home and Daddy is waiting for us," I said.

That night, what Ronnie said weighed heavily on my mind. I didn't sleep. I had everything—money, a beautiful home, wonderful children—but I was miserable. I was scared of Ron and I didn't want to bring up my children in this environment. I felt sad because I loved Ron, but things weren't changing. For all the good times we had together, the scary times outweighed them.

I told my mother and father I didn't want to go back to Ron. "I'm tired of walking on eggshells and having guns held to my head." They totally supported my decision.

The next day, I went to see a lawyer in Minneapolis who helped me hire a divorce lawyer in Pensacola. Ron at the time was at our home in North Carolina and told me to fly everyone there for a week. This was a solution to my problem. I told Ron that I wanted to stay for the opening of the Mall of America because I had an invitation to the exclusive party. I kept putting Ron off because I didn't want him to know what I was planning. I knew that if Ron was in Florida, he would never let me leave.

Susan and I flew back to Pensacola, and I left the children with my parents. I met with my lawyer, John Myrick, and we filed divorce papers and an order of protection. I was terrified to even attempt this. But I knew I only had a small window of time before Ron became suspicious and flew to Minnesota or came to Florida.

Susan and I rented a U-Haul. I packed up my clothes and my children's clothes in garbage bags along with the twins' cribs. That night, I lay on the couch and held a knife against my chest for protection, because I was convinced he would come that night.

Every hour, the home phone rang while we were packing and I didn't pick it up. I thought, "Does he know we're here?" Ron also called my parents' home asking to speak to me. My mother said, "I don't know where she is. She and Susan went out for the night." Ron became irate. She then called me on my cell and told me he was trying to find me.

We left the next morning at 5 a.m. and drove straight through. I was terrified; I just wanted to be back with the kids and feel safe. Susan and I kept switching off driving so that we could make it home. The whole time my heart was in my throat, and it was beating so fast I thought I was going to pass out. Ron was the kind of person who, in the middle of the night, could charter a plane and be at my parents' house when we arrived. Susan and I looked at each other with relief when we saw my parents standing outside the house. At dinner I went over everything that happened and I told my parents about the meeting with Mr. Myrick. I was exhausted from driving and went to bed right after I put the kids to bed.

At breakfast I was in a daze. I still couldn't believe I'd had the courage to do that. Ron called in the morning and no one answered the phone. Finally, my mother said, "Heather, you have to talk to him." The next time Ron called my cell phone, I told him I wasn't going back to Pensacola. I wanted a divorce. I had to hang up on Ron because he was screaming and wouldn't listen to anything I was saying. The harassment became so bad my parents changed their telephone number to an unlisted one. Somehow Ron got the new unlisted number and started calling again. I was exhausted from trying to avoid his calls. I needed time to clear my head.

Chapter 15

Being in Minnesota was definitely different but the children and I were happy. Lauren and Joe were only a year old and Ronnie was three. The transition for them seemed natural because they loved my parents and Ron had always been working. Susan was supportive of my decision to leave; she obviously could see what was going on. She continued her duties and helped me unpack. Three weeks later I had to fly back to Pensacola for my first hearing. My girlfriend Dawn picked me up at the airport and we had lunch. She drove me to the courthouse to meet John Myrick. I was anxious about seeing Ron.

Judge Rasmussen was assigned to our case. The hearing took about an hour and it was emotional. Ron told the judge that he did not want a divorce and sobbed uncontrollably. I told the judge there was no way I could be with him after everything that had transpired between us. He granted me the right to live in Minnesota with my children. Ron would have to fly to Minnesota once a month to see the children because of their young ages. I left the room quickly with my lawyer and Ron followed us and grabbed my arm. I said, "Please, Ron. Let me go." I felt bad for him but didn't want him to influence my decision. Flying home, I kept picturing Ron crying and felt terrible—but I also wondered if it was an act for the judge, or his true feelings.

At home, everything was peaceful and the children filled their days playing, running through sprinklers, and wading in a small pool in the yard. My parents had eleven acres of land right off the Rum River. It had been a great place to grow up. My sister, Tiffany, and I would climb trees, ride bikes, build forts, and ride our horses. The best part of being home was that we had a large family and a lot of cousins the same ages as Ronnie, Lauren, and Joe. The children looked forward to the weekends when we would all get together and have picnics. Eight little kids running around was a bit hectic, but they had fun. The end of the month was approaching quickly, and soon Ron would be coming to see the kids.

I explained to the children that their daddy was coming to see them and they seemed excited. Ron drove up in a minivan and, to my surprise, Ben and Helen Bentfield were with him. They both gave me a big hug and said they missed me terribly. Susan had packed up the diaper bag for the day. The kids were excited to see Ron, who was hugging and kissing them. Their plans were to go to the Mall of America for the day and then bring the children back after dinner. Susan and I hopped in the car and went to Rosedale Mall to do some shopping and have lunch. The day was enjoyable, although I was worried about the kids. Ronnie, Lauren, and Joe came back around seven o'clock. Ron brought them up to the house and said good night. They came back with bags of clothes from Baby Gap and Nordstrom. Ronnie said he'd had a good time with Daddy. I gave them baths and put them to bed, because they were tired from the big day. They had to do it all over again the following two days. During the exchange of the children, Ron kept trying to talk to me and say, "I love you." The second night he asked me to come to dinner with Ben, Helen, and him but I declined. Overall, I thought the visit went fine.

The summer went by quickly and soon it was fall. Ron continued his visitation every month, bringing Ben and Helen with him. He continually sent me flowers, gifts, and cards. I kept asking him to stop. Then he sent me the soundtrack to *The Bodyguard*, circling the song "I will always love you" and signing it with his name. I didn't know how to make him understand that for me, it was over.

My mother and I bought the kids winter jackets, mittens, scarves, and boots. Halloween was approaching. Ronnie wanted to be Batman, and Joe had to be Batman just like his brother. Lauren was the Little Mermaid. That night, trick-or-treating was so cold, we drove from house to house. I would jump out of the car each time with the kids, while my mom kept the car warm. We all had a nice time and I made hot chocolate for the kids when we got home.

The next week I flew to Pensacola for my first deposition. I met Mr. Myrick for lunch beforehand. I was a little nervous but he did a good job explaining the process. T. Sol Johnson, Ron's attorney, questioned me for two hours straight. It was exhausting. I was glad when it was over and Mr. Myrick said I did fine. He dropped me off at the airport that evening.

The next day, after I finished the kids' laundry, I got dressed to meet my girlfriend Terry for lunch at Friday's. I passed by the window in the living room and saw a strange car parked across the road. We lived on Seventh Avenue and it was a busy street. On the way to the restaurant, I looked back and noticed the car was following me. At first, I thought I was imagining things. But as I made another turn the car turned too. I didn't know what to do. The minute I arrived at Friday's, I told Terry what had happened. She was concerned and said, "If you see that same car again, you need to call the police." Our lunch was long and we spent time catching up. Terry Vevea had been my best friend since sixth grade, when we met in gymnastics. I had missed her ever since she moved to Houston, and it was nice to see her.

Driving home, I noticed the same car and became scared. I called 911 and told them I was being followed and gave them the car's license plate number. Immediately, a police officer drove up behind both of us and questioned the male driver following me. I was informed by Officer Rogers that the driver was a private detective paid to follow me.

I was shocked. I immediately thought, *What is he up to now? Why can't he just leave me alone?* I told my lawyer and parents immediately.

This harassment didn't stop. Cars were parked by our house all the time; I became paranoid and was always looking over my shoulder. One time, during one of Ron's visits, my father noticed Ron and a gentleman taking pictures of our house. Ron was doing anything he could to make me uncomfortable. I just wanted to start my life over and get divorced.

Christmastime was approaching; I was excited to buy a live tree, and Ronnie and I picked out the biggest one in the lot. We all decorated the tree and I was excited to be home for Christmas. This was the first time Ronnie, Lauren, and Joe were able to play in snow and make snow angels. Mom was planning to have everyone over for Christmas—all our relatives, cousins, and close friends. For three days, Mom and I baked bars and cookies and prepared appetizers. On Christmas Eve, Uncle Ken, my mom's brother, knocked on the window from outside and surprised the kids as Santa. They all started screaming in excitement as he entered the front door. After we opened our gifts together, we then went to midnight mass. It was so nice to have a normal Christmas, without Ron's theatrics.

Chapter 16

In the spring of 1993, my friend Shane and I were having dinner at the Pickled Parrot in Minneapolis. As we were leaving the restaurant, Shane saw his friend John Grossman and introduced him to me. I said hello and told him I had just moved back to Minnesota from Florida. Little did I know he would end up becoming a major part of my life.

I never went out much, but my girlfriend Katie came into town that summer, and Katie, my friend Ginny, and I went to dinner at the Palomino restaurant. While waiting for our table at the bar, I ran into John Grossman again. He came over with his friend Kevin Nelson and we talked for half an hour. He was funny, charming, and seemed to be interested in me. Our table was ready, so we said good-bye. After dinner, we walked to a lounge called The Living Room, sat down, and ordered some wine. On the way back from the bathroom, I looked over and saw John and Kevin with two women, laughing and having a good time. I ran back to the table before he could see me. "Guess who's here?" I said to Ginny and Katie. "John is over there and I'd really like to talk to him, but they're with two women." Ginny told me to talk to him anyway. I said "That's okay. I have too much on my plate—all the problems with Ron and caring for the kids. It's just too much." Driving home that night, I was surprised to find myself thinking about him.

Two months later I saw John again when I was out with Shane and Ginny at a private party in downtown Minneapolis. John immediately came up to me and asked, "What are you doing here?" "Shane invited me," I said. He replied, "Are you two dating?" I laughed and told him we were just good friends. At that point he asked for my number, and I wrote it on a napkin and gave to him. I told John to have a nice evening, and that I needed to get back to my friends. John seemed a little surprised at my remark. Later Shane asked about my conversation with John and seemed jealous. I felt uncomfortable; I didn't want to hurt Shane's feelings, but truthfully, I was attracted to John.

Two days later, John called to see if I would like to go for a walk around Lake Harriet and have dinner after. I was really excited and couldn't wait to see him. It was five thirty and the weather was beautiful. Lake Harriet was busy, filled with people biking, rollerblading, and walking around the picturesque area.

John and I walked for over an hour. It was the perfect time to talk and get to know each other. I couldn't believe how much fun I was having. Later we went to an Italian restaurant for dinner and continued to laugh and talk for hours.

John had been in the music business and was now running a marketing company. He had been divorced for several years and had two boys. Ben, his oldest, was in his first year of college at Boston University, and Matthew went to Edina High School. I had no idea John was older than me because he looked so young and athletic. I told John that I was separated and going through a divorce, and that I had three young children. He seemed empathetic and said, "A divorce is hard to go through, especially with children involved." He told me, "It's all about the babies."

I had a wonderful time with John. At the end of the evening, we kissed and I went home. The next morning, my mother asked me if I had a good time. I said, "I had a fantastic date with John. He's a great guy. We'll see what happens."

In July, Susan's mother, Mary, flew from New Zealand to stay with us and visit with her daughter. Mary was polite and excited for her first trip to the United States. I gave Susan a whole week off to spend time sightseeing and shopping with her. I in turn spent all my time with the kids, taking them to the Minnesota Zoo and Camp Snoopy at the Mall of America. Before Mary left, she thanked me for giving her daughter such a wonderful opportunity, and I knew she felt confident that Susan was doing well and living happily, even after all the changes that had taken place.

Over the next few months, my relationship with John developed quickly. We got along wonderfully and had a lot in common. We liked to Rollerblade and run around the lakes together. On the weekends, we enjoyed going to the symphony or Broadway shows. Every moment we spent together brought us closer.

It had been fourteen months since I last had sex with Ron. The first time John and I made love I was extremely nervous. After passionately kissing for weeks and controlling our excitement, John took my hand and led me to his bedroom. He unbuttoned my blouse; I couldn't control myself and proceeded to rip off his shirt. "Hold on," he said. "You're so beautiful; I want to look at you." So John took off my clothes piece by piece. Each time he touched my skin it made me quiver. I loosened his pants and he placed me on the bed, saying, "I can't wait to be inside you." After my third orgasm I could hardly breathe. John and I lay holding each other, my body still trembling. It was the best sex I had ever experienced. John asked me to stay the night and although I wanted to, I had to be home for the children. I went home, and John was all I could think about for days.

Chapter 17

It was the end of the month in August, and Ron drove up with Ben and Helen. I didn't have the children ready, so Ron came to the front door. I had tried to distance myself from him because I wanted him to know it was over. He knocked on the door and then barged into the house. I told him to please wait outside. He responded, "I need to talk to you."

"Give me a minute," I said. "Susan and I will meet you outside when the children are ready." When we got out there, I helped Helen buckle them into their car seats and kissed each one good-bye.

I turned to Ron and said, "What do you want?"

He grabbed my arm. "I'm miserable without you! Please come back! I can't work. I can't sleep. If you come back, I promise everything will change. I love you so much. Don't you still love me?"

"Ron, please, not in front of Ronnie. You know I care for you, but I can't change what's happened."

He replied, "Do you need anything, Heather? Money for you or the kids?" He whipped out a huge pile of cash.

"No thank you," I said. "I don't want your money."

He then put his hands on my shoulders, begging, "Please have dinner with me tonight, so we can talk."

My heart was broken. I looked back; everyone was watching from inside the van. "I'll think about it, Ron, and let you know." I left and went back inside the house.

I was an emotional wreck. I felt sorry for Ron and didn't know what to do. I hopped in the car and drove to the gym to meet my dad at our biweekly step aerobics class. After it was over, we talked about the situation, and I knew what I was going to do. When Ron dropped off the kids that night, I told him I would meet him at the Palomino restaurant at eight o'clock and gave him directions.

When I arrived, Ron was well-dressed and looked handsome. He told me I looked beautiful. "Hold on," I said. "This isn't a date. We're just here to talk." We shared an appetizer and ordered our meal. Ron, of course, was charming and on his best behavior. He tried to convince me to come back to him and wanted me to fly to Hawaii with him for a Southeast Toyota dealer trip.

"The trip sounds lovely, but I just can't go with you," I replied. I explained that we had to go on with our lives. I would always care for him, but it was over.

"Who would ever want you?" he said. "You're a single woman with three little kids." Ron seemed desperate to change my mind but I held my ground. We finished our dinner cordially but Ron was not happy. He was used to getting what he wanted.

The next two days, Ron picked up the kids as planned. I had Susan bring them out to avoid further conflict. John called and we made plans to go boating on Lake Minnetonka with his brother Andy and a friend. Andy was one of John's four brothers. When I first met him, he seemed friendly, intelligent, and arrogant. He was curious about me and asked me many questions. Andy lived on Lake of the Isles and was recently divorced with two children, Noah and Eileen. I had a relaxing time boating and really needed to laugh and have fun. Afterward, John and I went to the band shell at Lake Harriet, where we sat on a blanket and listened to classical music. We ordered a pizza and had wine. It was a perfect day.

Chapter 18

In August, I signed up the kids for Montessori preschool in Anoka, just ten miles from my parents' home. School started in September, after Labor Day. Ronnie was excited to meet the other children in the class, and the twins followed happily along. It was a half-day program, from 8:45 until noon. I would drop off the kids, go to the gym, shower, and go grocery shopping or run errands. Then I would head back to pick them up.

The mornings flew by, and after school I made the kids lunch and put them down for their naps. When they woke up, it was playtime, and soon after I would prepare dinner for everyone. I did most of the cooking; I enjoyed it and it allowed my parents to relax after work. After dinner I fulfilled my motherly duties. Although John wanted to see me nightly, my children were my top priority. I would only see him on the weekends, unless something special came up.

That fall, I took the children to pick out winter coats. Ronnie wanted a Green Bay Packers jacket. Joseph picked out the Minnesota Vikings, and Lauren chose a girlie one with a cute pattern.

In November, Ron showed up for his visitation and came only with Ben. I was surprised that Helen did not make the trip. I asked Ben if she was okay and he said yes. Helen had always had a special place in her heart for Ronnie when he was growing up in Pensacola. Ronnie would call them "Papa Ben" and "Granny Helen."

On the last day of the visitation I was absolutely livid. When the children returned Ronnie had on a new navy-blue winter jacket. Lauren had on a rabbit fur coat, and Joe wore a used hand-me-down jacket. I asked Ronnie, "What happened to the jackets I bought you?"

He said, "Daddy threw them away."

"He did what? Why does Joe have a used jacket and you and Lauren have new ones?"

Ronnie replied, "I think Daddy said that Joe looks too much like you to have a new one."

I controlled my temper but was pissed off that Ron would do this. Ronnie and Lauren went back to the porch and were acting withdrawn and pouty. Lauren seemed almost mad. Joe, however, was acting like his usual self.

"Mom," I said. "Something is wrong. Could you come back to the porch with me?" We both talked to the kids to see if they were okay. It took about an hour to calm them down and bring them back to normal. I felt so bad, I wanted to cry.

My mom said, "See, honey, they're okay now."

We sat down to dinner and I could hardly eat. I kept thinking about Ron emotionally messing with the kids during their visitation and couldn't understand why he would do this. A couple weeks later, I went out and bought the same jackets the kids had picked out and let them wear them while they were with me. During visitation I sent them in the jackets Ron had bought.

I was still seeing John on the weekends. It didn't matter whether we were going out to dinner and dancing, or just sitting around his house, we always had an amazing time together. However, my main focus was my children. I met John's oldest brother, Richard, when John invited my mother and me to a reading in downtown Minneapolis. Richard had just written his first novel, *The Alphabet Man*, a book about purgatory. There were many people there, including some of John's family members. After the reading, John introduced us to Richard and I said hello to Andy. My mother and I then left, because John had plans with his brothers. I had been seeing John for several months, but I hadn't told him much about Ron. Ron was still obsessed with me and I was scared to tell John the extent of his harassment, because our relationship was still new and casual.

December was a hectic month. I had to negotiate divorce issues with Mr. Myrick and it was exhausting and upsetting. Ron would not stop trying to cause problems. He kept postponing the divorce from going through. My girlfriend Terry came into town again. I picked her up at her parents' house to watch the Bulls game and have dinner at the Mall of America.

We started off talking about the drama with Ron, and then I told her about meeting John. Soon after I called John and asked him to meet us. The three of us spent the night talking and laughing at the restaurant. Then we walked over to a country western bar, where we line danced for two hours. On the way home, Terry said she liked John and I was happy because I knew she had my best interests at heart. I could always tell she didn't care for Ron.

That same week, Ronnie and the twins had a Christmas program at their preschool. It was cute to see their class sing. My mom invited the whole family over for Christmas again that year. The kids had fun seeing their cousins and opening their gifts. In the morning, we woke up and the kids opened their presents from Santa and then we got ready for church. I was dreading Ron coming into town for his Christmas visitation that was scheduled for four days. After the last episode with the coats, I was worried about the kids and if they were going to be okay with him.

John asked me to dinner. I was excited because I hadn't seen him for two and a half weeks. I waited for Ron to bring the children home from his visit and then drove to John's. We went to dinner at Ruth's Chris steakhouse, and were having a great time catching up. After our main course, we ordered cappuccinos and a crème brûlée to share. Then, my jaw dropped and I felt sick to my stomach. Walking toward our table was Ron. I immediately turned to John and said, "Ron is here."

"What?" he replied, and before I could open my mouth, Ron interrupted.

"So you're the person my wife has been seeing."

"Ron," I said, "What are you doing here?"

"Oh, just having dinner."

I turned to John and excused myself. I took Ron by the arm and walked him over to the bar with embarrassment. I knew Ron's temper and I did not want him to cause a scene in the restaurant. He told me that he had been having me followed and asked me how long I'd been seeing this man. He said, "Do you know he is breaking up our family?"

I told him, "Ron, I'm just dating him, and I don't want to discuss this here. What do you think you're doing? Could you please leave?"

He said, "I need to talk to you and I don't want to leave."

I told him I was going to call the police if he didn't. I turned around and walked back to the table. Ron stayed for about fifteen minutes and then left. I was apologetic to John and embarrassed that Ron was even there. John was visibly disturbed. "I can't believe him," he said.

The drive home was quiet. I thought to myself, "I can't believe that just happened." By the time we got back and were seated in John's living room, I decided that it was time to tell John what I was really going through with Ron. I explained that I was unhappy in my marriage, that Ron had been both physically and verbally abusive to me. I told John that Ron wanted to get back together and was trying to delay the divorce process. I assured John that it was over and that Ron and I would never get back together.

I said, "I didn't bring this up before because we were just getting to know each other." We talked for hours. John was understanding and supportive. He eased my mind and asked if there was anything he could do. I told him, "No, I just want to get divorced."

He pulled me close and kissed me. John said, "Please stay tonight."

"I would love to, but I can't," I answered. I left John's house at three o'clock in the morning and was emotionally exhausted driving home.

I woke up at six to get the kids ready for preschool and when I returned home I told my mother about the stunt Ron had tried to pull. She could not believe it and was worried that Ron might be watching my every move. "He's stalking you," she said.

"I don't want to leave our driveway," I said. "I'm always looking behind me and worrying that somebody is watching me. It gives me the creeps! What if Ron doesn't ever stop?" My mother told me to stop worrying, that hopefully everything would change after the divorce.

John had season tickets to the Timberwolves and invited my parents to the Target Center to join us for a game. I was glad he wanted to meet my parents because I wanted their opinion of him. The Timberwolves played the Clippers that evening, and our seats were in the fourteenth row, dead center. I love basketball and even though we lost the game, it was enjoyable. Afterward, we walked to an Italian restaurant across the street.

My father and John hit it off right away. They had a lot in common and talked about business, politics, and tennis all night long. I was happy because my father is a hard person to impress. I kissed my parents good-bye and told them I would be home later.

We entered John's car and kissed passionately. As he drove us back to his house he told me, "You have great parents, and I had an excellent time tonight."

Our passionate kisses continued when we entered his house, but I pulled back a bit. He said, "Don't worry Matt is spending the night at a friend's house. We're alone." Instantly we locked lips and progressed up the staircase, stopping only to remove pieces of each other's clothing.

Together we had the best orgasm of my life. Gasping, I snuggled up against John. He wrapped his arms around me and I started to shed tears because I had never experienced this type of emotional connection before.

John asked, "Are you okay?" I explained that he was an amazing lover and I was overwhelmed thinking of what I had missed by being with Ron. I also shared with him my increasing fear of the upcoming trial with Ron—a trial that was only weeks away.

Chapter 19

It was late February of 1994 when my parents, Susan, the children, and I boarded the plane for Pensacola. I brought Ronnie, Joe, and Lauren along so they could stay with their father during our divorce proceedings.

When I saw Ron at the airport he looked tired and had gained several pounds. He was irritable and wanted to start arguing in front of the kids, but I ignored him. I was worried about leaving the children with him because he was incapable of taking care of them by himself. I hoped Helen would come over to the house to help him out.

My parents and I kissed the kids good-bye and I told them, "I love you and I'll see you real soon." I was nervous to let them go. Would he be able to take care of them? Would he be good to them?

We checked into the Hilton, and then met with my lawyer, Mr. Myrick, to go over our testimonies and prepare for court. Mr. Myrick terrified me when he told me he was receiving death threats. They were not directly from Ron but from associates of his. He said he was trying to trace where they were coming from.

Then came the bombshell. He told me that sometime during our separation, Ron got a court reporter pregnant with twins. If that wasn't bad enough, he told me Ron had started a relationship with Debbie Love, his lawyer's paralegal. "I'm trying to subpoena her for court, but apparently she's in hiding and we can't find her."

I looked at him and said, "Why didn't you tell me any of this sooner?"

"I didn't want to worry you, and I felt bad."

"You felt bad? Come on, you have no idea what I've been going through." I had felt sorry for Ron, with all his crying and begging—and there he was with another woman, with twins on the way!

The next morning we went downstairs and had an early breakfast at the hotel. I hardly ate anything because I was so nervous and upset. Dad drove us to the courthouse in Milton.

Judge Rasmussen started the proceedings. My mother testified first, while Susan and my father waited in a room adjacent to the courtroom. They questioned my father next and then after lunch Susan was called to testify. The day was long and exhausting and on the way home we stopped for dinner. When we returned to the room the phone rang and my mom answered it. The caller said, "Ron is going to kill Heather. They are liars, and you can't let them win."

I was terrified and immediately called Mr. Myrick and told him what happened. My attorney was worried for my safety. However, he didn't advise me on what I should do. I called John and told him about our day and the strange call we received.

John was concerned. "You should call the police," he said. But I never did. I was afraid people would think I was blowing things out of proportion. Possibly Ron just wanted to scare us.

The next day I was disgusted by the testimony of people I had thought were my friends. Ted Ciano, John Hall, Betty Bancroft, and Ronnie Jones said bad things about me to make Ron look like the victim. While on the stand, Ron put on a big show for the judge and whined and cried about my leaving him. In the end, however, nobody could say that I was not a good wife and mother.

Judge Rasmussen awarded Ron and I joint custody. I kept physical custody, meaning the children would live with me. I was happy with the outcome, but Ron was so angry I'm surprised he contained himself in the courtroom.

Ron met us at the airport and I was relieved to see the kids with big smiles on their faces. It was nice to go home and even though I was exhausted, I felt relieved that it was all over. I was thrilled at the possibility of getting on with my life.

      The next day John and I went to a Timberwolves game. I was excited to see him. It had been weeks since our last sexual encounter and I found myself yearning for more. John held me in his arms and said, "I missed you terribly while you were gone. I'm happy your divorce is over and that everything went well." That night was the first time I stayed at John's house. We talked intimately about many things, and then made love. He held me all night long and I felt the safest I had in a very long time.

      I drove to John's because we were going out dancing. To my surprise, he had planned a birthday party at Rupert's, a restaurant with dancing and live music. My mom and dad, close friends, and John's two brothers, Andy and Joe, were there. Joe lived in New Zealand with his wife, Jeanine, and their two children. He was in town visiting for a couple of weeks.

      Joe was funny and laid back. I really enjoyed meeting him. After we ate, John and I danced the night away with everyone. It was the perfect birthday party and I had a really good time. Just being around my friends and John made me feel content, something I hadn't felt in a long time.

Chapter 20

Only two months after my divorce, there was a knock at my front door. When I opened it, I was served papers by a process server. My jaw dropped. Ron was filing for full custody of the children.

My dad, enraged, took his hunting rifle and ran down the driveway after him. He didn't do anything, but he too was fed up. I could not believe this was happening. I knew Ron would always be in my life because he was the father of my children. But he never spent quality time with them and was incapable of taking care of them. I felt like he wanted to hurt me all over again. I put on my tennis shoes, ran out the door, and kept running with tears pouring down my face. Was he ever going to leave me alone?

I had to tell John what Ron was up to now. He was supportive and asked me if there was anything he could do. He said, "You know I love you! Please let me help."

I was shocked when he said those words, but I said, "I love you, too." That's when I decided to ask John if he'd like to meet Ronnie, Lauren, and Joe. I had been seeing him for over a year and was confident it was an appropriate time.

My mother and father grilled steaks that weekend and I invited John over for dinner to meet the kids. The weather was perfect and the kids played outside on the swing set.

John was good with them and they warmed up to him quickly. Over time, John began asking to take the kids with us and planning fun things for us to do together. That was something Ron had never been interested in when the kids were younger.

I enjoyed meeting Matt, John's younger son. He was in high school, and during the week John and I would go to his baseball games. Matt was the sweetest kid and was always respectful to me. I met Ben when he came home for summer break. He went to Boston University and was interning that summer at a local television station. I was impressed with how smart and driven he was. He had a great personality and we hit it off right away. Ben was always concerned with his father's happiness. When he saw us together, he was delighted to see his father in love.

After considering my options regarding the custody papers, John's lawyers in Minneapolis found an established lawyer in Pensacola, Florida, named Laura Keene. After reading over all the documentation, Mrs. Keene did not seem concerned. I told her I was alarmed. Then I went on to explain Ron Samuels and the lengths to which he went to be vindictive. I said, "You don't understand. This is not about the children; he is doing this to hurt me." Mrs. Keene assured me that I was in good hands and she would get back to me soon.

In August, John invited me to go to Dick's fiftieth birthday party in Los Angeles. It was a black-tie event and Ben and Matt were coming too. I made sure my parents were okay with helping Susan care for the kids and started to pack.

When we arrived in LA, we stayed at the Beverly Wilshire Hotel off Rodeo Drive. It seemed that every Grossman was staying at that hotel and I would soon be meeting the rest of the family. That night we drove up to Sunset Boulevard and had Chinese food with the boys and took them to the Comedy Store. On the way back we stopped at a local convenience store so that Ben and Matt could stock up on chips, sodas, and snacks for the room.

The next morning I called my mom to check on the kids. I was upset to learn Ronnie had come down with chicken pox and my mom thought Joe and Lauren might be getting them too. My mom said she had everything under control, but I still felt awful that I wasn't there. We woke up Matt and Ben and went for breakfast at a deli on Rodeo Drive.

Afterward, we drove to Dick and Lisa's house, and we all rented bikes and rode along Venice Beach for a couple hours. Later the kids hung out together, and we sat by the pool with Dick, Lisa, and Andy while they reminisced about growing up and life changes. I was glad to learn about their family values, and glad the trip was bringing us closer.

The next afternoon, I called and checked on the kids, and started to get dressed for the evening. When I heard John enter the hotel room, I turned around and melted. He looked amazing in his black tux. I guess I've always liked a well-dressed man.

Dick's birthday party was held at a private club, where at least a hundred of his friends and family members celebrated the night with fine dining, a live band, and dancing all night long. I met John's father, Bud, for the first time and also his second wife, Beverly. Mr. Grossman was very cordial to me and Beverly was simply beautiful, like an older version of Grace Kelly.

John and I had a marvelous time, and when we returned to the hotel, we talked openly about his family dynamics. He told me about his mother, Alene, dying of leukemia at the age of sixty-six, and how he loved and missed her so much. We discussed his father, Bud, a proud Jewish businessman who built a Fortune 500 car-leasing company with his brother, Harold. John then went on to tell me about his father owning the Minnesota Vikings football team. I was astonished because John was always so private about details of his family. He explained that after being single for several years his father had married Beverly and was happy. I was pleased he was confiding in me. We made passionate love for hours and fell asleep in each other's arms.

I was excited to see my children when John dropped me at the house. They were over the chicken pox and greeted me with big smiles. I picked each of them up for a big hug. Joseph had peanut butter all over his face, but I didn't care.

That night I made popcorn, and we sat together and watched *The Lion King*.

Chapter 21

Per our visitation schedule, I had to fly the children to Ron for Thanksgiving. It was hard for me to face him after he had filed for custody, so my sister, Tiffany, volunteered to accompany Ronnie, Lauren, and Joe on the plane ride.

When they arrived in Pensacola, Ron was with a brunette standing at the gate. My sister was surprised to see him with a woman. Tiffany watched as the children ran to their dad. She proceeded to take her flight back and I picked her up at the airport. I told her, "Thank you for taking them. Was everything okay?" She said, "I felt uneasy leaving them with Ron and that woman. It was disgusting." I later found out that it was Debbie, the paralegal from his attorney's office.

John and his boys invited me to Thanksgiving dinner at Bud and Beverly's residence on Lake Minnetonka. Their home was decorated impeccably, and displayed artwork of Beverly's face painted by Andy Warhol. Beverly greeted me with a hug and graciously introduced John and me to her two sisters. I then met John's brother Tom and his wife, Pat, who were there with their two children.

Tom owned and operated all of the Grossman car dealerships. I could tell right away that there was tension between John and Tom. He had a pompous air about him, which stunned me because his wife was down-to-earth and personable.

Andy brought his new girlfriend, Lynn, whom I had met over the summer and liked. When everybody sat down to eat, a Lutheran minister appeared and blessed the meal and said a prayer. Andy and John looked at each other, astonished. Then they started to complain, "Doesn't she know we're Jewish?"

When dessert was finished, we said our good-byes and headed to the movies with Matt and Ben. Driving in the car, I thought to myself, "That was a bit over the top!" but I enjoyed myself.

I was excited for the holiday season. Christmas music, decorating the tree, and baking always put me in a happy mood. This year, John and I took Ronnie, Lauren, and Joe to downtown Minneapolis for the big Christmas parade. Dad and Mom met us at Dayton's department store for dinner and we watched the festivities together. The next weekend we planned to take the children sledding. Everyone was getting along well.

Unfortunately, problems always seemed to arise. Ron had not sent my child support payment, and it was already December 8. I called Ron and did not receive a response, so I was forced to call my attorney. Ron knew I needed to buy Christmas presents for the kids. I was at his mercy again—it was one of his ways of trying to control me. I never received any money that month. But I refused to let it upset me. I kept moving forward with our holiday plans.

On Christmas Eve, Mom and Dad threw their usual dinner party for our family and friends. John came and I introduced him to everyone. The children were excited to see him. Uncle Ken was Santa again and gave the little ones their gifts. I thought it was nice that John brought gifts for Ronnie, Lauren, and Joe. Everyone had an enjoyable evening and my relatives were impressed with John.

On Christmas morning I prepared chocolate chip pancakes, sausage, and eggs for my family; then my mother and I took the children to mass. When we returned home the kids wanted to play with their new toys. John celebrated Hanukkah, so on Christmas day he took Ben and Matt to the movies and dinner.

John and I had planned to meet that evening to exchange gifts. When I arrived he had candles burning throughout the entire living room, and my favorite song by Natalie Cole, "Unforgettable with Love," was playing. The setting was very romantic. We exchanged our gifts. John had ten gifts for me, and I was a little embarrassed—I had only two for him. John said, "Would you like to dance?"

"Of course," I said. "I love this song." We danced for the next hour. We kissed goodnight and, while driving home, I thought perhaps this was my second chance at happiness.

The following week John introduced me to Rick and Cathy Plessner. Rick was a close friend and associate. We had dinner at Champs Sports Bar; the guys talked about US Direct, the marketing company John owned, while I got to know Cathy. It was obvious that John valued Rick's opinion by the questions he was asking. They were talking about relocating John's company to a warmer climate.

Even though I kept chatting with Cathy, I was able to hear what they were talking about. Of course, I added my opinion and said, "California is nice, but Florida is amazing." I had no idea that John was even thinking about a change. John explained that he was tired of the winters and had always planned on moving after Matthew graduated. I was surprised; he had never mentioned this to me.

After we finished our meal, we walked to the Target Center to watch a Timberwolves game. I enjoyed meeting Rick and Cathy and we made plans to have dinner at their house in St. Paul next time. John and I chatted lightly about him moving. "Don't worry," he said, "You will always be in my future if you want to be."

Ron continued to withhold child support from our kids for several months, but Mrs. Keene assured me this would not go over well with Judge Rasmussen. His lawyer flew in from Florida to depose the children's Montessori preschool teachers for the child custody case. I was embarrassed that this was even happening. Carol and Teresa were highly respected teachers in Anoka, Minnesota, and did not know any personal information about my divorce. They had never met Ron Samuels.

John, being supportive, traveled to Pensacola with me for my custody hearing. We stayed at the Hilton hotel, despite the disturbing phone call I received the last time I stayed there. We met my attorney for the first time in person at her office. I was impressed with her. She was bright and confident. After speaking to her, I knew I had somebody who would fight with conviction for my children and me.

The next day, John dropped me off at the courthouse to meet Laura. He didn't come in because of Ron's unpredictable behavior—he didn't want there to be any conflict. During court, both sides produced their evidence.

Judge Rasmussen did not take custody away from me. We were to continue joint custody and Ron was to pay all of the back child support in one lump sum within seven days or he would be in contempt of court. The judge was not happy with him and said, "If you cared about your children, you would be paying your child support." Ron was enraged and stormed out of the courtroom. I turned to Laura, hugged her, and said "thank you so much."

John was waiting outside the courthouse. I couldn't wait to tell him what had happened. He was ecstatic for me. That night we had dinner at Jubilee's on Pensacola Beach to celebrate. We were in such good spirits, believing Ron might go away finally, that John tipped the server a hundred dollars that evening.

The next morning we had breakfast by the airport and caught our flight. My mom and dad picked us up when we arrived, and I told them everything that had happened. They were overjoyed.

Chapter 22

    The next couple of months flew by quickly. I assisted John with planning Mathew's high school graduation party. I sent out invitations, picked up catered platters, and prepared specialty dishes that Matt requested. I had grown close to him and wanted everything to be perfect. The party was a success. Matt's friends were excited, loud, and hungry. I met John's ex-wife, Susan, and her husband, Doug Greenberg. They were polite and complimented me on arranging the joyous event. Everyone left the party saying they had a great time.

    In June, Ben came home from college. John and I decided to plan a trip to Cancun, Mexico, and took the boys. We stayed at the Ritz Carlton right on the beach. Ben and Matt could not wait to put on their swimsuits and head to the ocean. John and I had cocktails and read our books by the pool. The ocean view was breathtaking and inviting. After a while, the boys came over to horse around in the pool, throwing each other around and doing cannon-balls into the water.

    I found myself feeling upset. The book I was reading was Nicole Brown Simpson's *The Private Diary of a Life Interrupted*. I could hardly put it down. I turned to John and said, "This is scary. O. J. Simpson sounds just like Ron. There are things in this book that are identical to him." I wasn't sure that I wanted to finish the book.

    I made reservations at Bogart's, one of my favorite restaurants in Cancun. I thought Ben and Matt would get a kick out of the waiters wearing turbans and knew they would love the food. Everyone turned in early that night. Holding each other, I could feel the breeze and smell the salty air move through the room as we fell asleep talking. The next few days were busy, as we toured the Mayan Ruins in Tulum, shopped for gifts for the kids, sunbathed, swam, and danced at clubs at night.

One morning, when John woke up, he looked green and wasn't feeling well. The boys too, seemed to be affected by the water and had Montezuma's Revenge. John looked at me and asked, "Why are you laughing? Why aren't you sick?" I replied, "I guess I have an iron stomach. I've eaten all around the world and never been sick like this!" So that day, I escaped to the pool. I had dinner downstairs alone that night. I ordered soup up to the room for the guys and listened to them moan and complain. I felt sorry for John, and I stayed up and took care of him all night.

The three of them were well again by the next day. We all agreed that we were tired of sunbathing and decided to explore the local market. I was shocked to see the guys dive into street tacos after their horrible sickness. Since it was our last night there, John and I dressed up and went to Señor Frogs with the boys to see a live band and dance. When the trip was over, my relationship with Ben and Matt was stronger than ever and John said to me, "Everyday I'm with you, I love you more and more." His words made me feel overjoyed and hopeful for a future together.

I was happy to be home and the children jumped up and down as I walked through the door. I immediately kissed all of them and after unpacking gave them their gifts. They were out of school for the summer, so Susan and I brought them to Bunker Beach Water Park, a place Tiffany and I had enjoyed when we were younger. They enjoyed splashing and playing for hours. We all feasted on hot dogs and popcorn and the kids finished with snow cones. As I wiped blue and red syrup from their giggling faces, I thought how much gratification I got from being their mother. That night Grandpa grilled his famous steaks while the kids played in the yard.

Unfortunately, my time with the children that summer was limited, as I had to fly the kids to Pensacola for summer visitation with Ron. They would be there until the end of August, and I dreaded every moment they would be away. When we arrived at the airport, Ron was waiting with Ben and Helen. I was shocked when I saw Ron: he had gained around a hundred pounds and looked terrible. I kissed and hugged my kids and sadly said good-bye.

John was adamant about moving, so we discussed our options between California and Florida. I was delighted we were planning a life together. Both states were equally attractive places to live, but the deciding factor was the children's visitation schedule. John quickly booked our tickets the following week for Florida. We stayed at the Boca Raton Resort on the beach. Greeted with champagne and fresh strawberries, we were escorted to our beautiful room with a balcony overlooking the ocean.

Sitting on the balcony, I was relaxed and content. John stated, "We're perfect together. I love you and want to marry you. So, why don't you and the kids move in with me?"

I told John that I loved him too, but I didn't think it was the right time because he needed to relocate his businesses and figure out where he was moving. He said, "I want you involved in all these decisions. Please think about it, because I want to spend every day with you." I wanted to say yes, but I was afraid of Ron's reaction and knew this was a big commitment. I could tell John was disappointed, but I assured him that when the time was right we would be together.

We decided to go out to dinner, so I called the concierge and he recommended Maxwell's Chophouse right down the road from our resort. Maxwell's was packed with local patrons and vacationing guests. There was a wait so John suggested we go to the bar and have a cocktail. John asked the piano player to play "The Nearness of You," and we danced together for the next hour. Whenever we were together, each moment was precious.

The next morning John and I drove around West Palm Beach, Boca Raton, and the surrounding areas looking for prospective places to live. Later that afternoon, John had scheduled an appointment with a commercial realtor, Jerry Lehman, to look at several office locations.

When I returned to the room, I immediately called my mom to see how everything was going. I was excited to tell her how much I loved being with John and how much I enjoyed South Florida. My mother was genuinely happy for me. She said, "All I want for you is to live in peace and to find love again. After all you've been through with Ron, you deserve that and so do the children." I was glad to have her support. At twenty-eight years old, I was opening my heart again to true love and happiness.

During dinner that night, John was excited to tell me about the office properties he saw during the day. He was confident that Boca would be a great place to relocate his businesses. His enthusiasm thrilled me; each day our lives were coming closer together.

We relaxed and slept until noon the following day. I wanted to take John to South Beach in Miami to my favorite Cuban restaurant, Lario's on the beach. We unwound while drinking mojitos and watching the people. John said, "We'll have to come back here when we move."

When we returned to the hotel, we changed clothes and took a walk on the beach. As the sun went down we were holding hands. John stopped to face me and said, "We should look at homes together tomorrow. I love you and I don't want to wait to be together." He pulled me close to him and we kissed. I didn't hesitate this time. I told him, "I love you and want to be with you, too."

John smiled at me and said, "Then it's settled. We'll go look at homes tomorrow." I felt delighted as we walked to the room. We celebrated that evening, making love, drinking champagne, and holding each other.

We were up early the next morning and John called Jerry Lehman and asked him if he could recommend a good realtor to show us houses. Jerry contacted Candy, an associate in his office, and she called us immediately. John told her we were looking for a five-bedroom home in a gated community, in a good school district for the children, with a price range of $1–$1.5 million.

Candy drove us to see various properties. After viewing six homes she took us to Wood Bridge Country Club. We pulled up to a new model home. In the front was a beautiful courtyard, impeccably landscaped, with bromeliads, bougainvillea, and flowers. John stated, "I'm impressed!" He grabbed my hand and said, "Let's check out the inside."

We walked into the main entrance and saw vaulted ceilings, marble floors, massive windows that overlooked the pool, and a hot tub in the backyard. The master bedroom was immaculate with a large sitting area, a fireplace, and walk-in closets. John was quiet but I could tell he was looking at every detail in the room. We followed Candy into the kitchen. It was spacious and seemed as if it were designed just for me. The home office walls were covered with dark oak shelves and cabinets, ideal for John to work in.

I turned to Candy and said, "Could we see the other bedrooms?" Just as I expected, the three rooms were perfect for Ronnie, Lauren, and Joe.

We walked down the staircase and Candy asked, "Do you like it?" John and I looked at each other and we both knew this was the one. John immediately responded, "Yes we love it!" and I said, "It is absolutely perfect for us!"

We met with the builder that same day, picked out a lot, and signed a contract for purchase. The architect assisted us in customizing our floor plan and increasing the size by 2,000 sq. ft. John was determined to have everything done before we flew back home.

Candy interrupted the meeting and said, "Hold on. We're going to have to find you a rental property while your house is being built. Should I start looking immediately?" With all the excitement we hadn't even thought about that. I told her to get on it right away. John and I thanked her, and Candy said, "No, thank you! This is the fastest sale I've ever made."

Candy found us a nice rental in New Port Bay Club in Boca Raton. It was a gated community with lots of families and kids. Flying home we talked enthusiastically about plans for our house. John was the happiest I had ever seen him. Everything was coming together for us, and I felt blessed to have him in my life.

I was excited to tell my parents our plans. Over dinner we showed them the blueprints for our house and talked about how nice Boca Raton is. They were happy and felt it was a positive move for all of us. I was glad when I heard their response because I knew they would miss Ronnie, Lauren, and Joe terribly. We also told Bud, Beverly, and John's two boys our news. They were all pleased and supportive of our decision.

John put his house in Edina up for sale. The first couple who viewed the home purchased it. The house was only on the market for four days.

John called me and said, "I'm going to have to fly to Florida to set up the business, so that everything is ready for the move. Could you please call moving companies for us while I'm out of town?" I said of course. I was under a lot of pressure, because everything was happening so quickly. I dreaded calling Ron to tell him about our plans. I knew he would flip out when I told him that the kids and I were going to live with John.

Later that evening I made my weekly call to the kids. Ron answered and passed the phone to them. I talked to Lauren and Joe first, and they were doing well. When I talked to Ronnie, he was upset and said he missed me and wanted to come home. I comforted him by saying, "It will be okay. You'll see Mommy soon!" Once Ronnie felt better, I asked him if I could speak to Daddy.

"Yes, Heather," Ron said. "What do you want?"

"I'm concerned about Ronnie. Has he been okay?"

"I was going to call you," Ron said. "He misses you all the time and cries to see you. I want to send him home early. Is that okay?"

"Yes, that's fine.," I said. "However, I need to talk to you about something else. John and I are moving to Boca Raton in August. We've decided we want to start our life together."

"Are you crazy?" Ron yelled. "You bitch! My wife and kids—moving in with him!"

"Stop screaming. In the first place, I am not your wife. And we thought being in Florida would make it easier for visitation. We could have moved to California."

Ron said, "I don't care. I don't want you to do this."

"I want to start my life over," I told Ron calmly. "Why can't we all just try to get along for the benefit of our children?" There was a long pause on his end of the phone.

I asked, "Are you there, Ron?"

Ron finally said, "I'll call you with Ronnie's flight information" and hung up. I was trembling after the call was over. It stayed on my mind for hours.

Three days later Ron called and gave me Ronnie's flight information, saying he would fly Ronnie back on Monday. He was composed as he added, "I'll fly Lauren and Joe to Fort Lauderdale at the end of our visitation. My girlfriend, Debbie, will be bringing them." I said, "That is fine. Thank you, Ron." But I wondered to myself why he couldn't accompany his children.

Chapter 23

The next three weeks were hectic, as I organized the move and tied up loose ends. Ronnie was especially happy to be home with us and enjoyed playing with his cousins. Our families and friends wanted to see us before we left for Florida, so each day was spent with different people, saying our goodbyes.

When we arrived in Boca Raton, it was sunny with a light breeze. We checked in at the hotel, and the next morning, met the movers to unload and place our belongings. Ronnie was eager to explore each room of the house and choose his bedroom. While I began organizing the kitchen, John arranged his office. By seven o'clock that night, the truck was empty and both of us were exhausted.

John started working immediately. He and his staff were busy interviewing potential employees and meeting with new clients. I had the big job of unpacking our things and caring for Ronnie. After two weeks everything was in place and it finally felt like home. I took Ronnie to enroll him in kindergarten at Calusa Elementary School.

The month of August had passed quickly and it was time for me to pick up Lauren and Joe from the airport. As Ron had stated, Debbie Love accompanied the children off the plane. Lauren and Joe came running toward me with open arms. I kneeled down, wrapped my arms around them, and said, "I missed you so much. I'm glad you're home."

I turned to Debbie, introduced myself, and said, "Thank you for coming with them."

"You're welcome," she responded in an unfriendly manner.

The first thing I noticed about Debbie was her strong Southern accent. She was about ten years older than me with short, dark-brown hair, and about five feet, five inches tall. Although she was well dressed, I could tell she was a simple woman.

When we arrived, Lauren and Joe were curious about their new home. After unpacking their clothes, I made them lunch. They were happy to see each other and they played together the rest of the afternoon.

John came home early from work, eager to see the kids. They, too, had been asking for him all day. John kissed me and asked, "How was your day?"

"Interesting!" I replied. "I'll have to tell you about it later."

At dinner it was obvious the twins had missed me, demanding my attention and wanting to be next to me. John kindly held Lauren so I could eat while Joe sat on my lap. I smiled at John, grateful for his interest in my children.

The kids were exhausted by the time we returned home, so I tucked them into their beds. John was relaxing on the sofa. I cuddled next to him and said, "I'm upset about Debbie Love's attitude toward me. I wonder if she's nice to the children. When I met her today, I was shocked at how unfriendly and cold she was."

John responded, "Well, you don't know what Ron has told her about you. Honey, don't worry. She's probably someone he's just dating." Talking to John gave me some relief.

The next day I was on a mission to find a good Montessori preschool for the twins. On a ninety-degree day, with 100 percent humidity, I took all three children to look at three schools. Get Ready, Set, Grow on Jog Road was our choice. Lauren and Joe really liked the teachers and I thought their program was exceptional. John met us for a quick lunch, and we then shopped for the kids' school clothes. John went crazy and we ended up leaving with eighteen bags. That evening we hung out in the backyard. John grilled burgers and we all played in the pool to stay cool.

A few months passed and everyone was settling in nicely. I hired a great nanny named Jasmine to care for the kids when John and I went out for the evening.

While waiting at the bus stop with Ronnie, I met Donna Nussbaum. Within weeks we became close friends. Donna was a cute, bubbly, slender blonde full of energy. John nicknamed her "Diamond Lil" because of her passion for jewelry. She had two children, Bret and Ashley, who were close in age to Ronnie, Lauren, and Joe. After school our kids played together almost every day. Donna's husband, Harvey, worked as a prominent divorce attorney in West Palm Beach County. He stood six feet tall with salt-and-pepper hair, wore glasses, and was intellectual. Donna and I were happy the guys had similar interests and formed a friendship. The four of us enjoyed each other's company and we all went out to dinner once a week.

The week of Thanksgiving, my parents came to visit. Ronnie, Lauren, and Joe were excited to see them. While John was at work, I took my parents sightseeing and showed them around town. We went to Del Ray Beach, and my mom and I lay in the sun while my dad played with the kids in the ocean. The kids laughed as they jumped in the waves. My mom said, "Heather, it's wonderful to be on the beach, instead of walking through slush and shoveling snow back home." I responded, "I'm so glad you're here." That night, our whole family met Donna, Harvey, and their kids for lobster on the beach.

On Thanksgiving Day, my mother helped me prepare our traditional holiday dishes, while John, Dad, and the kids lounged around the pool. When the table was set, we all joined together to say grace and share what we were most thankful for. At that moment, when I looked around at everyone I knew, I was thankful for having my family together and for our good health and happiness. After dinner, we went outside to watch Ronnie ride his bike for the first time without his training wheels. He was proud and smiled as everyone clapped and yelled, "Good job!" We all went to bed early that night, because my parents had to catch a seven thirty flight in the morning.

Ron came to Boca for his first visitation at the end of the month. I was stressed getting the children's things together for their three-day stay with him. I hoped the transition would go smoothly.

John came into the room and asked, "Are you okay? Do you want me to go with you?"

"Yes, please," I said. "I would feel so much better if you did."

We waited at the guard gate. Ron pulled up and we walked the children over to him. "Hi, I'm Ron," he said, shaking John's hand. "It's nice to meet you."

Ron turned to me and said, "I'll have the children back by six o'clock Sunday evening. Here's my cell phone number if you need to reach us."

"Thank you," I said. Then John and I kissed the kids good-bye. I sighed with relief as we walked away, pleasantly surprised things had gone so well.

On Friday night John and I met Jerry Lehman and his wife, Elizabeth, at Mezzanotte, a trendy new restaurant and bar. When we arrived, the place was packed. Jerry waved at us, John took my hand, and we made our way through the crowd. Over the surrounding music and chatter at the bar, Jerry introduced us to Elizabeth. Eventually the restaurant transformed into a dance floor, and I took hold of John's hand and said, "Let's go!" As we danced, I noticed Jerry and Elizabeth watching us from the table. I quickly ran over, grabbed them by their hands, and said, "Come on, guys, join us!"

We all danced for hours, and it was obvious that Jerry was enamored with Elizabeth. "You're amazing tonight," John said. I kissed him on the cheek and replied, "You are too." Driving home that evening, I was thrilled we were making friends—if our life was a puzzle, then another piece had just fallen into place.

Over the next two days John and I planted flowers in the yard and relaxed by the pool. On Sunday, Ron drove up with Debbie, and with Frank and Joan Butel. The kids jumped out of the car dressed in turquoise and orange Miami Dolphin gear. Frank was a well-known sports broadcaster in Minneapolis who now worked for the Miami Dolphins football team. Joan and Frank were also friends of mine and came over to greet me.

"It's good to see you," I said. "How are you doing?"

"We're doing well. We just became grandparents."

I congratulated them and introduced John.

All of a sudden I turned around and saw Ron on his knees, hugging Ronnie, Lauren, and Joe while weeping and telling them, "Daddy's going to miss you so much." Debbie had a camera and was taking pictures of the production.

I immediately left John and told the kids to say good-bye, because it was time for us to leave. I knew I had to get them out of there because Ron was upsetting them. The children were smothered in Ron's cologne and the smell made me nauseous. The moment we entered the house I put them in the bathtub and then dressed them in their pajamas.

John said, "Let's go to Baskin-Robbins for ice cream."

Ronnie yelled, "Ice cream party!" and we all hopped in the car.

I was up at six o'clock in the morning to get the kids organized for school and pack their lunches. I headed to the gym for a workout, and then went home to shower, change, and meet John. During lunch John told me we were invited to Christy and Jay Johnson's wedding in New Jersey.

"I know we just met them," he said. "But he's a great guy who handles my financial account, and I feel it's important for us to go."

"It sounds fun," I said. "Let me see if Donna can watch the children."

"Let's leave early and spend a couple of days in New York," John suggested. It sounded perfect. When I left John, I started to plan our trip.

Chapter 24

New York was wintry and chilly. We stayed in Manhattan at the Plaza Hotel. Our room overlooked snow-covered Central Park. During breakfast, John looked at me and said, "I want to take you to look at diamonds for a ring." I responded, "Really? Right now?" He held both of my hands, looked into my eyes, and said, "I'm crazy in love with you and can't wait to get married."

I kissed him and said, "I love you and can't wait to be your wife."

We took a taxi to the Diamond District. John and I walked around the busy area, talking to different venders, educating ourselves about the cut, color, quality, and carat weight of the stones. John smiled at me and said, "Which cut do you like?"

"I definitely think the emerald princess cut is my favorite." Then I asked him, "What do you like, honey?"

"Whatever makes you happy," he said. "I'm just trying to get an idea of what you like so I can surprise you."

I said, "You're so thoughtful and good to me."

The next day, John and I went ice skating at Rockefeller Center. To my surprise John was an excellent skater. As he glided around me, I asked him, "How did you get so good?" He replied, "I played hockey in high school!" Then he grabbed my waist and started twirling me around. We laughed and played like teenagers in love.

A few hours later, we were back at the hotel getting dressed for a night out on the town. Our evening started with dinner at Le Bernardin, a French seafood restaurant in midtown. Then we headed to the theater district to see the Broadway show *Chicago*. Afterward, John and I met up with his nephew Max, who lived in the city. Max suggested a nearby coffee lounge, which was the perfect place to relax and sip hot cappuccinos while taking in the New York scene. John and Max reminisced and talked. It was late driving back to the Plaza and, resting my head on John's shoulder, I said, "I really enjoyed the time we spent with Max."

Saturday morning we arranged for a driver to take us to Summit, New Jersey. We checked into the Holiday Inn and started getting ready for the wedding. The ceremony was held at a quaint Presbyterian church in the middle of town. Approximately 150 guests attended. At the reception, John and I joined the receiving line and congratulated Jay and Christy.

Although we did not know many people, Jay introduced us to their family and friends. During dinner several champagne toasts were made to the happy couple. John stood up, held his glass in the air, and said, "Congratulations, Jay and Christy! I hope you enjoy the rest of your celebration today and the rest of your lives together!"

When everyone was finished the band started playing music. The newlyweds danced to the first song and soon everyone joined them on the dance floor. John and I danced, shared a piece of cake, and said good-bye to everyone. The next morning we flew home and picked up the children from Donna and Harvey. We had really missed Ronnie, Lauren, and Joe, and wanted to spend the rest of Sunday with them.

Chapter 26

I was on cloud nine and happier than ever. It occurred to me that, strangely enough, I had not heard from Ron or received any child support in three months. I called Ron Samuels' Toyota and asked to speak to Ron. The receptionist informed me he no longer owned the dealership.

As my jaw dropped I said, "When did he sell it?"

She responded, "The sale went through in November."

I hung up in dismay and tried calling Ron's cell phone, but there was no answer. I immediately called my attorney, Laura Keene, and told her the information I had just found out. She too was in disbelief and asked, "Where do you think he is?"

I said, "I have no idea. The last time I was in contact with him, Ron had just married Debbie and they were leaving for their honeymoon in Belize."

"You're kidding me!" Laura said. "I'm going to make some calls and look into this." I thanked her and told her to let me know what she found out.

We were invited in April to Scottsdale, Arizona, to celebrate the birthdays of Bud, Harold, and Marian Grossman. Donna and Harvey were kind enough to watch the kids so we could attend. There were forty family members staying at the La Posada Resort. The first night Harold's wife, June, hosted a catered dinner. Their elegant home was on Camelback Mountain overlooking the downtown Phoenix lights. The next day John spent the day with Ben and Matt by the pool. Beverly picked me up at the hotel and the two of us went for manicures. Afterward, we met the girls for lunch and shopped for a while.

When I returned I put on my swimsuit and met John and the boys by the pool. I was excited to see Ben and Matt. I had missed them and wanted to find out how they were doing in college. By three o'clock the entire family had gathered around the pool to relax and enjoy the afternoon. Andy introduced me once again to his new fiancée, Lynn, a pretentious, petite redhead. Lynn asked, "Would you like to see my engagement ring?"

I said, "Sure!" She held out her hand wanting to compare our rings. I instantly sensed she did not care for me. Around five o'clock John and I went to our room to get ready for the evening.

Ben and Matt knocked on our door and spoke to their dad. The boys were upset. They had overheard Lynn making derogatory comments about me. John came into the room clearly irritated. He said, "Lynn made some insulting remarks and she is not going to get away with this. I'm going to talk to Andy now!" "You don't have to be my hero," I said. "Please let it go. I don't want it to ruin the weekend." He said, "Heather, I'll be back!" Andy had Lynn write a letter of apology to me the next day.

The party that night was at Mary Elaine's in the Phoenician Hotel. Everyone was dressed beautifully. I was excited to see John's reaction to the classy, sexy black Chanel dress I had purchased in New York. As I walked toward John, he said, "My fiancée is the most gorgeous woman in the room tonight! I am a lucky man!"

I replied, "Yes you are—and you better not forget it!"

Dinner was followed by a dedication to Bud, Harold, and Marian. Everyone raised their glasses, toasting them, and the celebration continued with music and dancing.

Sunday morning John and I awoke around eight o'clock and phoned the boys so they could pack and meet us downstairs. We checked out of the hotel and drove to Bud and Beverly's home in Gainey Village Country Club. Beverly had prepared a special brunch for all of Bud's family. The food was served under cabanas overlooking the golf course. Everyone sipped mimosas and chatted about how great it was to have the relatives together. When it was time to leave, John, the boys, and I thanked Bud and Beverly for the wonderful weekend and drove to the airport.

In June the children were out of school for the summer. Our lives had been peaceful for the past seven months. John and I were more in love than ever. We had settled in as a family and Ronnie, Lauren, and Joe were happy and carefree. My attorney and I had no idea where Ron was. The only thing she had found out was that Ron had sold his home in Gulf Breeze, Florida. Although I wasn't receiving any child support, I felt my peace of mind was more important.

John and I had already decided months ago to stop the construction of our home in Wood Bridge Country Club because the builder was so behind schedule. Our next endeavor would be to find a new home. I met with Candy to begin looking. Within two days we found a beautiful home in the Seasons Development, just five minutes from where we were living. The day before we moved I received a large box addressed to the kids. When they opened the box, it was filled with gifts from Ron and Debbie. I immediately looked at the label to see where it came from. There was no physical address: it said only "KY091378." After some research I found out the package came from the Grand Cayman Islands.

I called John right away and said, "Ron just sent a package to the kids and you won't believe where he is. He's in the Grand Cayman Islands."

"What would he be doing there?" John said.

"I have no idea."

"Well," John said, "at least we know where he is. You need to call Laura and tell her." After I hung up with him I placed a call to Laura.

The following week we had dinner in Fort Lauderdale with Donna and Harvey. When we returned home, the kids were in bed and Jan, our new babysitter, was sitting on the couch reading. I had hired Jan two months before. She was fifty-five years old, caring, and responsible. I paid Jan and asked, "How were the children tonight?"

She said, "Everyone was just fine. However, the security guard called from the front gate saying there was a man requesting to enter the community. He wanted to see you and John."

"Do you know who it was?" I asked.

Jan responded, "No the person wouldn't give his name." I thanked Jan and walked her to the door.

That night, lying next to John in bed, I said, "Who do you think came to the gate? It's very strange they didn't want to give their name."

"Oh, honey," John said. "It could have been anyone."

The next morning I was up early. I made blueberry pancakes and bacon for everyone. While John and I were reading the paper and having our coffee, the phone rang. It was Tom, the security guard at the gate. He said, "There is a man ranting and screaming, saying his name is Ron Samuels and he wants to see his children. Heather, he is causing a huge scene out here. What do you want me to do?"

I immediately told John what was going on. John said, "Tell him not to let him in; it's not his visitation time. We need to call Laura first thing Monday morning."

With my heart racing, I told Tom, "Please don't let him in."

"No problem!" Tom said. My anxiety was instantly heightened just hearing Ron was back in town. That Sunday we spent the day around the house, playing tennis, swimming in the pool, and watching movies.

I informed my attorney about Ron. Judge Rasmussen removed Ron's visitation due to him being in contempt of court. A hearing was set to find out where he had been for the past eight months. John and I went to Harvey Nussbaum's office a week later for our phone hearing. Laura Keene was present in Judge Rasmussen's chambers in Pensacola, Florida, when they placed the conference call. Ron was also on the line with his new attorney, Don Sasser.

The judge started the hearing by asking, "Ron, where have you been?"

Ron said, "My wife, Debbie, and I have moved to the Grand Cayman Islands. I have sold my dealership in Pensacola and I want to take the children to the Grand Caymans for visitation."

The judge replied, "You are not to take the children out of the United States. If you have passports for them you must turn them over to Ms. Stephens. Your visitation will be in Florida. You are in contempt of court for not paying child support. Why haven't you paid it over the last eight months?"

Ron was mad as hell and I could hear it in his voice. In the background, his attorney was trying to get him to settle down. Ron said, "Your Honor, when I sold the dealership it was upside down. It was a complete loss and I have no money. That's why I haven't paid child support."

"It's hard to believe that," Judge Rasmussen said. "I'm going to have Ms. Stephens's attorney subpoena the documents of the sale." The judge ordered to reinstate Ron's visitation at the end of the month and told him to start paying his child support.

When we hung up the phone, we all looked at each other in disbelief. I said, "He is such a liar. The dealership is worth $8–$10 million."

"Don't worry, Heather," Harvey said. "It will all be discovered in the records. Why do you think he chose the Grand Caymans?"

"To hide the money!" I said. "It's so obvious."

Ron and Debbie came for Lauren, Ronnie, and Joe on Friday morning. They were taking the children to Disney World in Orlando. Included in the visitation order Ron was to inform me of their location during the trip and I was able to call them once a day. They were staying at the Disney Grand Floridian Resort. John checked it out online and said, "This is the most expensive resort on the grounds. So much for him being broke." We both laughed.

I sat on John's lap and put my arms around him. "I just want the children to have a great time," I said. "They were really excited when they left."

John kissed me and said, "Don't worry. I'm sure everything will be fine."

We met Jerry and Elizabeth that evening at the movies and saw *Independence Day*. Over dinner there was so much to talk about with them. The conversation and company were great, but the entire time I couldn't help but think about Ronnie, Lauren, and Joe. I wondered if they were doing well.

Our weekend flew by quickly. I tried to call the children three times while they were gone but Ron would not answer his phone. On Sunday morning we met Jay and Christy for breakfast and went to Costco before the kids were scheduled to return at one o'clock.

Ron did not bring them on time. I went into John's office and said, "I'm worried, John! The children are not back and it's one thirty. I've tried to call Ron but there's no answer."

John said, "You better call Laura to let her know."

I immediately called Laura. "Don't worry," she said. "He's probably running late."

By three o'clock, John and I were pacing the house and frantic. The phone rang and John answered it. Ron screamed uncontrollably, "You are a cowardly, motherless son of a bitch!"

"That's not very nice," John replied.

"No, I want to speak!"

"Don't you care about the children?"

"No," Ron said. "I care about what you put your hands on . . . the children . . ."

"You know darn well I would never put my hands on your children."

"All three of them here told me differently," Ron said, hanging up the phone. Both of us were hysterical and had no idea where the children were or what Ron was doing.

Another hour passed. The phone rang and I answered it. The man identified himself as Detective Sanchez of the Boca Raton Police Department. He told me Mr. Samuels brought Ronnie, Lauren, and Joe in to be interviewed and asked, "Can you please come to the department and speak with me?"

"Yes," I said. "I'll be there right away." Stunned, I turned to John and said, "You won't believe this. Ron brought the kids to the police department and I have to go down there and get them."

"Do you want me to go with you?"

"No," I said. "I'm nervous but I don't want you to run into Ron."

When I entered the police department, Ronnie, Lauren, and Joe were sitting in a room by themselves. I checked to see if they were doing all right. Detective Sanchez walked toward me, introduced himself, and led me into a room for questioning. He started by telling me, "Mr. Samuels is concerned for the well-being of his children. While sobbing, he inferred that your fiancé, John Grossman, is abusing the children."

"That's absurd!" I said. "Ron is a liar. He's always trying to cause problems. John is kind and wonderful to my children. He would never hurt them. If you're done talking to me, I am leaving and taking my kids with me." Driving home, I held back my tears to avoid upsetting the kids. John was waiting anxiously by the door. He put his arms around me, gave me a hug, and asked if I was feeling all right.

I said, "I'm scared, John." Then I explained everything that had happened with Detective Sanchez. John told me not to worry; the most important thing was the children were with us and out of harm's way.

With John, 1994.

Wedding to John Grossman 1997

Chapter 27

The next morning I called Laura and told her what happened. She was sympathetic about our situation and understood Ron's agenda. Four days later detective Sanchez came to our house to let us know he was starting an investigation and Child Protective Services (CPS) would be involved. He asked us questions pertaining to the children. I immediately defended John and provided court papers showing Ron's history of being in contempt of court and his continual harassment toward me.

Detective Sanchez said, "Mr. Samuels is being very persistent. He has been in my office every day upset and making sure we stay on top of this." We walked him to the door and said, "Please let us know if you need anything else from us."

I turned to John in disbelief and said, "I'm so sorry this is happening to you." John replied, "Don't worry. I have already spoken to my dad and I'm going to retain an attorney in the morning. We know what Ron is capable of and need to protect ourselves."

I kissed him and said, "I love you. Thank you for being supportive."

"I love you, too," he said.

That evening I went for a six-mile run. I struggled to get through it, which was unusual for me. I couldn't relax; I started hyperventilating and almost passed out. The stress was getting to me.

John and I met with Bruce Goodman at his law firm in Fort Lauderdale. Mr. Goodman was a prominent criminal attorney. He stood about six feet tall, and had dark, curly hair and a polished appearance about him. After discussing our case, John and I were very impressed with his character. The plan was to attack Ron's credibility. To do this John hired Ken Hawkins, a private investigator at the law firm.

Although things were becoming complicated in my life, I stayed positive and hoped that this too would pass. I needed someone to talk to, so I reached out to Donna. We met at McDonald's with the kids. While the children played in the ball pit, we sipped on our sodas. As my eyes filled with tears, I told Donna, "I don't know if I can take much more. Ron is at the police department every day trying to force them to file charges against John. I feel terrible because this wouldn't be happening to him if we weren't engaged. I don't know what to do."

Donna asked, "Is everything okay with John?"

"Yes," I replied. "He's holding up fine, but we've had our first fight and of course it was over Ron."

"Don't worry. I know John loves you and wants to marry you."

"I know that, but Ron won't stop until he gets what he wants."

Donna replied, "The love you two have for each other is strong. You'll make it through this."

After speaking to her, my spirits were lifted and soon we were laughing.

Two weeks later there was a knock at the door. When I opened it, I was served with papers stating Ron was filing for full custody of Ronnie, Lauren, and Joe for the second time, due to the abuse allegations he had filed against John. I immediately felt sick to my stomach and called John at work to tell him what Ron had done.

"Please, honey, stop crying," John said. "Don't let him get to you. There is no way that asshole is going to take the children from you."

"I'm worried," I replied. "I don't understand why he keeps doing this."

"He's reaching for any way to hurt us."

As if that wasn't bad enough, two days later, a woman from CPS called and wanted to set up an interview with me at her office. By this time John and I were both alarmed at how quickly the situation had escalated.

Stepping off the elevator, my heart was racing and my nerves were shot. I was meeting with caseworker Bernice Jones. When the door opened a slender, soft spoken, African-American woman introduced herself and asked, "Would you care for something to drink?"

I answered, "No thank you."

Mrs. Jones started the conversation by asking questions about Ronnie, Lauren, and Joe. She continued by inquiring about myself and John. She then had some interesting questions about Ron.

I asked her if she was going to be interviewing the children or John. To my surprise she said, "No, I have already spoken to the kids' teachers, your neighbors, and close friends. I will not be filing any charges against John Grossman."

I responded, "Oh, thank God! I have been so worried about John and the effect this is having on our relationship."

She said, "I can understand. Mr. Samuels has been in my office every other day trying to push me to do something. When I wouldn't file charges of child abuse against Mr. Grossman, Mr. Samuels became angry and threatened me by saying, 'You have a nice home. It would be a shame if it happened to burn down.'"

"You have got to be kidding," I said. "I can't believe he said that."

Mrs. Jones then expressed her concern. "Be careful of Detective Sanchez, because he is also being pressured by Ron." I thanked her and left, relieved.

I called John at work to tell him the good news. He was relieved to hear the outcome of the meeting. He came home early that day to take us all to dinner. We went to Wilt Chamberlain's restaurant, a favorite of the children's because of the arcade. During our salads, while the kids played, John and I talked about our wedding plans. We decided that the Ritz Carlton in West Palm Beach was the perfect place for our event.

Now all we had to do was pick the date. John kept joking, saying, "You sure are dragging your feet. Did you find a new man?"

"Stop saying that," I said. "We've been a little busy lately. You know I love you."

"Can you make an appointment with the hotel's wedding consultant," he asked, "so we can look at menu selections for the reception?"

I responded, "Sure, honey, I'll get right on it." After finishing our meal John shot some hoops with the kids. As I watched them laugh and play around, I thought to myself how nice it was to finally have an evening not overshadowed by Ron Samuels.

Chapter 28

I started focusing on the wedding arrangements. That week, Donna and I met with a highly recommended photographer. When we returned home, I invited Donna in for a glass of iced tea. While chatting, the phone rang. It was Rob at the front gate. He said, "Ms. Stephens, there is a Detective Sanchez here to see you. Can I let him in?"

"Yes," I told him. After my warning I was scared.

I turned to Donna and said, "Detective Sanchez is on his way here. Will you stay with me?"

She replied, "Of course I will!"

When Detective Sanchez talked to me he was curt and unfriendly. He said, "I am here regarding a report of abuse of your daughter, Lauren."

"What are you talking about?" I asked.

"Where did she get the marks on her leg?"

"Lauren was riding her bike with the two girls from across the street when she fell and scraped her leg," I explained. I walked Detective Sanchez outside, pointed at a white house, and said, "If you would like to speak to the girls and their mother they live right there."

"I will follow up with them and get back to you."

I kept our conversation short and said, "Good-bye."

Donna looked at me. "That guy's a jerk," she said. "I can't believe he drove all the way over here just for that."

"I know," I replied. "This is embarrassing for us."

When Donna left I didn't bother to call John this time. I started making dinner, while the kids played outside.

When John came home I kissed him and asked, "How was your day?"

"Very busy," he said, "but I accomplished a lot."

"I need to speak to you in the office," I said. "Detective Sanchez was here today." I took his hand, shut the door, and told him what happened.

"You should have called me right away," John said. "What were you thinking?"

"We've been dealing with so much lately. I didn't want this to interfere with your day."

John raised his voice and said, "This is my life! I'm getting tired of all this shit! Ron's never going to stop, is he?"

"I'm so sorry this is happening to you." I hugged him and said, "I feel absolutely terrible, but I know he's not going to get away with these lies."

"Yes, but look at what's happening. I need to call my attorney. Can you give me a little privacy?" I walked out with tears in my eyes.

Over the next couple of days, I continued to notice the stress and tension in John. I could tell the pressure was beginning to affect him. He wasn't sleeping well and we had a more arguments over Ron. We weren't even making love as much.

I called my mom to tell her that things were getting worse. She was sympathetic and asked, "How are you and John holding up?"

"Not well, Mom. I love John and I can't help but feel I'm responsible for his anguish. If we weren't together, Ron wouldn't be trying to hurt him."

She said, "I'm sorry you are going through this."

"I know things are going to get worse. I just found out Ron and Debbie are moving to Boca."

"What!" Mom said. "Oh my God, Heather. What are you going to do?"

"I don't know."

"If you need our help, your dad and I are here for you."

"Thank you," I said. "I love you, Mom. I'll talk to you soon."

Still holding it together, the next morning I dropped Ronnie, Lauren, and Joe off at school and went to the gym for a workout. Afterward, I drove to John's office and we went to lunch. While we were eating our sandwiches I hesitated to tell John the bad news. Holding his hand, I finally said, "John, Laura informed me that Ron and Debbie are moving here."

His jaw dropped. "I can't believe he would do this. Is he stalking you?"

"I don't know!" I responded. "I was just as shocked as you when I found out."

John decided to take the rest of the day off. As soon as we arrived home, he placed a call to his attorney. I made a cup of hot tea, sat on the couch, and thought about everything that was happening. Somehow, every day Ron's actions were affecting our lives and it was becoming unbearable.

I called Donna and asked her if she could pick up the kids from school. Two hours later John appeared, relieved. He put his arms around me and said, "Don't worry everything is going to be fine. Bruce feels it's better to have Ron here in Boca, where Hawkins can keep an eye on him." I kissed him and said, "I love you!" Before I could finish what I was going to say the front door opened and the kids ran into the room. They were excited to see us. All three of them sat down on the couch and told us about their day. That evening, after we kissed the children goodnight, I followed them upstairs to tuck them in.

When I came downstairs I went to our master bedroom. John was sitting on the couch watching television. He said, "Come over here, honey, and sit by me."

"Hold on," I said. "I want to take off my jewelry." I walked into the bathroom where I had my jewelry box. John followed me and put his arms around my waist. He kissed me on the side of my neck and caressed my breast. I turned around and started kissing him. I pulled back.

John said, "Is everything okay?"

"We need to talk."

"What's going on?" We sat on the bed next to each other.

"I don't know if we should be together," I said. "You're having all these problems because of me. Ron is a monster and I don't think he's going to stop."

John said, "I love you. Everything is going to be okay. Stop talking like this."

I started to cry and said, "I love you too, but I have to let you go. It's the only way he'll leave you alone."

John took his hand and wiped away my tears. "You're the love of my life," he said. "I don't want to lose you; I don't care about Ron or what he does."

"I'm trying to protect you. Please understand."

"I have it under control. This is why I hired Bruce. Don't worry!"

"Are you sure?" I asked.

John pulled me close and said, "Yes." He started unbuttoning my blouse. I could feel his breath on my neck as he whispered, "I love you." He kissed me passionately. We undressed slowly, gently kissing and caressing each other's bodies. John's touch made my thoughts melt away. We made intense love and it felt incredible. Lying in John's arms I thought about our lives and knew what I had to do.

Two days after our discussion, John was leaving for work and I kissed him good-bye, knowing I was leaving my soul mate. I felt crushed inside but I knew it was for the best. My father flew into town. He and Donna helped pack my and the children's belongings. I left John my ring and a letter explaining my deep love for him and the reason I was leaving. I was devastated but knew this was the only way I could shield John from Ron's harassment. I said good-bye to Donna. As my father, the children, and I left for the airport I had tears rolling down my cheeks. My father asked, "Are you going to be okay?"

"I don't know," I said, knowing my future happiness with John had vanished.

Chapter 29

Being back in Minnesota at my parents' home was comforting. I was hoping to have all three children in the same school, but they didn't have room to accommodate Ronnie. I put him in Washington Elementary and enrolled Lauren and Joe at St. Stephens Elementary School in Anoka. I finally had the courage to answer one of John's phone calls after having avoided them for five days. When I spoke with him he was clearly upset and hurt.

"Why did you leave like that?" he said. "I told you everything was going to be okay."

"John, you don't get it! This is the way it has to be."

"No, I am not going to accept this. I never will!"

"You have no choice. You have to accept this."

"I love you."

"I love you, too," I said. "Please try to understand." Feeling overwhelmed, I hung up the phone.

A few weeks had gone by and I had developed a routine. I felt sad and missed John terribly. I kept myself busy with the kids and my family and tried my best to hold it together.

Lauren and I were shopping in downtown Minneapolis when I ran into Tony, an old friend. Tony hugged me and said, "What have you been doing lately? Last I heard you were living in Florida."

I told him, "I've moved back home and I'm bored to death."

"Would you like to go to a Timberwolves game tomorrow night with me?" he asked.

"Yes!" I said. "That sounds like fun." I gave him my phone number and told him to call me. The next night he picked me up; we had a nice dinner and enjoyed the game. I was glad to finally get out and do something with someone my own age.

The next morning I was woken by a phone call. It was John and he was extremely upset. He said, "Ben called me this morning and told me he saw you at a basketball game with a handsome man. Is this true? Were you on a date?"

"No," I said. "I was not on a date. He was just a friend. I've known him for years."

John said, "I was really hurt when Ben said he saw you with another man."

"You don't have to worry; that's the last thing I want right now. I have to focus on the court case coming up at the end of the month." John kept trying to talk to me but I told him I was busy. I was really just avoiding talking about us.

A couple of days later, I dropped the kids at school on my way to Simonson's Salon for my appointment with Kyle. I was introduced to Kyle at Ronnie's preschool Christmas pageant. Not only did she give the best facials, but we had also become close friends. Right away she hugged me and said, "I am so glad you're back."

"I'm happy to be back," I said, "but I wish it was under different circumstances." We continued to catch up with each other's lives during my facial. By the time my appointment was over I felt revitalized.

When I returned home, I was completely taken aback to find John sitting at the kitchen table talking to my father. In a stern voice I asked, "What are you doing here?"

"I can't take it anymore," he answered. "I had to talk to you face to face. Can we go somewhere?"

"Yes," I said. "Let's go have lunch."

We went to Applebee's. When we sat down I could tell John was serious. He told me how much he missed me, how he was miserable without me, and how he worried about me and the children all the time.

"I miss you too," I said. "I'm trying to be strong because I couldn't take it if anything happened to you."

"I don't care," he said. "I love you!" He leaned across the table and kissed me. After talking for over an hour I decided our relationship was worth fighting for. That evening we went to dinner. John put my engagement ring back on my finger and jokingly said, "You better not ever take this off again, or the next time you might not get it back."

I laughed and said, "Oh really! I wouldn't push my luck if I were you."

Then John leaned over, kissed me, and said, "Hawkins found a needle in the haystack. It's going to help your case tremendously." He then went on to tell me the details. After dinner we both felt blissfully in love and positive about our future together. John flew home to Boca Raton the next day.

My attorney, Laura Keene, was hard at work preparing for the upcoming hearing on the child abuse allegations. I was on my way to Pensacola to face Ron once again. John insisted on meeting me at the Atlanta airport, and we flew into Pensacola together.

The next morning my stomach was queasy. John dropped me off at the courthouse to meet Laura; she thought it would be best if he didn't attend. When we entered Judge Rasmussen's chambers, Laura and I were seated directly across from Ron and his attorney, Don Sasser. Ron had a pompous look on his face as if he were untouchable. Don Sasser immediately filed a petition trying to change jurisdiction of the custody case from Pensacola to Palm Beach County, Florida.

Judge Rasmussen looked at Ron and asked, "I see you're wearing a sticker. Did you vote here in Pensacola?"

Ron said, "Yes I stopped on my way here."

Judge Rasmussen replied, "Well, if you voted here you must still be a resident of Pensacola, right?" He angrily denied the petition for change of jurisdiction. I felt a tinge of happiness knowing that Ron was not going to get his way on this.

Don Sasser then stated, "The reason we are here today is because my client, Mr. Samuels, is concerned for the well-being of his children. He believes they're being abused by Ms. Stephens's new fiancé, John Grossman."

Mrs. Keene stood up and said, "Your Honor, these accusations are all fabricated by Mr. Samuels. I have filed documentation with this court from both CPS and the Boca Raton Police Department stating that the allegations were unfounded. There was no abuse." Laura played the tape of Ron screaming at John for Judge Rasmussen. She said, "I would like to enter this report into evidence."

Laura then handed the judge and Don Sasser a copy of a police report from 1984 in Daytona Beach, Florida. The report stated that Ron had been arrested for child abuse, for beating his then-girlfriend's son so badly he had to be hospitalized. You could tell by the look on Ron's face he was shaken. Judge Rasmussen instantly called for a fifteen-minute recess.

Judge Rasmussen returned to his chambers and stated, "Mr. Samuels, in light of your recent behavior and the discovery of past charges against you, I am ordering you to undergo a psychological evaluation before you will be awarded visitation with your three children."

Ron blew up and started ranting and raving. Don Sasser put his hand on Ron's shoulder and calmed him down. Laura and I left the courthouse. I turned to her and said, "Thank you for all your help. Finally, I'm satisfied with the judge's decision on this matter."

She said, "I'm glad I could be here for you."

I smiled and said good-bye to Laura.

John was waiting outside the courthouse. I quickly walked to the car and jumped in the passenger seat. I hugged him and said, "You won't believe what judge Rasmussen did. He ordered Ron to be psychologically evaluated before he can see the kids again."

John said, "That's great news!"

"Thank you again. Without your help, we wouldn't have uncovered this information."

"Honey, I'm here for you. I told you things would get better."

As soon as we arrived at the hotel we called Harvey and Donna to tell them what had happened. Harvey, being a lawyer, thought it was a smart move by the judge. They both were happy for us. Later that evening John and I went out to dinner. In high spirits we shared a bottle of wine and ate seafood by the water. We made love that night. The next morning John and I flew to Atlanta. We kissed each other good-bye and sadly went our separate ways. I went home to Minneapolis and John went back to Florida.

Chapter 30

The next couple of months were peaceful and quiet. The children had adjusted to their new schools and were happy to be home with Grandma and Grandpa. John flew in every other weekend to see us and we talked on the phone every day. I was enjoying the cool fall weather and seeing the leaves change color. I had missed that when I was in Florida.

I received a call from Laura telling me that Ron's psychological evaluation was done. She said, "You won't believe this! That psycho passed."

"That can't be right," I said in disbelief. "Who did he see?"

Laura replied, "A doctor here in Pensacola. I think the doctor is a friend of Ted Ciano's. Heather, I'm sending you a fax of the evaluation. I want you to read through it and pull out any lies or things that don't make sense."

"I'll look over it as soon as I receive it and call you back. Thank you." Right away I called John and told him.

I looked over the evaluation. I found inconsistencies and fabricated answers. Ron had told the doctor Sam Samuels was not his father. After doing some of my own investigating, I pulled Ron's birth certificate. To my surprise, Sam Samuels was not listed as his father— Anthony Maloney was. I thought to myself, why would he keep this a secret?

I informed Laura of all the discrepancies. "I'm sorry," she said. "Judge Rasmussen has already reinstated his visitation for Thanksgiving weekend."

My heart dropped. "I'm so tired of all this," I said. "Now I'm going to have to worry about the kids again."

I was happy that the judge had ordered Ron's visitation to be in Minnesota. I was feeling anxious that morning just thinking about the kids leaving. I was getting ready when the phone rang.

When I answered it a man said, "Don't let Ron take the children. He's going to run away with them and leave the country."

"Who is this?" I said. "What are you talking about?" They hung up.

I turned to my mother and told her what they said. She said, "Quick! Dial star-six-nine to trace the call!" I did and a man answered, identifying himself as Don Pollock, Ron's friend who worked in Southeast Toyota's finance department. I told him someone had called me from this number, saying my children were going to be kidnapped. "No one called you from this number," he said and hung up on me.

I frantically called 911 and an officer came to the house. I explained the phone call and he made a report. I asked him, "What should I do? If I don't let the children go I will be in contempt of court." "Then you have to follow the visitation order," he said.

I asked him to stay until Ron arrived to pick them up. Not trusting Ron, I asked the officer to check each child's body for any signs of abuse. Knowing how Ron's mind worked, I was afraid he would say one of us was hurting them. When Ron and Debbie arrived, I hugged and kissed the children and said, "I love you."

They all replied, "Bye, Mommy. I love you." As the door closed behind them I felt terrified.

My father and I raced to the airport so I wouldn't miss my flight. I was flying to Florida to spend Thanksgiving weekend with John. After all the commotion I finally had time to call him. When John answered, I broke down, crying and upset. I told him what had happened. In a consoling voice he said, "Don't worry, honey. You did the right thing. Just get here so we can be together."

"I can't wait to see you," I said. "I love you."

John was waiting by the gate with a bouquet of red roses. I ran into his arms and kissed him. I felt like a wounded puppy in need of tender loving care. When we drove up to the house, seeing the beautiful impatiens planted in the front yard and feeling the warm sun hit my face, I realized how much I missed being there. I had not visited Boca since I moved back to Minnesota.

The moment we walked through the door John put down my luggage. He pulled my body close to his and kissed my lips. Almost instantaneously we started undressing each other.

"Why do you make me feel so alive?" I said.

"Our bodies feel like they were meant for each other."

After we made love, we lay next to each other as we both tried to catch our breath. I looked over at the time and said, "I have to get ready."

John grabbed my hand. "I don't want you to go."

"I'll only be gone a couple hours, love."

He grinned and said, "I'll be waiting for you."

I kissed John goodbye and drove to Peter Coppola's salon for my hair appointment. My stylist foiled and cut my hair as I relaxed and enjoyed my iced cappuccino.

On my way home I stopped to see Donna. We had been keeping in touch by phone but I missed her. When I returned home, John was in the office working on the computer. I opened the door and said, "I'm home, hon. I'm going to make iced tea. Would you like some?"

"Yes that would be nice." John got up and followed me to the kitchen. We poured our iced tea and went to the patio to relax. It was a beautiful, calm afternoon, but my mind kept wandering to the kids.

We went to dinner at New York Prime, a new steak restaurant John wanted to try. When we entered, the vibrant bar area was packed with people dressed to the nines. We sat down and ordered our drinks, as we listened to the pianist. Looking into my eyes John said, "I am so thankful you are here with me. I miss you when we're apart."

"I know," I said. "I wish it didn't have to be this way. I just don't trust Ron."

"I don't give a shit about Ron. We can't live apart forever because of him."

"I promise we won't have to," I said.

The waiter approached the table and asked if we were ready to order. The conversation changed from frustration to delight as we ate. John and I stayed later to enjoy the music and sip cappuccinos. Driving home, exhausted, I fell asleep with my head on John's shoulder.

The next day we went to Mizner Park to do some shopping and walk around the outdoor mall. We walked to the theater and decided to watch *Ransom*, the new Mel Gibson movie. After the show I felt sick to my stomach. I'd had no idea the movie was about a kidnapping.

We arrived home around five-thirty p.m., which gave us plenty of time to get ready for the evening. Donna and Harvey were picking us up to have dinner at Maxwell's Chop House. Our table was in the bar area near the piano player. John and I enjoyed listening and dancing to the music. The topic of conversation, of course, was my court case and when I was moving back. By this time, these were two topics I was tired of talking about. When they dropped us off I felt sad, knowing I wouldn't be seeing them for a while.

Chapter 31

Over the next few days, John and I spent quality time together, just he and I. Before I knew it, I was packing my bags. We were both upset. I didn't want to leave John, and just thinking about dealing with Ron made it worse. We arrived at the airport; he parked the car and walked in with me. When I was checking my bag, John said to the agent, "She's changed her mind. She's staying." Then he grabbed my bag and started walking away with it.

I stood there laughing and said, "C'mon! Bring that back here!"

He smiled and said, "No! You're staying!"

I said to the agent, "Please excuse him, he has separation anxiety." Then John and I looked at each other and laughed. We sat and had coffee until I had to leave; then we kissed and said good-bye.

Mom picked me up at the airport. On our way home we stopped at the grocery store to do some shopping. When we got to the house, I went upstairs and unpacked my things. Mom asked me to help with dinner. When 6:00 p.m. arrived there was no sign of the children. Thirty minutes later they still weren't home and I called the police.

The police took the information over the phone. Ron showed up with the children forty-five minutes later. My mom said, "He's up to his old tricks again. He finally gets his visitation back and he's already pushing the limits and not bringing them back on time."

"I know, Mom, but I'm just glad they're home."

"He could have at least called," she said, "so we didn't have to worry."

The children were happy to be home. We all sat down to dinner and I could see the kids weren't the same. They were quiet and seemed distressed. It took a few hours for them to get back to their normal selves, before they were running around and laughing again. I tucked them into bed and kissed each one of them good night.

The next morning I was up early making breakfast and getting the children bundled up for school. After I ran some errands, I stopped by the Anoka Police Department to get a copy of the police report that was filed before Thanksgiving.

The clerk behind the window said, "There are two reports here. Would you like them both?"

"What do you mean there are two?"

"There is one dated November 27 and the other is dated yesterday."

"Thank you," I said. "I would like them both, please."

When I read over the police report dated the day before, I was livid. Ron had met the police outside of the Anoka Ice Arena. He had the children questioned regarding any abuse by myself, my parents, or John Grossman. I immediately called my attorney, Laura Keene, and told her what was going on. She told me to fax the police reports to her and not to worry.

Driving home I felt sick to my stomach. When I entered the house, I told mom and dad what Ron had done. They were upset and my dad said, "I am so tired of that lying asshole terrorizing us!"

"Me too," I said. "I can hardly stand it anymore." I went upstairs to call John to let him know. John was sympathetic and tried to console me. While we were on the phone, Lauren ran upstairs and came into my room. She was agitated and said, "Mommy, I need your help!"

Alarmed, I said, "What's wrong?"

She replied, "Joe is asleep on the bus and I can't get him up."

I quickly hung up with John and ran outside to the end of the driveway. I picked Joe up and carried him out of the bus. The bus driver looked at me and said, "Thank you for getting your son."

I smiled and said, "You're welcome."

We had spaghetti and meatballs for dinner. I never questioned the children about the incident with the police because I felt terrible they'd had to experience that.

The holidays were approaching quickly. This year was Ron and Debbie's Christmas with the children. I was informed by Laura Keene that Ron would be spending Christmas in Bloomington, Minnesota, where he was renting an apartment. When I heard this information I felt uncomfortable with him being so close. My whole family had Christmas with the children a week early.

Mom and I were getting the kids ready for the St. Stephens Christmas program. Lauren and Joe were singing angels in the choir. They were excited to dress up in white robes and wear big gold angel wings. While we were waiting for the show to begin, Ron and Debbie walked in and sat right in front of us. I was shocked and pointed them out to my mom. The show lasted for about forty-five minutes. When it was over Ron and Debbie went to see the kids. I could see that Lauren and Joe were surprised and not thrilled to see them.

Then they walked up to the teachers and introduced themselves. I could see Ron was being friendly and jovial to everyone around him. When they were leaving, Ron said hello to my mother and me. We greeted him back and kept walking.

Once we were in the car, I received a call from Ron. He started yelling at me because the kids hadn't been excited to see him. He also said my mother and I had been rude to Debbie. I told him, "I don't have to take this from you anymore," and hung up the phone.

The morning that Ron was picking up Ronnie, Lauren, and Joe for Christmas, as much as I hated to, I had the police check them for any signs of abuse. I felt that was the only way to protect myself and my family from his continued allegations. I was worried about them being with Ron. I kissed them good-bye and told them that I loved them. That night I prayed to God, asking him to protect them during their visit.

The next day I flew to Boca to spend two weeks with John. When he picked me up at the airport, he seemed anxious to get home. As I entered the house it was as if I had walked into a Winter Wonderland. The entire living room was covered from floor to ceiling with Christmas decorations. A twelve-foot tree with an assortment of gorgeous crystal and silver ornaments stood against the windows.

I looked at John and said, "This is so beautiful! Did you hire someone to do this?"

He said, "I had a little help with the lights; other than that, I did the rest. This is something I wanted to do for you. I know how much you love Christmas and I knew you'd be sad the kids aren't here."

I hugged him and said, "I can't believe you did this. It's amazing."

"I'm glad you like it."

"I love it, and I love you!" We ordered in dinner and ate our meal by the Christmas tree.

We spent Christmas Eve with Donna and Harvey, their children, and Donna's siblings. When we entered their home, Donna came right over and gave us both a big hug. She said in her bubbly voice, "I'm so glad you guys could join us!"

"Thank you for inviting us," I said. "Is there anything I can help you with?"

"Yes, come with me and I'll put you to work." Once in the kitchen, I helped her arrange the appetizers, and placed the wine glasses on the table for dinner. John and I had an enjoyable evening and stayed until 10 p.m. As we were leaving, we gave Donna and Harvey hugs and wished them a Merry Christmas. When we arrived home, we sat by the tree and opened our gifts to each other.

The next morning we slept in late, made love, showered together. We sipped our coffee and ate as we read the newspaper. I tried to call

Ron's cell phone because I wanted to wish the kids Merry Christmas and see how things were going. There was no answer so I left a message.

Two hours later I tried again, and still no answer. I did not let it upset me. This was a typical Ron move.

That evening John and I had Christmas dinner with Norman Gurstel and his family in Miami. Norman was a friend of ours who practiced law in Minneapolis. We enjoyed catching up on the Minnesota happenings. It was wonderful to be able to spend time with them.

We woke up early the next morning and were excited to pick up Ben and Matt for a weeklong visit with us. After everyone settled in we lay by the pool and had a relaxing afternoon. John and I enjoyed catching up with the boys' news. Ben was in his senior year at Boston University, and Matt was attending the University of New Hampshire. Both were enjoying their studies and were transforming into responsible adults.

The prior month I had booked reservations in Key West for John's birthday weekend, on December 31. It was supposed to be a surprise, John found out. We left Boca at noon with Ben and Matt. We were all excited to be together. The estimated drive time was four hours; however, it took us over five hours due to holiday traffic and the one-lane road.

We stayed at the Pier House Resort and Caribbean Spa. The hotel was in the heart of Old Town and overlooked the Gulf of Mexico. We could walk or ride the trolley to restaurants, shops, and local attractions. After we checked in, the boys came to our room and jumped on their dad. They wrestled around in good fun.

I couldn't stop laughing. "Hey, leave the old man alone!" I said.

Then they came after me. I ran behind John and said, "Okay! He's all yours!"

Over the next three days it rained and rained. We were still able to visit the Key West lighthouse and tour the Hemingway House and Museum. We decided to leave a day early because it continued to be cold and wet. We finished off John's birthday celebration by going out to dinner with the boys and friends in Fort Lauderdale. At midnight we toasted to 1996.

Two days later I made breakfast for everyone. John and I drove the boys to the airport and sadly said good-bye. I had a nice time with Ben and Matt and knew I would miss them being around. On our way home, John stopped off to buy some computer supplies for his office. While I was waiting for him I received a call from my mother. She said, "There's a package here for you. It arrived today. It's from the law firm of Bill Mullen, attorney at law."

I asked, "Is he a Minneapolis attorney?"

"Yes, he is!" she said. "I wonder what Ron is up to now."

"I don't know, but this worries me. I'll deal with it when I get home. Thank you for calling me, Mom." And I hung up.

I found John in the store and told him about the package. He could tell I was upset and tried to comfort me. "You can't do anything about it now," he said. "Whatever happens, we'll get through it." I smiled at him and held his hand as we walked out of the store.

Our evening was quiet. John ordered Chinese takeout for dinner. I helped him take down some of the Christmas decorations. After I started packing, an overpowering feeling of sadness came over me. I didn't want to leave John. But then I thought about seeing my children's smiling faces, and suddenly felt it was time to go home. When we went to bed John and I held each other close, knowing it was our last night together.

When I arrived back in Minnesota, my anxiety was high. Ron was returning the children at six o'clock and I wanted to open the package. When I read it, I became so mad I could hardly contain my emotions. There was a cover sheet explaining that Mr. Samuels had retained Bill Mullen as a custody attorney in Minneapolis. Following that was a doctor's report stating that during their visitation Ron had taken Ronnie, age seven, and Lauren and Joe, age five, to be interviewed and examined for physical and sexual abuse. In the papers, Ron stated John Grossman and the children's grandparents had been abusing the children. When I looked at the fine print, Joe said absolutely nothing. Lauren said John had touched her birthmark on the side of her body, and Ronnie had said Grandma and Grandpa could be mean. There were no signs of physical, sexual, or emotional abuse. I was livid that Ron would put the kids through this.

I brought the papers to the kitchen and showed them to my parents. They, too, were enraged; my mother sat in the chair and held her head. She looked up at me and said, "Ron is a lunatic! He's never going to stop."

I started crying, knelt down, and said, "Mom, I'm so sorry you're going through this, but your support means the world to me. You are the best grandma ever!"

"It's not your fault," she said. "When the kids come back, we'll act like this never happened."

"I agree, they have been through enough."

This time the children arrived on time and we greeted each one of them with hugs and kisses. We had a nice dinner together, and after I asked them what they got for Christmas from Daddy and Debbie. They told us about their Christmas and Ronnie said, "Daddy made us leave our presents at the apartment for next time."

I thought this was strange but said, "I'm glad you had a nice time. You have plenty of toys to play with here."

"I know, Mommy," he said. That evening, after their baths, I read to them and tucked them into bed. I called John and told him everything that was going on. He empathized with me, but he was also furious and said, "He's not going to get away with this."

The next morning I faxed all the papers to Laura Keene. She told me not to worry but that didn't really ease my mind. Three weeks later Ronnie's school called me to come in because Ronnie had bumped his chin on the monkey bars. Being paranoid because of Ron, I told the school nurse to document everything that had happened. Things were not getting any better.

Two months later, Ronnie, Lauren, and Joe were at a friend's birthday party. There was a knock at our door; I answered it and it was Ron.

"What are you doing here?" I asked.

"I'm here to pick up the kids for visitation."

"You know your visitation starts tomorrow."

"No, it doesn't!" he said. "It starts today!"

"The children are at Aaron's birthday party. They won't be home until later."

"I'll be back for them tomorrow," he said.

Within an hour I received a fax stating I had to appear at Anoka County Courthouse for contempt of court. I thought to myself, "Here we go, the bastard strikes again!" I had one hour to get to the courthouse. I immediately told Mom and the two of us drove down there. I had no time to change into a suit; I was embarrassed to be in jeans.

When we entered the courtroom Ron was standing next to his attorney, Bill Mullen. He was a tall, gray-haired, older gentleman. Mr. Mullen told the judge I was in contempt of court for not following the visitation schedule. He explained that Mr. Samuels had attempted to pick up his three children earlier that day and I did not comply.

The judge asked me, "Is this true, Ms. Stephens?"

"I did not know Mr. Samuels was coming in a day early," I replied. "The children are at a birthday party right now."

Mr. Mullen interrupted and said, "Your Honor, Ms. Stephens was sent a notice that Mr. Samuels would arrive in town a day early and pick up the children by noon."

The judge asked me if I had received the notice.

"Absolutely not, Your Honor," I replied.

The judge said, "Since Mr. Samuels is in town now, he can pick up the children at six o'clock this evening."

I responded, "Yes, Your Honor."

I looked over at Ron, who was smirking, and thought to myself "another corrupt judge."

I decided to have an officer once again check the children before they left. This was becoming a routine. I hated doing it but needed to protect myself and my family.

Ron arrived to pick up the kids, and I kissed them all good-bye. John was in town the next three days. We met Bud and Beverly in downtown Minneapolis and had dinner at a new restaurant, The Whittier. Bud and Beverly were gracious and friendly. They were concerned about everything we had been going through. John and I assured them it would be over soon, and the children and I would be moving back to Boca.

Ron was supposed to return the children by six o'clock. Around four o'clock we received a fax of an official court document stating that Ron Samuels had been granted temporary custody of Ronald, Lauren, and Joseph Samuels on the basis of abuse. Custody was awarded until a hearing could be set for all parties involved.

I ran to my mom sobbing. I couldn't get out the words to tell her. She grabbed the paper from my hand, read it, and said, "Call Laura Keene right now!"

"Mom, it's Sunday."

"I don't care. Call her at home."

I dialed her home number. Laura's son answered and I asked if I could speak to his mother. She got on the phone and after hearing my voice said, "Heather, calm down. What has happened?"

I took a deep breath and told her, "Ron was granted temporary custody of the children. How could this happen?"

She said, "I need you to fax the court documents to me right now."

I stayed on the phone as I faxed the papers to her. She looked them over and explained that Ron's lawyer, Bill Mullen, went to a side judge and he granted Ron temporary custody without having any prior knowledge of the case.

"What do we do now?" I asked.

"Heather, don't worry!" she replied. "I will call Judge Rasmussen first thing in the morning and will take it from there."

"Thank you, Laura. Please call me as soon as you find something out." I hung up the phone and started crying again.

That evening I sat at the kitchen table in disbelief. I looked at my parents and said, "How could this be happening?"

My mom came over and hugged me. "Ron has a lot of money and uses it to get what he wants from people," she said. "Do you actually think he wants the children? He's just doing this to hurt you."

"Mom, this is killing me! I can't take any more."

"Yes, you can," she said. "You have to be strong for your children."

After dinner I went upstairs and called John to tell him what Ron had done. He had just arrived home from his flight. John was worried about my emotional state and stayed on the phone with me for hours. I did not get any sleep. I was terrified and tossed and turned all night.

The next morning I came downstairs in my robe and made a cup of coffee. I was still shaken up over the children and had hoped it was all a bad dream. Mom tried to comfort me but it didn't help. Taking Laura Keene's advice, I drove to the Anoka Police Department and met with the chief of police, Philip Johanson. We discussed what was going on with Ron and the children. After talking with him I felt even worse.

"Mr. Samuels has been in my office and at Child Protective Services numerous times claiming abuse against the children," he said.

"Who is he accusing of abusing them now?" I asked. "He did the same thing in Boca Raton. There were never any charges brought against anyone because they never found any signs of abuse."

"Mr. Samuels brought Ronnie, Lauren, and Joe in for questioning, a few days ago," Chief Johanson said.

"He's trying to hurt me. He's behind on his child support by $20,000! He's been in contempt of court numerous times."

"I'm sorry, Ms. Stephens," he said, "but there is nothing I can do."

I started to cry. "If I end up dead just know Ron Samuels is responsible."

He put his hand on my shoulder and said, "Don't talk like that Ms. Stephens."

I looked at him. "He told me he would destroy me and I'm beginning to believe it," I said.

After I left the station I called John. With a shaky voice, I shared what Chief Johanson had told me. John said, "I've already talked to my father and we have found an attorney in Minneapolis to represent you. His name is Robert Levy."

"That's wonderful," I said. "When can I meet with him?"

"I'm coming there to be with you. We can meet with him Wednesday at 11 a.m."

"I don't know what I would do without you."

"You'll never have to find out," John said.

When I arrived home I sat my mom and dad down at the kitchen table and explained to them what I had found out. I looked at them and said, "You won't believe this. Ron told the police that Ronnie told him Grandma pulled him out of the bathtub by his penis."

I thought Mom was going to pass out, her face was so pale. "How could he say something like that?" she said.

My dad stood up and shouted, "Ron is one sick bastard!"

After about thirty minutes, when we had all calmed down, we laughed. My dad said, "He's the only person I know who could come up with something that delusional."

The phone rang, and it was the principal of St. Stephens Elementary. "How are you doing Ms. Stephens?" he asked.

"Not well! I'm sure you know what is going on with Lauren and Joe?"

"Yes, that is why I'm calling. Is there anything I can do?"

"The kids are going to need their uniforms," I said. "Can I bring them by the school, so you can give them to their father?"

"No problem," he answered. "I'll take care of that. I am sorry you're going through this. Everyone here at St. Stephens is behind you."

"Thank you for your kind words," I said.

I went upstairs and gathered Lauren and Joe's school uniforms. Around three o'clock I drove to the school. I accidentally passed Main Street, so I turned on the back road by Washington Elementary. I was shocked to see Ron and Debbie sitting in their car as I drove right by them. I wanted to stop the car and scream at the top of my lungs. I wanted to confront Ron, but I didn't. At that moment I realized I was still afraid of him. I dropped off the children's clothes and hoped they hadn't seen me.

Chapter 32

John flew in the next morning. He drove straight to my parents' house. I was so happy to see him. He held me in his arms and assured me everything would be fine. On the way to attorney Robert Levy's office John looked over at me and said, "Stop that! You're not going to have any nail polish left."

"I can't help it," I said. "I'm a nervous wreck."

We met with Mr. Levy. We told him details about the case and presented him with past legal documentation to bring him up to date. We were both impressed with his integrity and genuine concern. Before leaving the meeting, Mr. Levy shook my hand and said, "You're a strong woman. I can't believe you've gone through so much. Rest assured it all comes out in the wash."

I opened my purse and reached for my checkbook. John touched my hand and said, "No, honey, I'm going to pay the retainer fee."

"It's $15,000."

"Don't worry about it. You need your money for you and the kids." John wrote him a check. We thanked him for everything and drove back to John's hotel.

John stayed for three days. He wanted to stay longer but had scheduled sales meetings he couldn't miss. I missed the children terribly. I felt lost; my whole routine was out of balance.

Mr. Levy called and gave me tasks to complete for the case. First I was to speak to Child Protective Services in Anoka and provide them with documentation of the case in Florida, giving them detailed information describing Ron Samuels's past behavior. The next task was to contact Laura Keene to keep her in the loop. I did what he asked as quickly as possible. It was difficult for me to wait two weeks for the scheduled court date. I had problems sleeping, I had no appetite, and I felt miserable. The only thing that kept me going was the one-day visitation that the Minnesota judge had ordered.

My day for visitation was a Sunday. Ron dropped off the children in the morning. We all had lunch together. Afterward, Aunt Judy and I took them to an arcade to play games. Later on we walked along the Mississippi River in Anoka. The kids threw rocks into the river and skipped with each other. We sat down to have a snack and Ronnie asked, "Why are we with Daddy?"

"You'll be home soon," I replied. "Mommy has to go talk to a judge." They kept saying they didn't understand why they couldn't come home. It broke my heart, but I told them, "Mommy loves you so much, and everything's going to be fine." I just wanted us to have a nice afternoon. Ron picked up the children at six o'clock. I hugged them and tried to hold back my tears.

I got up earlier than usual to get ready for court. I was sick to my stomach and my anxiety was at an all-time high. When I came downstairs I could see that my parents were also feeling the same. I took their hands and said, "Here we go!"

The drive to the courthouse seemed to take forever. When we walked into the courtroom I was surrounded by smiles. My grandparents, aunts, uncles, cousins, and friends from high school were all there to support me. Their presence made me feel confident. I looked over at Ron and Debbie; they were sitting with just their lawyer. Ron looked haggard and old. As for Debbie, she was his puppet and did anything she was told. I wondered where my children were. I asked my lawyer to find out.

Court was now in session and Ron's attorney called him to the stand. He took the oath and began to put on a show. He started crying and stated the children were being abused. His performance was somewhat convincing, which worried me, but there was no proof; it was all hearsay. No one else testified on their behalf, not even Debbie. Next, Mr. Levy called my mother to the stand to question her about Ron's allegations against her. She testified that she would never hurt Ronnie or any of her grandchildren. My mother continued by telling the judge about Ron's continued harassment of our family.

The hearing lasted three hours. When court adjourned the judge scheduled everyone to return at one o'clock the next day. I was disappointed because I wanted everything to be finished. I didn't want to worry about the kids for another night.

The next day the courtroom was filled with my family and friends once again. I noticed Ron's appearance had changed overnight. All his grey hair was gone; he had dyed it dark brown. When court started, Mr. Levy called me to the stand. I told the judge, "Your Honor, Mr. Samuels's accusations are false! He is determined to take my children away from me by fabricating lies. He also accused my fiancé in Florida of abuse. After CPS and the Boca Raton Police Department investigated, they didn't file charges against him."

"When did this happen?" the judge asked.

"About six months ago," I replied.

The judge had no more questions for me. I stepped down from the stand and sat next to my attorney. The judge took a forty-five-minute recess, stating he was going to place a call to Judge Rasmussen in Boca Raton, Florida.

Everyone walked outside the courtroom to wait together. Ron and Debbie walked by us and I could tell he was nervous. I, too, had anxiety, but when I called John to update him on what was happening, he gave me positive feedback and was grateful that Judge Rasmussen was involved. When we returned to the courtroom it was quiet; everyone was waiting to hear what was going to happen.

"After reviewing all the documentation and speaking to Judge Rasmussen," the judge said, "I am ruling in favor of Ms. Stephens. The children are to be returned to her by four o'clock this afternoon."

I was elated. As I turned to walk toward my family, I saw Ron pointing his finger and yelling at his attorney. I just smiled and kept walking. After everything was over, I met my family and friends outside. They were all happy for me. I wanted to talk but I had to get ready for the kids to come home.

When we returned home, I immediately called John and told him the good news. Then I called Laura to inform her of the judge's decision. She said. "Heather that's wonderful news. I don't want to scare you but, I'm afraid he might try to run with the kids." She asked, "Do you have their passports in your possession?"

"No, I don't. Ron's lawyer is supposed to have them."

"I don't trust Ron's lawyer, Don Sasser."

"What should we do?"

"There's really nothing we can do until it happens," Laura said.

I thanked Laura for everything. I told her I would call her as soon as Ronnie, Lauren, and Joe were home. I was an emotional wreck and Mom, Dad, and I were on pins and needles waiting for the kids to come home. It seemed as though four o'clock would never come.

I was surprised and happy that Ron was right on time. He drove up with Debbie and his private investigator. Of course he made a huge scene in the driveway. He began to cry and yell out to the kids, "I will always love you." The kids didn't even look back at him. They came running into my arms. I turned around and took the children into the house. I could not believe how easily they adjusted to being home. They were playing with their kittens, laughing, and running around. I called Laura and John to tell them the kids were home safe. We spent the rest of the evening at home. I cooked them dinner and we watched *The Lion King*.

Chapter 33

Within the next week I was packing and moving us back to Florida. John desperately wanted us to come home. Laura Keene thought it best that I reside in Florida because I'd be in Judge Rasmussen's jurisdiction again. She did not trust Ron and his Minnesota lawyer, who could possibly stir up more trouble. I was sad to leave Mom and Dad again, but I knew their life would be more peaceful.

John and I were thrilled to be living together again. Everything fell back into place rather smoothly. I enrolled all three kids at Calusa Elementary. They were excited to start school again. There were a lot of kids in our community. Their friends were glad to see them back, especially Bret and Ashley. It was mid-April and I was back in time for my thirty-first birthday. We celebrated at New York Prime with a few of our friends.

When we arrived home, John opened the door and said, "C'mon, birthday girl, the night is still young." I walked into the bedroom and there were candles lit all around the room. When I looked at him it only took a few seconds before we were undressed and in bed. It was the perfect ending to an amazing day.

The next day John and I met with the wedding coordinator at the Ritz Carlton in West Palm Beach. We chose the menu and the rooms for the wedding and reception, as well as the date: June 8, 1997. That did not give us a lot of time, but we wanted to do it right away; after all, we had waited so long already.

It was easy to plan the finishing touches because I had done most of the work eight months ago. I appreciated how involved John was. When I married Ron he wasn't involved in any of the planning. He had told me to do whatever I wanted and he would show up. John and I couldn't wait to tell our friends and send out the invitations. On the drive home John said, "I think we should inform Laura Keene and Judge Rasmussen of the wedding. I don't want any publicity—let's keep the date from being disclosed to Ron."

"That's a good idea," I said.

"You never know what that psycho might do."

"I can't believe we have to go to these measures," I said. "I will call them first thing in the morning."

On May 3, John and I had a birthday party for the twins. I couldn't believe they were turning six. Twenty-five of Lauren and Joe's friends attended with their parents. We played video games, miniature golf, and raced around in go karts. When we returned home everyone was exhausted. The rest of the month Donna and I stayed busy trying to finish up everything for the wedding before the guests started to arrive from out of town. John was a peach; he offered to pick up the children from school every day so I didn't have to rush home.

A week before the wedding I had to travel to Pensacola for a hearing in front of Judge Rasmussen. When I told John he became very upset. "I can't believe you have to go now," he said. "Ron is always causing us problems."

"I am so sorry this happened," I said. "Mom will be here early so she can help take care of the kids."

"That's fine but I'm not happy about you going."

"I don't want to go either, but I don't have a choice."

"I know," John said. He turned around in his slippers and stomped away.

I flew into Pensacola and returned the same day. The judge would not reinstate Ron's visitation with the children because of what he had tried to do in Minnesota.

Our out-of-town guests flew in on Wednesday and Thursday. John and I were busy showing them around and getting everyone settled. On Friday we hosted a dinner for thirty people at Max's Grill in Mizner Park. Saturday morning I woke up early, kissed John good-bye, and went to my hair appointment. When I was finished, the Grossman girls—Beverly, Lynn, Jan, and Lisa—picked me up in a limo and we drove to West Palm Beach.

We had lunch on Worth Avenue at a French restaurant. We shared three bottles of Dom Perignon and everyone was a little giddy. To top off a wonderful day with the girls; as I was leaving, I saw Michael Bolton eating lunch. I used to love it when he would sing, "How Am I Supposed to Live Without You?"

When I stepped out of the limo, John was waiting by the door. He said, "I thought you would never get home. Did you have a good time?"

"Yes," I said. "It was amazing." John replied, "I'm glad you had such a great time. Everyone has been calling to talk to you all day."

We both ran into the house. I quickly returned some phone calls, grabbed a glass of wine, and changed for dinner. I then began getting Ronnie, Lauren, and Joe ready. The kids were excited and kept asking "When are we going to go, Mom?" We all hopped in the car and headed to West Palm Beach for our party.

Our groom's dinner was hosted by Bud and Beverly Grossman at Morton's Steakhouse. When I walked into the room I saw Terry Vevea, my maid of honor, and her boyfriend, Mike. She gave me a big hug and said, "I'm so excited to be here. I've missed you; I haven't seen you in months."

I replied, "I'm so glad you are here! It means so much to me."

Everyone mingled and had cocktails. At dinner John and I sat with Bud and Beverly, Donna and Harvey, and John's brother, Dick, and his wife, Lisa. It was a lovely evening with numerous toasts to our future together. The night ended with everyone commenting on what a nice time they had.

On Sunday morning I awoke with butterflies in my stomach. I dropped Ronnie and Joe off at my parents' hotel. I drove to the Ritz Carlton with Lauren and met with Terry. We then checked into our room. Terry and I reminisced about old times while Lauren jumped up and down on the bed. Marcus, my stylist, styled my hair in an updo of large curls with small Stefano flowers tucked inside. I wore a Badgley Mischka floor-length wedding gown designed with lace and pearls.

As I peeked into the room, it was beautifully decorated. There was a trellis covered in white orchids at the end of the walkway. Every row had a flower arrangement and a lit candle at the end. As my dad walked me down the aisle I looked at John, and he had a big smile on his face. There was no doubt this was the man I wanted to spend the rest of my life with.

My father kissed me on my cheek and said, "I love you honey! I hope this one's better than the last one." I held back my laughter and kissed him back. John and I exchanged our vows and it wasn't long before we kissed and the rabbi introduced us as Mr. and Mrs. Grossman. As we turned we could see all the happy faces of our friends and family. While our guests moved to the reception we took our photos with our families.

The reception hall looked more exquisite than I could have ever dreamed. The chandeliers shimmered over the tower vases filled with thousands of calla lilies and orchids. The white tables and silver bamboo chairs added to the splendor of the room. John and I danced our first dance to "Unforgettable." We looked into each other's eyes. "You looked so beautiful today," he said. "You have made me the happiest I have ever been."

"I love you so much," I said.

"I will love you forever," he replied.

John twirled me around, dipped me backward, lifted me up, and kissed my lips. Everyone joined us on the dance floor. By the end of the night Ronnie, Joe, and Lauren had everyone doing the Macarena. I could not have asked for a more perfect wedding. We said good-bye to everyone around midnight and John and I headed to our suite.

We walked hand-in-hand to our room. When we entered our suite, there were heart-shaped rose petals on the bed. I looked at him and said, "When did you have time to do that?"

He said, "I had a little help from a friend." There was a knock. I opened the door and room service delivered a bottle of champagne and fresh strawberries. We enjoyed the champagne, strawberries, and each other.

We met Ben and Matt for breakfast downstairs. We saw some of our friends at the restaurant and they looked tired as could be. The boys told us they had all ended up in the hot tub after the wedding.

After breakfast we checked out. We met Mom, Dad, and the kids in the lobby. I hugged and kissed Ronnie, Joe, and Lauren and said good-bye before we left for our honeymoon.

When we arrived in San Francisco, we checked into our hotel in Ghirardelli Square, one of the city's most beautiful and historic areas right by Fisherman's Wharf. When we entered the room John embraced me as soon as the door closed behind us. We continued to kiss as we moved toward the bedroom. He unzipped the back of my dress and helped me out of it. "Come on wife!" he said, laughing.

Over the next few days John and I enjoyed walking along the wharf and eating seafood. The highlight of our trip was spending two days in Napa Valley touring different vineyards and wine tasting. We sat outside on a beautiful, sunny day with a light breeze hitting our faces while we listened to an acoustic band. We enjoyed a bottle of wine with French brie and a baguette. We had so much fun the time flew by. Our seven-day trip was over too soon and we began packing for the flight home.

Chapter 34

The kids went crazy when they saw us walk through the door. Aunt Donna and Mom had taken care of them while we were gone. Everyone wanted to hear about San Francisco, so we sat in the living room and talked about our honeymoon. We gave the children the gifts we had gotten them at Fisherman's Wharf. That evening I called Donna and Harvey and invited them out to dinner. John treated everyone to lobster at one of our favorite restaurants. We returned home and I tucked the children into bed. I realized how glad I was to be home.

The next two months were blissful for John and me. Our relationship was stronger than ever. We lived in a beautiful home and the children were happy. Our lives were focused on each other and our family. The summer heat didn't stop us from playing tennis, learning country line dancing together, and going out on the town.

One evening we went out to dinner with four other couples at the Boca Raton Resort for a fund-raising event. As we walked out of the resort, Harvey said, "You two look the happiest I've ever seen you. What's going on?"

John replied, "We're in love." We both smiled at each other and walked out holding hands. He leaned over to me and whispered in my ear, "Let's get out of here! I'll go get the car." We drove home and spent the rest of the evening together.

The next night John and I were up late lying in bed. We were watching television and saw breaking news about Princess Diana's car accident. She died on August 31, 1997. The whole world was sad because everyone loved her. I told John another bad thing was going to happen, because they always come in threes.

A few days later I was cleaning the kitchen when the phone rang. When I answered it, all I heard was somebody breathing. I kept saying "hello," but there was no response. I hung up the phone and went into the bedroom to finish getting dressed for the day. As I was leaving the house the phone rang again. I answered it and the same thing happened; no one was there. I hung up the phone and left the house. I drove to John's office and we went to lunch at Houston's. I told him about the strange phone calls. He thought maybe it was a wrong number. We finished our lunch and thought nothing about it.

The following month, I received a few more of these anonymous calls. I began to worry. One day I was leaving John's office, heading home on Federal Highway. I heard loud music and a car honking. I looked in my rearview mirror and saw a yellow Corvette with two men in it. I kept driving and turned down Yamato Road; they turned behind me and kept honking. I was nervous and suddenly the car swerved and raced right by me. I swear I saw Ron in the driver's seat, but I didn't recognize the passenger. I kept driving and thought maybe I was wrong, second guessing myself about what I had seen. Later that evening, when we were having dinner, I didn't mention anything to John about the yellow Corvette. I didn't want to alarm him; after all, everything had been going perfectly.

The next morning John yelled from the office, "Heather, would you come to the office, please? I want to talk to you."

I went in and John said, "I just spoke to my private investigator, Ken Hawkins. He told me he had a conversation with Ron's attorney, Don Sasser, and Ken is concerned."

"Why?" I said. "What's going on?"

"Don was asking how much you love your children. He also said if Ron doesn't get his way, things might get messy." John looked worried.

"I love my kids," I said. "I will never let that sick psycho hurt them."

John hugged me and said, "They're just trying to intimidate us." I tried to shake it off, but I couldn't. My peace of mind was gone.

Chapter 35

It was October. I woke up early to make lunch for the kids. As usual I wrote and placed individual notes in their lunchboxes. John dropped them off at school and I went Halloween shopping to decorate the house.

When I returned home there was a message on the machine from Laura, alerting me to a child support hearing in Pensacola on October 6 at 1 p.m." I called Laura back and confirmed that I would be there.

When John came home I told him about the hearing. He was not happy that I had to go and felt everything was starting all over again. That night while John and I were sleeping the phone rang. John answered it and a man said, "You're gonna die. Someone is going to kill you; you're gonna die. Someone is going to kill you!" They hung up.

"Who was it?" I asked.

"It was a man saying 'someone is going to kill you.'"

"John! Oh my God!" I said. "We need to report this!" We dialed star-six-nine to trace the call, but it was blocked. We stayed awake the rest of the night. In the morning John called the Boca Raton Police Department. They came to the house, took a report, and traced the call through the telephone company. The operator told the police officer the call had come from Chicago at 2:25 a.m. John and I looked at each other in disbelief.

"That can't be right," I said to the officer. "I know my ex-husband, Ron Samuels, is behind this. He's trying to scare us and he lives here in town."

The officer said he would document this information in his report and added, "If anything else happens give us a call."

It was hard to function normally over the next few days. I called Detective Sanchez to tell him about the death threat we'd received and the strange anonymous calls. His response was nonchalant and he spoke to me as if I were overreacting. I was upset and met with Donna to tell her what was going on. Donna was upset, too. "I can't believe you guys have to deal with this," she said.

"Hopefully things will get better," I said. "I'm just worried about these prank phone calls." John and I were strong and moved on from that night. Every day we spent together was better than the last. He was working hard and I enjoyed volunteering at Calusa Elementary in the library and cafeteria.

John and I woke up early on October 6. We dropped the kids off at school and then headed to the West Palm Beach Airport. My anxiety was high just thinking about the hearing. John knew I was nervous when he dropped me off. He hugged me tight and reassured me everything would be okay.

On my way to the gate I stopped at Starbucks to buy a latte. I turned around and saw Ron and his lawyer, Don Sasser, approximately twelve feet from me. My jaw dropped and my stomach turned. They didn't see me. I quickly hid by the phone booths and called John. When he answered I said, "They're on the same flight as me!"

John said, "Calm down. Who are you talking about?"

"Ron and Don Sasser! I don't even want to get on the plane."

"I'm so sorry I'm not with you," he said, "but you can do this, honey."

After talking to John I felt more confident. I walked right past them with my head held high, without looking their way. I boarded the plane, thinking forty-five minutes would fly by quickly. Halfway through the flight I looked up and saw Ron walking toward me. As he passed me we made eye contact. He smirked and laughed at me. He made me physically sick. I was glad when the plane landed and I was on my way to the courthouse.

Laura was waiting for me outside the judge's chambers. I told her that I had flown on the same flight as Ron and Don Sasser. "You poor thing," she said. "You must be a nervous wreck."

"I am!"

"Don't worry, Heather," she said. "Ron is the one in contempt of court."

The hearing began with the judge asking Ron about his delinquency in paying child support. "You are $38,000 behind in child support," the judge said. "Why haven't you made any payments?"

Ron answered, "I can't afford to pay it. I have no money."

The judge questioned Don Sasser, asking, "How much has Mr. Samuels paid you in legal fees?"

Don Sasser responded by providing Xerox copies of hundred dollar bills, stating the cash payments amounted to $60,000. Then Judge Rasmussen looked at Ron and said, "Obviously you have money to pay an attorney. You have paid your attorney more than what you owe in child support."

Ron didn't say anything and just shrugged his shoulders. Judge Rasmussen looked at me and said, "Mrs. Grossman how is this affecting the children?"

"Your Honor," I responded. "I need some help. Not only are the children suffering, but Mr. Samuels continues to be in contempt of court. He has the money to pay, but he refuses to. John and I are receiving death threats in the middle of the night and I believe Ron is going to kill me."

Judge Rasmussen looked shocked. When I looked across the table at Ron he was laughing hysterically. I started to cry and Laura Keene put her arms around me. "Heather," she said, "please calm down. Everything is going to be fine."

The judge called for a thirty-minute recess and asked for everyone to leave his chambers. When Judge Rasmussen resumed the hearing he ruled that Ron was to pay all of Laura Keene's legal fees and ten thousand dollars in child support within seven days of the hearing. Also, his visitation would not be reinstated until the child support to me was caught up.

Laura and I left the courtroom and she walked me to my rental car. We both felt content knowing that Ron was finally being held accountable.

On the flight home I read a book and tried to avoid Ron and his attorney. When the plane landed John was waiting for me at the gate. I gave him a hug and a kiss and said, "I am so glad to see you!"

John said, "Ron and Don Sasser walked right by me and it took everything I had to not say something to them."

"I am really glad you didn't," I replied. "They're not worth it." On the drive home I told John everything that had happened in Pensacola. He was happy to hear the outcome and said, "Judge Rasmussen is finally holding him responsible for his actions."

"I was hoping he would put him in jail for not paying his child support," I said.

John responded, "Oh, honey, be thankful things are going our way."

Chapter 36

Over the next week my spirits were up. Ron had paid Laura Keene's legal fees and I was waiting for the child support check to come. John had a meeting with Ken Hawkins to find a local attorney. We met with an attorney in Fort Lauderdale and told him about Ron and the problems we had in the past. He was reluctant to take our case because we already had Laura Keene as a lawyer. But he said, "I will help you two because I can see the fear in your eyes, Mrs. Grossman." We were trying to be a step ahead of Ron. Hopefully this second attorney would never have to represent us. Ron seemed to be following the court order this time.

That evening, when I returned from my run, John had put the kids to bed. I went upstairs to kiss them all goodnight and Lauren was still awake. "Mommy," she said, "can you stay and talk with me?"

"Sure, honey." I lay next her. We talked for about twenty minutes. The last thing Lauren said was, "Mommy, will you put my hair in a bun for school tomorrow?"

"Yes, of course, honey. We'll have to get up a little earlier."

"OK, Mommy. I love you."

"I love you, too."

I walked downstairs into our bedroom and John was relaxing reading a magazine. He looked up at me with a smile and asked, "How was your run?"

"It was amazing," I said. "I feel so good, I'm going to hop in the shower!"

I got out and got ready for bed, putting on a light pink silk and lace chemise. It wasn't long before it hit the floor. We made love and, with a feeling of fulfillment, I fell right to sleep.

I woke up suddenly not knowing what time it was. The alarm was going off; I had slept right through it. In a panic I jumped out of bed and ran upstairs to wake up the kids. I quickly got ready and started breakfast for Ronnie, Lauren, and Joe. After breakfast Lauren said, "Mommy, what about my bun?"

"Oh, honey, we have to leave right now for school. I promise I'll do your hair tomorrow."

"Okay, Mom," she said.

We rushed out the door and I managed to get them to school on time. When I came home I went into the bedroom and heard John waking up. I walked over to the bed and said, "Hey, sleepyhead, aren't you going to get up?"

John held my hand and said, "Come back to bed."

I leaned over and kissed him and said, "I wish I could but I have so many things to do before I meet Donna for lunch."

In a disappointed tone he said, "Alright, I better get ready for work."

I finished getting ready and kissed John good bye. I drove to Walgreens and the deli. Right next to the deli was a boutique with children's clothing. I saw a cute little dress for Lauren in the window and had to get it for her. When I arrived back home I put everything away and went to Laruen's room to place the dress on her bed to surprise her. The phone rang; when I answered I could hear breathing but no one responded. I hung up and didn't think much about it. As I was leaving the phone rang again. It was John.

"Baby," he said, "come meet me for lunch."

"You know Donna and I have plans."

"Pretty please? I miss you."

"I'll be there in thirty minutes," I said. I called Donna to cancel our lunch date and headed out the door.

When I arrived at John's office around noon I went upstairs to say hello to some of his staff. As we came down the elevator, John said, "Let's take your car. I'll drive."

"Okay, that's fine honey," I said.

John pulled out of the parking lot and headed south on Federal Highway. "I'd like to eat at Flakowitz Deli," he said.

"I'm kind of tired of that place. Can we go to the new Thai restaurant?"

"Yes," he said, "that sounds good."

John made a U-turn at the intersection and headed north on Federal Highway. There was a lot of traffic and we got held up at the stop light on Yamato Road. John and I were chatting and laughing as usual.

I leaned over to get something out of my briefcase. When I came back up I felt an explosion in the back of my neck. I instantly thought, "I've been shot." I tried to yell for help but the words would not come out. I felt my body shutting down as if it were a machine being turned off. My head, guts, and blood fell onto John's lap.

John, terrified, immediately stopped the car. The driver and shooter turned around and drove by our car again. They fired the gun once more directly in the car, and the bullet grazed John's chin. He began to bleed. John looked down at my head on his lap and realized I wasn't breathing.

Numerous witnesses called 911 to inform the police about the shooting. The police and ambulance showed up on the scene before John could grasp what had happened. They pulled me out of the car and cut my clothes completely off. A paramedic intubated me and brought me back to life. They placed me on a gurney and put me in the ambulance. On the drive to Del Ray Hospital I opened my eyes and heard a man's voice saying, "If you can hear me, blink your eyes!" I blinked my eyes and passed out.

John was also placed in an ambulance and rushed to the hospital. He only had a wound to the chin. While the nurses were cleaning and dressing John's wound, Detective Sanchez entered the emergency room. John, seeing him, jumped off the gurney and punched Detective Sanchez in the face, yelling, "We told you this would happen! Now my wife is lying there dying!"

Detective Sanchez said, "Please, Mr. Grossman, sit back down! Finish the medical attention you need. We're going to get to the bottom of this, I promise." John sat back down and began to sob uncontrollably.

When John walked out of the emergency room he was still in shock. Detective Sanchez approached him and softly asked, "Do you remember anything that happened, Mr. Grossman?" John told him what he remembered and then went to check on me.

While waiting outside the trauma room, John called his father and told him what had happened. Then he called my mom and dad, and then Donna to pick up the kids from school. He continued to wait and pace up and down the hallway.

The emergency room doctor came and said, "We have been working on stabilizing your wife. She sustained injuries to her cervical spine. The bullet penetrated at the C3 level, which means your wife will be paralyzed from the neck down."

"Oh my God!" John said. "Is my wife going to die?" He continued to cry.

"She's still in critical condition," the doctor said. "Due to the severity of the injuries, it would probably be best if she died."

John became angry; he couldn't believe what the doctor had said. After hearing that I had been shot, Bud and Beverly Grossman immediately chartered a plane and brought my parents with them from Minnesota to Boca Raton.

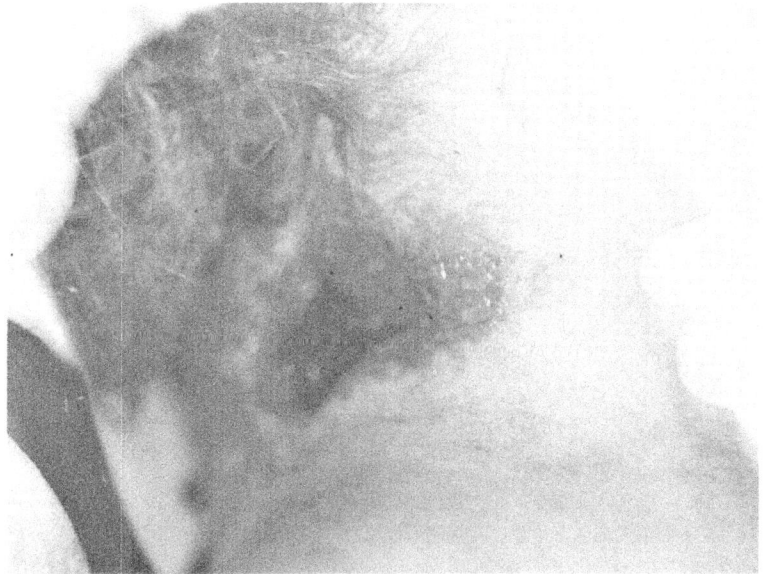

The car and the hole in Heather's neck.

169

The 3-inch rifle bullet that hit Heather.

Chapter 37

Two days later I woke up and saw a police officer at my bedside. When he noticed I was awake he got up, left, and returned with a nurse.

The next thing I remember is Bud and Beverly, my parents, and John standing over my bed. The first thing that came to my mind was: did somebody pick up the children from school? When I tried to ask them, nothing came out and I began to panic and cry. I then realized that I couldn't move my arms or legs, and I started to cry even harder. I didn't know what was going on and I was terrified. I looked back up and saw tears in my mother's eyes. That is when I knew that at the age of thirty-one my life would never be the same.

I had tubes up my nose, IVs in both my arms, a collar on my neck, and medical equipment all around me. I began to panic even more. I couldn't breathe and alarms started going off. A nurse came running in; I could see she had a tube in her hand. Suddenly, I felt an object going from the inside of my throat down in my chest and it hurt. I began to gag, and when she pulled out the tube I could breathe again. I had been suctioned for the first time while conscious and it was disgusting.

When the doctor entered the room, he held my hand and explained my condition to me. He said, "Mrs. Grossman, you were shot and the bullet hit you in the neck and severed your spinal cord at C3. You are paralyzed from the neck down."

I began to sob uncontrollably. John leaned down and kissed my forehead. "Honey, I love you!" he said. He sat by my bed and held my hand until I fell asleep.

When my parents left the hospital they went to pick up Ronnie, Lauren, and Joe. When they saw Donna and Harvey they informed them of my condition. Ronnie heard my parents' voices and all the kids came running out. The children were so happy to see Grandma and Grandpa. They kept asking, "Where are Mommy and John?"

On the drive to the Boca Raton Resort, Lauren said, "Was there an accident? We saw something on TV."

Grandma said, "Yes, honey."

"Did R.O.N. do it?" Lauren asked.

Grandma avoided the question. "Don't worry," she said. "Everyone is going to be okay."

The next morning I was awakened by nurses checking my vitals and drawing my blood. John came into the room with Detective Sanchez and another investigator. They asked me, "Do you know who shot you?"

I tried to mouth the answer but Detective Sanchez could not tell what I was saying. He held up an alphabet board and asked me the same question again. He asked me to blink when his finger was on the right letter. By the time we were finished I had spelled out Ron Samuels. They asked me other questions and I answered a few of them. My body was so weak; I became exhausted quickly and could not continue with the questioning.

A plastic surgeon was called in to assess the gunshot wound. He came in every day and cleaned the wound and packed it with gauze. The hole in the back of my neck was so large the plastic surgeon could fit his fist from one side of my neck to the other. They were medicating me with morphine because of my extreme pain. I was still in the ICU in critical condition. My family and friends came to see me but I still had not seen my children. Every time the police officers came by they would say, "We're going to put Ron in jail for this."

No arrests had been made yet and the police warned us to be careful. Bud hired a security team to watch over John, Ronnie, Lauren, and Joe. My mother and father stayed at our home to help run errands and take care of the children. My mother made tapes of the children talking to me so that I could hear their voices while I was in the hospital. A police car was stationed outside our home for our safety. The children were not afraid of the officers who came. They were friendly and would play basketball and Go Fish with them.

It took eighteen days before I was stable enough for the doctors to remove my intubation tube and do a tracheotomy. I started speech therapy where they taught me how to drink water and talk with my trach.

The first time I tried to speak I was excited, but it was not as easy as I thought. You could hardly hear my voice or understand what I was trying to say. I developed pneumonia. I also had morphine psychosis so bad I was afraid to sleep. One time I dreamed I was fighting off Al Qaeda in the hospital. I thought the nurse was trying to poison me through my feeding tube.

Every time the police came to see me they would tell me they were working hard on the case, but they could not arrest Ron yet. It was discouraging that they could not make an arrest. I was worried that he would try to kill me while I was in the hospital.

The hole in my neck was still open and I was not doing any better. I needed surgery desperately but I was still not stable enough for it. One evening my plastic surgeon came in and called John and my family. "We are going to do surgery immediately," he said, "because your wife's fever has broken. This is the best chance we have to save her life. She is still in very critical condition, so everyone should come see her before the surgery in case she does not pull through."

I was terrified when my doctor told me they were taking me to surgery. Everyone came in to say their good-byes and I hoped and prayed that everything would turn out okay. During the surgery everyone waited in the chapel with the children.

When the plastic surgeon came out of the operating room to speak to my family he said, "When I went in the bullet wound was clean. She had a good, strong artery that I attached to her trap muscle. I closed the wound using skin grafts. It's a miracle she has made it this far."

"That's great news," John said. "Thank you so much! When can I see her?"

The doctor answered, "You can see her as soon as she is out of recovery and back in her room, but please understand she needs time to recover and we are not completely out of the woods yet."

Over the next few days, I got stronger. I had spent five-and-a-half weeks in the ICU and my doctors decided I was stable enough to be transferred to a rehab hospital. In the middle of the night, under witness protection, the police had a jet waiting to fly John and me, along with a doctor and a nurse, to Englewood, Colorado. When we landed I was transported by ambulance to Craig Hospital.

When I woke up that morning everything was a blur. The doctor came into my room and said, "Hello, Mrs. Kaufman, my name is Dr. Rodger Luke. I will be in charge of your care during your rehabilitation, here at Craig Hospital."

My nurse came in and deflated the balloon to my trach so that I could speak. Softly I said to him, "It is nice to meet you. I'm very scared."

He touched my hand and responded, "Don't worry, Mrs. Kaufman. "You are at one of the best spinal cord hospitals in the nation and I am one the best doctors here."

Doctor Luke was six-foot-two with gray hair. He was soft-spoken and kind. After doing numerous tests, he and my nurse, Helene, left the room. I turned to John and said, "How did you come up with the name Kaufman?"

"It was the name of my German shepherd that passed away," John answered.

"When are the kids going to be here?"

"Your mother is flying them up today. I'm going to pick them up at the airport and we will come straight back to the hospital."

"I can't wait to see them. I miss them so much!"

"I know you have," John said. "They've missed you, too."

When my mom and the children arrived, they were excited to see me. John lifted Ronnie and Joe to the bed so that I could give them each a kiss. As he was lifting Lauren to the bed she hit a button and my whole bed lost its air. She became scared.

"Oh, honey," I said, "don't worry. The bed just deflated. We'll get the nurse and she will help us."

John and I had to explain to the children that because of the shooting their last name was now going to be Kaufman. I felt awful doing this to them, but we had no choice. That night everyone went to the cafeteria and brought back their food so that we could eat dinner together. I enjoyed just being with my family, even though I couldn't eat because I still had my feeding tube in.

John rented a house close to the hospital. The WITSEC agent put the rent and all the household bills in his name, so as not to disclose where we were living. To keep their lives as normal as possible, we enrolled the children in school right away.

My doctors at Craig started me on a program of speech, physical, and occupational therapy and classes on how to live with my disability. The first day they transferred me out of bed into my wheelchair, I had a binder around my waist to help control my blood pressure. We were going to physical therapy and my mother was coming along. I could only endure fifteen minutes before I started to pass out and panic. They had to take me back to my room.

I hadn't sat up for two months and I didn't realize my body would react that way. Once I was able to sit up in my chair for more than two hours, I asked my nurse, Helene, if I could wash my hair. She said, "Yes, but I will need your mother to help me."

My mother and Helene drove my wheelchair over to the sink and leaned it back. While my mother supported my neck, Helene removed my collar and started to wash the blood from my hair. Helene said, "Oh my gosh, Heather, you have a terrible sore from the collar back here and your hair is coming out in that spot."

When she told me that, tears began to roll down the sides of my cheeks. "Please don't show me," I said. "I can't bear to see it." I looked up at my mom and started to cry even more.

"Oh, honey," she said, "don't get upset."

I tried to stop crying, but so much had changed in my life I couldn't handle it. I was paralyzed from the neck down and would never be able to put my arms around my kids again. I had to be fed every bite of food and drop of water by someone else, washed and dressed by strangers, and depended on a ventilator for every breath I took. I'd be forever beholden to others, asking them for everything I needed, rather than doing it myself.

Why had they revived me? What was I good for now? Who could live like this? Who would want to? I was a total burden to everyone. I had seen and read about people with this type of injury, like Christopher Reeve, and had pitied them. I had wondered how they and their families handled it. Now I was one of them. Never in my wildest dreams had I envisioned this would be my life.

I went through all five stages of grief: denial that this had happened to me, of all people, who had such a zest for life. I felt anger at Ron, at God, for putting me in this situation—after all, I had been a good person. I bargained with God to make it not true, to let me wake up and find out this was a nightmare and not my life. I would get depressed, and eventually I gained acceptance. I still had three great kids to raise and the support of a loving family and husband. I decided I would not let Ron win. I would live my life and do as much as I could. I moved on.

With the help of my speech therapist I was drinking water and had just started learning how to eat again. By the time Thanksgiving came around I was able to enjoy dinner in the cafeteria with John, my mom, and all the children. I was well enough to attend most of my therapy sessions and begin to meet the other quadriplegics and their families.

My mother went home to Minnesota, so John hired a babysitter named Glenda to help him with the children. She was a simple-looking woman in her fifties, with short brown hair and glasses. Every day after school Glenda would pick up the children and bring them to the hospital. They would hang out, do their homework, and then we would have dinner together. I felt guilty that John had to take on such a huge responsibility by himself. Every day he conducted business with his office in Florida. He dealt with the Boca Raton police about the investigation and at night he took care of the children. I could tell he was stressed but he handled it well. Every night when the children went to bed he would call me so I could tell them good night and I loved them.

One morning John came to my room and said, "We have a problem."

"What is it?"

"We need to call Laura Keene," he said. "Ron has filed a petition to take full custody of Ronnie, Lauren, and Joe, stating it endangers their lives to be with you."

I started to cry. "You have got to be kidding! How can they even allow this to happen?"

John hugged me. "Don't worry," he said. "Everything will be fine. Ron is out of his mind. The hearing is today at one o'clock. Laura says you need to call and speak with the judge."

The hospital helped us with the equipment we needed to be on the conference call for the hearing. When the hearing started Judge Rasmussen asked me how I was doing. "I am doing fine," I said, "and recovering well."

Judge Rasmussen said, "I am throwing out this frivolous attempt to change the custody order. Custody stays with Mrs. Grossman." Don Sasser then tried to recuse Judge Rasmussen, stating he had a lack of impartiality. Judge Rasmussen said, "Absolutely not!" When the hearing was finished we were relieved at the outcome. I spoke with Laura for a few minutes. She told me not to worry about anything and to relax and get better.

In January 1998, Dr. Scott Falci preformed a ten-hour surgery on my neck. He placed a titanium rod in my spine from C4 through C8 to stabilize my neck. My parents flew back for the surgery. They planned to stay in Denver until I was done with rehab. The doctors stated the surgery was a success.

I felt better within two weeks and attended physical therapy and classes again. Three weeks after surgery I was ready to go on a group outing. John and the kids came along. There were ten people in wheelchairs loaded up on the shuttle plus their families. The occupational therapists, Randy and Sue, locked in our wheelchairs and made sure they were secure. We headed to the movies.

Halfway through the ride I started to cry. My neck was bouncing around on every bump, I felt sick to my stomach, and I was freezing. When we arrived at the theater I was so miserable, I didn't even want to watch the movie. I wanted to go back to the hospital, but I didn't want to disappoint the kids. With my teeth chattering and blankets piled on me, I stuck it out. I was glad to get back to the hospital and my warm room. I wasn't ready to be out in the world yet.

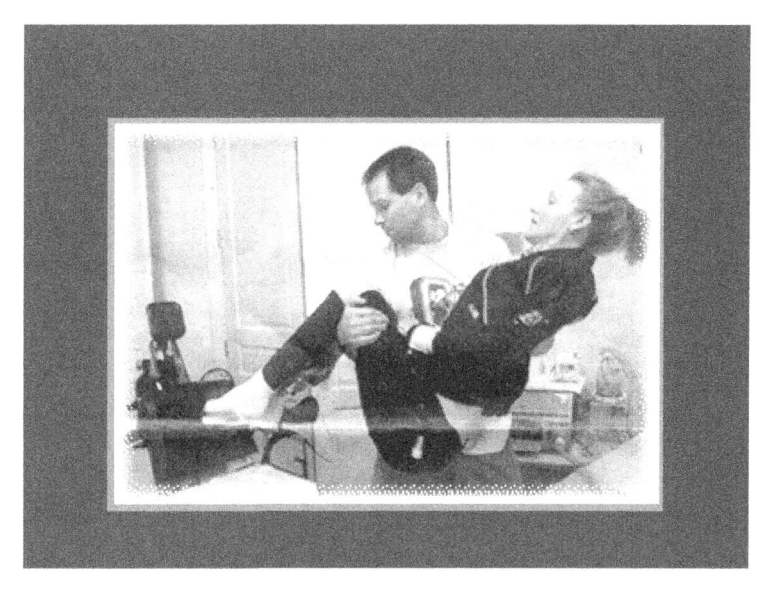

Heather being assisted by one of her nurses, Aron Belame.

Heather's new life as a quadriplegic on a ventilator.

Chapter 38

Over the next few months family and friends visited me. I was making progress with physical therapy and occupational therapy. I was feeling the results. I even learned how to drive my wheelchair with a sip and puff straw. In the process I put two holes in the wall. I ran into a decorative tree and knocked it over. I almost ran over Dr. Luke. Believe me, it's not easy learning how to drive a wheelchair. I kept trying even though the patients and staff laughed at me and called me Crash Kauffman.

John called Detective Sanchez and asked for an update on our case, but it was not good news. The police were still searching for the weapon that was used in the shooting. They were still interrogating the suspects, but they were not cooperating. Scott Richardson, from the state attorney's office in West Palm Beach, Florida, flew to Denver to meet with John and me. Mr. Richardson was six feet tall and slender with dark-brown hair and glasses. We sat in my hospital room with the door closed.

Mr. Richardson said, "I'm here on behalf of Barry Cusher, the state attorney. In order to prosecute Ron Samuels we must give immunity to the others involved in the shooting."

"Who would get immunity?" John asked.

Mr. Richardson responded, "Jeff Pollock, the stalker; Hugh Estes, who found the shooter; Eddie Stafford, the driver; and Roger Runyon, the shooter."

"Hell no!" John said. "There is no way they're getting away with what they did."

"We need their testimony to prove Ron is guilty," Mr. Richardson said.

"I don't care about the other three," I said, "but I want the shooter prosecuted."

Mr. Richardson said, "I'm here to make a deal and both of you have to sign off on it."

John and I asked Mr. Richardson to leave the room. When he walked out John said, "What do you think, Heather?"

"I think we have to take the deal and give the other men immunity."

"No," John said, "they all deserve to go to jail."

"Ron is the one who wanted us dead. He's the one who needs to rot in jail. Don't you agree?"

"Yes I do," John said, "but I think this is bullshit."

John opened the door and asked Mr. Richardson to come back in. We signed off on the deal. John and I were not happy. I felt sick to my stomach, but we had no choice.

My parents came to the hospital every day. On the weekends they would take Ronnie, Lauren, and Joe to amusement parks, Chuck E. Cheese, movies, and museums. It helped them to cope and let them be kids.

One afternoon my mom and I were sitting outside. "I don't want to upset you," she said, "but I'm concerned about the way John has been talking to you and how he's been treating the children lately."

"I've noticed a change in his attitude with me, but I thought it was due to stress. What's going on with him and the kids?"

"He's not being understanding with them. He's being downright mean. The kids can't be kids without being yelled at. He's also roughhousing with them in an inappropriate manner. He's putting them in headlocks between his legs and holding them until they cry and he laughs about it."

"That doesn't sound like him, Mom," I said. "I'm worried. I'm going to talk to him."

The next day my parents spoke to Dr. Luke and my psychologist, Lisa Pain, about John's recent behavior. I didn't even get a chance to speak to John before shit hit the fan. Dr. Luke and Mrs. Pain addressed the issues with John right away. John became enraged.

He saw my mom and dad standing in the hall outside my room. He approached them and started yelling at them. He was so loud I could hear him. "Get out of this hospital!" he screamed. "I don't ever want to see you here again!"

My mom yelled back, "That's my daughter in there! I have to be here to help her!"

"I'm her husband and I'll decide who's going to see her!" John said. My parents had no choice but to leave.

John came into my room; I was crying. I asked him, "Why did you do that? I heard everything."

"Your parents lied about me to the doctors."

"John, they're just concerned about you. You have a lot to cope with right now."

"I don't give a shit what they think," he said. "They embarrassed me."

I didn't say anything else to him, but I felt terrible. That night while I was watching TV my nurse, Mary Ann, came in and told me I had a phone call. She put in my ear piece and I said "hello." It was my mom and she said, "I'm sorry we had to leave today. I love you and I want you to get better. Please don't stress out about this. We're fine. The conflict between us and John won't help the situation, so your dad and I will be going home soon."

"I don't want you to go," I said. "I love you so much."

"What are we supposed to do?" she said. "John is determined to keep us away from you. I'll keep in touch; I'll call you at night. I love you."

"I love you, too," I said.

As soon as we hung up Mary Ann came in and said, "John's on the phone." The first thing he said was, "I've been trying to call you. Who have you been talking to?"

I paused for a minute, and then said, "My mom. She said they would be going home soon." I could hear anger in his voice.

"I don't want those people causing problems between us."

"John, I'm tired. I'm going to bed. Goodnight."

"Goodnight," he said. "I love you."

I couldn't believe this was happening. I was so upset I didn't even want to talk to him.

Bud and Beverly visited me consistently. I was happy to have their support, because having them around made John's mood better. John was always on his best behavior when his father was around. I only wished they would have been here when he erupted on my parents. I didn't say anything to them about what had happened. God only knows what he told them.

My rehabilitation was almost finished at Craig Hospital. John and I were planning on going home to Boca Raton. John called Berry Kusher, the state attorney, to inform him. He said, "Mr. Samuels has not been arrested yet. It is not safe for you to move back here with Heather and the children."

"How long do you think it's going to take?" John asked.

"We're working diligently on your case," Mr. Kusher said, "but it could still take a few months."

John hung up. "We have a problem," he said. "We can't go home. They haven't arrested Ron and they think it's too dangerous."

"What are we going to do? Should we stay here in Colorado?"

"No. We are going somewhere with nice weather. I will contact witness protection to inform them of what's going on."

"Okay," I said.

A few days later John flew to San Diego, California. He rented a five-bedroom home overlooking the ocean in La Jolla, California. We were still in the witness protection program so John's father, Bud, signed the lease. John furnished the home by renting everything from beds to wall décor. When John returned to Denver he told me everything he had accomplished.

"John you did a wonderful job," I told him.

He kissed me and said, "I can't wait to get out of here! I'm very excited. You're going to love La Jolla. It's beautiful."

"I can't wait!" I replied.

The truth was, I was afraid to leave Craig Hospital. I was surrounded by other people who were like me in wheelchairs. I was terrified to be out in the real world. I turned to Father John for guidance. He had visited me in the ICU a few times. I told him how I didn't think I could be a good mother. I was filled with fear and doubt about living my life in my wheelchair.

"There is a reason you're alive," he said. "God never makes a mistake. You may not understand right now, but you will. You're a strong person. Your faith will get you through this."

"Thank you, Father," I said. "I appreciate your advice."

When I hung up the phone I was disappointed. I wanted an answer. I knew I had faith, but I was angry. I questioned God—why had this happened to me? I'd been a good person and had never gone out of my way to hurt anyone. I just didn't understand.

Chapter 39

The day we left Craig Hospital we traveled out of there in a caravan, carrying me, John, the three kids, a registered nurse, a respiratory therapist, and a certified nursing assistant. Not to mention all of our luggage, my medical equipment, and supplies. We all flew to San Diego. John had already set up transportation.

Upon arrival there was a disability van waiting for me outside the airport. The kids jumped in the back of the van and everyone else took taxis. As we drove into La Jolla, I couldn't believe how beautiful it was. It was a sunny day; the temperature was eighty-five degrees. We had our windows down as we drove. I could smell the ocean and feel the humidity in the air.

We pulled up to the house. The first thing I noticed was a flower bed overfilled with impatiens of different colors. The lawn was nicely landscaped with lush green grass and palm trees.

When the nurse opened the van door the kids jumped out. As soon as John opened the front door the kids hurried inside the house, anxious to check it out. My nurse got me out of the van and I followed them inside. I loved the contemporary interior. My favorite was the living room. It had floor-to-ceiling windows overlooking the ocean. It was breathtaking.

Over the next week I enjoyed adding my personal touch to the home. I shopped for linens, bedding, plates, and cookware. Jeremy, John's office assistant, flew in from Florida to help us with the transition. John and I enrolled Ronnie, Lauren, and Joe in Torrey Pines Elementary School in La Jolla. Ronnie Kaufman was in third grade, and the Kaufman twins were in first.

My first task was to find and hire four nurses. I required round-the-clock nursing care. Two nurses would work days and two on nights. I interviewed for three days. The Colorado nurse and health team trained my new nurses before leaving. It was hard to say good-bye to them. After all, I had been with them for six-and-a-half months. I thanked them graciously for everything they did. The new nurses started immediately.

Terry and Mike came down from Los Angeles to celebrate my thirty-second birthday. We spent the afternoon walking around Seaport Village and had dinner at the Chart House. We sat by the window, overlooking the water. I could see the waves crashing on the rocks down below. The children were a little fidgety at the table and John seemed frustrated. Mike moved their chairs over by him and entertained them. It felt great to be out enjoying life, but by the end of the evening, I was exhausted.

In mid- May, Detective Sanchez called and spoke to John. "We are going to the grand jury to indict Ron Samuels," he said.

"It's been eight months since the shooting," John said. "It's about time. I can't wait to tell Heather."

Detective Sanchez said, "I'll call you as soon as we have the warrant for his arrest."

"Thank you so much," John said. He hung up the phone and looked at me with a big grin on his face. "It's finally happening, Heather," he said. "He's going to be arrested." That afternoon John, my nurse, Aaron, and I went to lunch at the Hard Rock Café in La Jolla. We discussed the news from Detective Sanchez. We were excited.

When the waitress brought our food, Aaron placed napkins on my chest and lap. He gave me a bite of my salad and put my fork down. I looked over at Aaron and thought to myself, I'm never going to have a moment alone anymore. A nurse will always be with me. Aaron reached over and loaded up my fork with salad. He gave me another bite and asked, "Would you like a drink of soda?" "Yes please," I replied. He lifted my glass and put the straw to my lips. I took a sip and said, "thank you."

After lunch, to pass the time, we roamed around the area and looked in a few shops. We picked up the children when school got out, drove to the house, and waited for the call. Thirty minutes later the phone rang. It was Detective Sanchez. "We have the warrant for his arrest," he said. "We are on our way to his house now. I'll call you when he's in our custody."

"That's great news," John said. "We'll be waiting to hear back from you." John hung up the phone and said to me, "They're on their way to pick up Ron right now."

An hour passed before the phone rang again. John answered. Detective Sanchez said, "When we arrived at Ron Samuels's apartment, his wife informed us that he had packed his things and left. He had to have been tipped off. He's on the run!"

When I looked at John I knew something was wrong by the look on his face. "How the hell could you let this happen?" he screamed. "You have to be the stupidest detectives I've ever known!"

I impatiently asked, "John what happened?"

"Heather, hold on! I have to finish talking to these idiots!"

John continued to scream into the phone for the next five minutes as I sat patiently waiting. The last thing I heard John say was, "You better find that bastard!" John turned to me and said, "Those assholes screwed up! After waiting eight months, when they went to arrest him, Ron was gone!"

"I kind of gathered that," I said. "What are they going to do now?"

"Chase him, I guess," John replied. "Sanchez said they're searching his apartment now."

Five days later, at seven in the morning I was awoken by the fax machine. I yelled, "John, there's a fax!" He pulled it off the machine and read it out loud:

A Boca Raton man whose ex-wife was shot and paralyzed eight months ago in an alleged murder-for-hire plot remains in a Mexican jail on Tuesday after police found six kilograms of cocaine in his luggage, authorities said. Ronald Samuels, 50, was arrested on Friday in Nuevo Leon state after a high-speed police chase through the streets of the northern Mexico City Monterrey. The chase ended when Samuels crashed his rental car."

I was in shock when John finished reading the article. "I can't believe he's dealing drugs!" I said. "What happened to him?"

"Did you ever know him to do drugs?" John asked.

"No, absolutely not. He obviously had to do something to make money after he put his money from the sale of the dealership in the Grand Caymans and paid no taxes."

"Thank God he is in jail and we know where he is."

"I'm happy they caught him," I said, "but it is Mexico. What if he pays his way out?"

"I'm going to call Sanchez to find out all the details," John said.

"I'm going to have the nurse get me out of bed and wash my hair," I said. "I will be out in a couple of hours."

When I came out to the kitchen John was sitting at the table having coffee. He said, "Detective Sanchez found cocaine, passports for the children, and phony passports for Ron in alias names. They also found an album with pictures of you and articles about your shooting when they searched his apartment."

"Oh my God!" I said. "It's really creepy that he would have an album with pictures of me."

"I told you he was obsessed with you."

"The whole thing makes me sick," I said.

"Detective Sanchez said Debbie Samuels was a key player in getting Ron arrested. She let the FBI tape her calls with Ron, which led to him getting caught in Mexico. I'm glad she cooperated with them," John said.

Two hours later the phone rang. John answered it. I was talking to my nurse, Aaron, in the family room. John came running into the room and said, "That was Sanchez. He said the FBI agent who interrogated Ron in Mexico just called him. Ron said that he paid someone to kidnap the children."

"If that's true, then what are we going to do?" I said. "We have to keep them safe."

"We're still in witness protection, so I don't know how he could have found us. We'll just have to be extra cautious."

"I can't believe this is happening," I said. "Ron is still haunting me from jail."

Over the next month John, the nurse on duty, and I watched over the children like hawks. We were extra careful whenever we went somewhere. I informed Torrey Pines Elementary that I would be picking up the children and dropping them off in the office. When they asked why, I had to tell them about the kidnapping plot. The principal was understanding and told all of their teachers to keep a close watch over them.

Chapter 40

It was summertime and the kids were out of school. Every day seemed like an adventure to them. We enjoyed going to Sea World and the San Diego Zoo, walking down the boardwalk at Mission Beach, and visiting Balboa Park. Our home overlooked the beach, where we enjoyed laying out while the kids swam in the waves.

On the weekends the kids would have a lemonade stand on the beach with their friends Zach and Alexis. John and I had become good friends with their parents, Jeannie and Mike Kushner. Whether we went to a San Diego Padres baseball game, the movies, or dinner we always had a nice time.

John's aunt and uncle, Harold and Gene, lived in Arizona but owned a condo on Coronado Island. When it would reach over a hundred degrees in Scottsdale they would escape to Coronado. John and I looked forward to seeing them. They visited us in La Jolla almost every other week. Bud and Beverly flew in from Minnesota to visit us every month. It was nice to have family support and I appreciated it, but I missed my parents. I had not seen them since the fight at Craig Hospital. My mom called me every night at the hospital, but I hadn't spoken to her since I was discharged. I wished I could see them, but it was not the right time.

Craig Hospital was superb in planning my after-care. They referred me to a San Diego-based physiatrist, who specialized in the nonsurgical treatment of painful nerve, joint, and muscle conditions. I called Dr. Lance Stone's office and made an appointment. A week later, John, Aaron, and I met Dr. Stone. We were waiting in the rehab area, when a man with light-brown hair and average build walked up to me and said, "Hello, I'm Dr. Stone."

I replied, "Hello, I'm Heather Kaufman." He was neatly dressed and there wasn't a hair out of place. When he examined me I noticed he was soft spoken. I could tell he was a caring doctor.

"Dr. Stone," I said. "I'm interested in buying an Ergys bike. I rode one at Craig Hospital and really liked it. Can you find a physical therapy place that has one?"

"I'll have to do some research," he said, "but I'll get back to you."

"I was a runner and always had a highly physical lifestyle. It's important to me to continue that."

"I understand," he said. "I'm a runner myself."

On our way out John and Dr. Stone chatted. John found out that he lived in La Jolla, only two blocks from us. What a coincidence!

The next day I was surprised when my new van arrived. John and I went outside and watched them unload it from the transport truck. It was a navy-blue Ford Econoline van with all-leather interior and a pro river ramp. A month before, when Beverly was visiting, she had offered to buy me a new van, and we'd chosen the custom features I wanted and needed. Once the van was unloaded John and I checked it out. The driver gave us the keys and showed us how to work the ramp. We went inside and called Beverly.

"The van just arrived," I said. "It's perfect! Thank you so much!"

"Oh, honey," she said, "you deserve it."

We drove to Los Angeles for a summer trip with the children and two nurses. We were staying for five days and planned on visiting the LA theme parks.

The first thing on our agenda was to visit John's brother, Dick, and his wife, Lisa. When we pulled up, I remembered the last time I had been there. I was able to walk in the front door. This time it was a challenge. John and my nurse, Chris, pushed the sides of my wheelchair through the grass uphill and around to the back of the house.

Dick was waiting for us with the back door open. He greeted me with a smile and a kiss on the cheek. He gave John a hug, said hello to the kids, and introduced himself to Chris. After lunch we sat poolside with fresh iced teas. The kids swam and played in the pool. Dick and Lisa were inquisitive of my case so John and I updated them on the recent developments. We talked mainly of Ron's arrest in Mexico. Dick, being an author said, "Heather, your story would make a great movie."

"Do you really think so?" I said.

John interrupted. "I don't think Dad would be too happy about that. He prefers our personal affairs to remain private."

After a few hours it started to get warm. I told the kids to get out of the pool and my nurse helped dry them off. When we entered the living room I said, "This is such a beautiful house."

"You know Dick," Lisa said. "He loves buying famous real estate. When we purchased this property there were two homes on it. This one was owned by Cecil B. DeMille and the adjacent one was owned by Charlie Chaplain."

"That's interesting!" I said. "Your home is a Hollywood landmark." Dick and Lisa walked us around and showed us the renovations they had made. They invited us to dinner but we declined because it was getting late and we had to check in to our hotel. We were staying at the Disneyland Resort.

The next morning our kids couldn't wait to go to Disneyland. They loved seeing all the characters and had fun on the rides. There were tons of people everywhere. The lines for the rides were long, with waits of one to two hours. We stood in line and the attendant approached us and said, "You don't have to wait in line due to your disability." He brought us to the front of the line and the kids got on. Finally, there was a perk to being paralyzed! This made the experience much more pleasant for me and the kids thought it was great.

We had BBQ for dinner and then walked to Main Street to watch the light parade. John bought the boys flashing light swords and Lauren a spinning Tinkerbell light and light-up Minnie Mouse ears. It filled me with joy to see my kids so happy. The next day we took the tram to Universal Studios and the following day we drove to Knott's Berry Farm. By the end of our Los Angeles adventure, everyone was exhausted and ready to go home.

It was September and the kids were starting a new school year. I signed up Ronnie, Lauren, and Joe at the Boys and Girls Club. It was conveniently located right across the street from Torrey Pines Elementary. Most of their friends were members so they liked going to the afterschool program. I signed them up to play basketball on the weekends with their friends Alexis and Zach.

Dr. Stone found a physical therapy place for me, called the Challenge Center. I started training on the bike three days a week. Every Monday, Wednesday, and Friday my nurses would dress me in my bike pants and workout clothes. We would drive thirty-five minutes to the Challenge Center. I was building my leg muscles so I could increase my endurance to ride. After I finished my rehabilitation I always felt great. It felt good to push myself.

My nurse got me ready for a day of shopping. I asked John for money and he gave me $2,000 out of the safe. He gave me a kiss and said, "I'll meet you at the mall."

It felt strange paying cash for everything. Nothing could be traced back to us. We couldn't use checks or credit cards.

Aaron and I left early for the anniversary sale at Nordstrom at Town Center Mall. I wanted to look at new fall clothing styles. He maneuvered me through the aisles as he pulled things from the racks and showed them to me. I had picked out a couple suits, sweaters, and some dress pants. John found us and I asked him, "What do you think of these?"

"They're nice," he said.

We checked out and left the bags for Nordstrom to hold in the back because it was too much to carry. We strolled around enjoying the weather. Town Center Mall was outdoors and had a dining plaza. We had lunch at a café and then we went to Starbucks for café mochas and dessert. When we arrived home everyone was laughing and in good spirits. What a nice day, I thought to myself. The last time I had been at Town Center Mall, I remember being scared and paranoid about the children's safety.

Ronnie, Lauren, and Joe woke me up to show me their Halloween costumes. They all looked so cute; Lauren was dressed as Dorothy with little red ruby slippers and braids in her hair, and the boys were ninja warriors. I kissed each one of them good-bye and said "John and I will see you at the school later. We're coming to the Halloween parade. I love you."

"We love you too," they said.

John drove them to school. Chris, my nurse on duty, put me in my chair, fixed my hair, and put on my makeup. We drove to the school and John got dressed up in his clown costume, complete with a big, puffy, multicolored wig and a red nose. Chris put my witch's hat on me and in the background I heard someone yell, "John, I like your new hairstyle!"

I asked my nurse to turn my wheelchair around and I saw Jeannie and Mike. "You guys look awesome," I said.

"Thank you!" Jeannie said. "Let me give you some finishing touches." She walked toward me and glued rubber warts onto my face. "Now you look perfect."

We all went to the back of the school and watched the parade. I was pleased that so many parents showed up to support their adorable children. The parade lasted half an hour and everyone had cake, coffee, and punch afterward. John gathered the kids together while Chris loaded me into the van and we drove back to the house.

As soon as we got home I had the children take out their homework. I told them, "Let's get your homework done before we go trick-or-treating."

While I helped the children finish their schoolwork, John placed a call to the FBI agent to make sure that Ron was still jailed in Monterrey,

Mexico. John's father had hired the FBI agent to monitor Ron's whereabouts at all times.

When John came out of the office, he looked at me and said, "We don't have to worry; everything is fine."

We had made plans to trick-or-treat with the Kushner family. At dusk John, the kids, and I were at Jeannie and Mike's, ready to go. We went in a group from home to home collecting candy. After a while the twins began to get tired so John carried Lauren and Joseph sat on my lap. The kids went home with more candy than they could ever eat, but we all had a wonderful time.

Chapter 41

December was my favorite time of the year. By now we had settled into our lives in La Jolla as the Kaufmans. The children were happy at school and John and I had made many friends. The nurses helped me decorate the house for Christmas and Hanukah.

I enjoyed buying Christmas presents, but it was more difficult this year. We had to use cash only and I kept running out and having to go back to the house to get more. For a person with a disability, running back to the house isn't easy. I would have to go up and down the ramp, get the packages out and try to hide them from the children, and then back into the van and off again. Finally, I decided I should just take a whole wad of cash with me each time I left.

By mid-month I was feeling stress free. I had finished my shopping and the nurses had wrapped all my gifts. John said, "Let's have a Hanukah party!"

We invited Brent, Jeremy, Dr. Stone, his son Chase, and of course our family. For dinner John made homemade potato latkes served with sour cream and applesauce, roasted chicken, and green beans with toasted almonds. After we exchanged gifts, we sang on Lauren's new karaoke machine.

John and I said good-bye to our friends. I told the children to get their pajamas on and I kissed them good night. Aaron brought me to my room and transferred me to bed. John came in the room and lay beside me. "How did you like your gift?" I asked. I had paid for sessions with a personal trainer at a local La Jolla gym.

"I'm really excited about it," he said. "I need to get back into shape."

"It's for three months with a personal trainer named Bruce. I know you were stressed while I was in the hospital and it caused you to gain some weight."

"It was too many late-night pizzas, I think."

"I just want you to be healthy and happy."

John kissed me and replied, "I love you!"

"I love you too!" I said.

The next few months were busy. I hired two babysitters to help take Ronnie, Joe, and Lauren back and forth to school. Bonnie was athletic with blonde hair and a bubbly personality. Ann was a tall, slender woman with dark hair and pale skin. Both women were good to the kids. The children enjoyed being with them and they behaved well.

John had done his monthly check on Ron and found out that he was still in jail and not going anywhere. The witness protection agency decided it was safe for us to make a trip back to Boca Raton. The moment we heard this, we started planning our eight-day trip. We figured the best time to go would be during the kids' spring break.

Traveling would never be easy for us again, and the expense was huge. We purchased tickets for John, the children, and I, along with four nurses and two nannies. John, the kids, and I would stay at our home but I had to make reservations for the nurses and nannies at a nearby hotel. We rented one disability van and two other rental cars. One car was for John and one was for the nurses.

We planned our trip for April. Three days before I left, I was a basket case, trying to pack my children's suitcases with the nurse's assistance. My nurses made a supply and travel list for my medical care. They kept coming to me and saying they didn't know if they had everything or if they had packed enough supplies. By the time everyone was ready to leave, there were eighteen suitcases lined up by the front door.

When we got to the airport we were able to pre-board first. John, Aaron, and I sat in bulkhead seats in first class. Everyone else sat in coach. I felt terrible when the plane took off because Ronnie was terrified of flying and I wasn't able to hold his hand and comfort him.

The flight took four hours and forty-five minutes. My forehead hurt because I had to tie my head to the back of the seat. Every hour my nurse stood me up and held me against him to shift my weight so I wouldn't get a pressure sore. When the plane landed, we were the last ones off. I had to wait for the agent to bring my wheelchair. Aaron transferred me into it and we all left the plane together. While the nurses collected our bags, John, Chris and Bonnie went to pick up the rental van and cars.

When we drove up to the house I could feel anxiety building inside of me. I had missed my beautiful home. The kids hopped out of the van and were excited to run inside and check out their old bedrooms. My nurse put down the ramp for me to go through the front door.

John brought me inside. When I looked around it was as if time had stood still. I started to cry. "Oh, honey," John said, "are you okay?" He wiped away the tears from my eyes.

"I'll be fine," I said.

Nothing was out of place. It was just like the morning I left, before I was shot. When I went by the coffee table I got a creepy feeling as I saw magazines dated October 1997. I asked John to take me to the bedroom.

When he wheeled me into the room it was sad to see our empty closets. I remembered John asking me to come back to bed that morning. I started to tear up again, thinking how our lives would never be the same.

"Honey, please don't cry," John said.

"I just realize how much I miss it here," I said. The rest of the day my nurse unpacked all the medical supplies and set up for my care. John and I sat on the patio and relaxed while the children swam in our pool. For dinner that evening we ordered in pizza for everyone. I woke up in the middle of the night to the vent alarm going off. I thought to myself,

"Here I am in our beautiful room alone and in this medical bed." I came to the conclusion that it sucked.

The next morning I called Donna and Harvey. They were shocked that we were in town. Donna wanted to get together right away, but I told her that John and I had a lunch date and we would have to do it another time. She insisted on picking up the kids and taking them for the afternoon to play with Bret and Ashley.

John, Aaron, and I met Bruce Goodman and Ken Hawkins at Houston's for lunch. After we ordered our food, we started telling them what had been going on in our lives. Bruce and Ken could hardly believe it. As we were eating I began to look around the restaurant and noticed that all eyes were on me. I asked them, "Do you notice people staring at me?"

Bruce answered, "I am sure they are wondering if you are Heather Grossman."

"I'm just not used to this," I said.

"Nobody ever gets shot in Boca Raton," Bruce replied.

We looked at each other and laughed. As we left Houston's and said our good-byes, a woman came up to me, patted my head, and said, "God bless you. Are you the woman that was shot?"

"Yes."

"How are you doing?"

"I'm doing fine," I replied. "Thank you for asking."

On the way home we stopped to have two plaques made. One for the police department and the other for the fire department to thank them for their service during my accident.

When we arrived at Donna and Harvey's house to pick up the kids, Harvey came out to the van. "Please come into the house, Heather," he said. "Donna can't wait to see you."

"Of course," I said. "Just give me a minute to get out."

Aaron drove me down my ramp; Harvey was waiting at the end of it. He gave me a big hug and said, "Boy, Heather, I missed you guys!"

Just then Donna came running out of the house with her arms in the air saying, "Oh my God, I cannot believe you are finally here." She placed her hand on top of mine and we all walked in together. Donna offered everyone refreshments. John and I sat down with Donna and Harvey and told them about our crazy life.

After a few hours of talking and laughing; Harvey said he was going to order Chinese food for dinner and John and he left to pick it up. Donna and I continued to talk as she set the table for dinner. The children came into the kitchen when John and Harvey returned with the food. Everyone savored being together; it was like old times.

The next morning John, my nurse, and I drove to Del Rey Hospital. I wanted to thank the doctors and nurses who had taken care of me. When we got inside it didn't look anything like I remembered.

John and I met with two of the doctors who had taken care of me. We talked with them and thanked them both. John took me to the nurses' station and I saw a familiar face. I smiled and said, "Hello, Sue, it's so nice to see you."

She recognized me without hesitation. "You look great!" she said. "How have you been?" We talked for a bit. Then she asked me if I wanted to see the room I had stayed in. John and I followed her through the ICU. "Here is your bed," she said. "You were here for five and a half weeks."

"You have got to be kidding," I said. "I thought I had switched rooms."

"No, you are the longest patient I have ever had in the ICU," she said.

We thanked Sue and the staff for all the care and help they gave me. We said our good-byes and left.

The following day John and I took everyone to breakfast. While we waited to be seated, they pulled together tables for our large group. By the time everyone finished their food, I realized that almost everywhere I went people would stare at me.

The nurses and nannies had the day off to sightsee. The next stop for John, the kids, and I was the Boca Raton Police Department. We went in to find Detective Sanchez; when he saw us, he walked over and greeted us kindly.

John said, "We'd like to present a plaque to all the officers who have helped with the investigation and thank them for their hard work."

With a surprised look on his face, Detective Sanchez said, "That is so nice! Let me get all the officers together." He brought them all into the room and we thanked them. Ronnie presented the plaque to Detective Sanchez as everyone lined up for a picture. We said our good-byes and headed to the fire station.

When we entered, John spoke to the chief and asked if he could see the paramedics who were on duty when I was taken to the hospital. The children asked if they could see the fire trucks. The chief had one of the firefighters give the kids a tour.

The chief made a couple of calls and out came three men. John and I introduced ourselves, thanked them, and presented them with the plaques. They all were appreciative.

One of the men said, "This is the first time anyone has ever done this!"

We stayed for a while and waited for the children to return. The chief said, "Mrs. Grossman, could I have your home number? I know Michael would love to come see you."

"Who's Michael?"

"He's the medic who rode in the ambulance with you."

"Sure," I said. "I would love to meet him."

John wrote down our number and handed it to the chief. When we got home, John went upstairs and tucked the children into bed. He came back down to spend time with me as my nurse got me ready for bed.

In the morning John and I were ready early. Detective Sanchez was coming to visit with us. I had Donna pick up the children to entertain them until Bret and Ashley got home from school. We were sitting at the kitchen table when Detective Sanchez arrived. John opened the door and the detective joined us at the table. John poured him a cup of coffee.

Sanchez began, "I'm here to go over your case and give you additional information that you may not be aware of."

"I would definitely like to hear it," John said.

"First of all," Sanchez said, "Mr. Samuels had people stalking you for two months before the shooting. He paid an ex-convict $25,000 to shoot you in September. You were lucky."

John gasped. "We had no idea someone was following us!"

"He saw your wife with the children and decided he couldn't do it," Sanchez continued. "So he took the money and ran. There were also two other plans that they had in store for you, Heather. The first one was to break into your home, tie John up, rape and then kill you, and steal your jewelry to make it look like a burglary."

"With the children in the house?" I said. "That would have been terrible!"

"With the guard gates and surveillance in your area they thought it was too risky, so they scratched that idea. The other plan was to kidnap you and rape and torture you until you died."

"Thank God they didn't do it," I said. "I wouldn't have survived it."

I didn't want to hear any more. I felt disgusted and sick to my stomach. I said good-bye and thanked Detective Sanchez for all his help. I asked Aaron to take me outside on the patio.

John and Sanchez talked for an hour longer. I came in at the end of their conversation as John walked the detective to the door. John and I sat and talked in disbelief. "Ron Samuels is an evil, disgusting man," I said. "I will never forgive him for any of this."

Just then the phone rang and John stood to answer it. He had a brief conversation and hung up. He turned to me and said, "Michael, the paramedic, is on his way to see you."

"Lucky me!" I said. "Two visitors in one day. That first one was hard to take but I am sure this one will be a pleasure."

When Michael arrived he had a big grin on his face and was carrying a bouquet of flowers. He was young, with sandy-brown hair, clean-cut, and cute.

"Hi," I said. "I'm Heather. It's so nice to meet you."

"The pleasure is all mine," Michael said. He handed me the flowers and kissed my cheek.

"Thank you so much for the flowers." I asked Aaron to put them in a vase for me.

"I want to thank you for saving my wife's life," John said.

"You are welcome. I'll never forget that day. When I train new paramedics, I talk about that day." He looked at me and asked, "Do you remember anything from the accident?"

"Not really," I replied. "Only waking up in the ambulance."

"Let me tell you what happened," Michael said. "I was buying my lunch and I received the call about the shooting. When I arrived on scene, I was nervous and my hands were shaking, I had only been a medic for six months. I looked at you and thought, 'Oh, you are so beautiful!' I checked your vitals and injuries and realized you were missing half your neck and you were dead. I took a deep breath and began trying to resuscitate you. When I realized I was unable to, I intubated but it was difficult because of all the blood. Once I got it in I started bagging you. We immediately got you into the ambulance. You were in shock and I continued to bag you all the way to the hospital."

"I am so thankful you were there," I said.

"I was just doing my job," he replied. We visited for a few minutes longer. I thanked him again and John and I said good-bye.

Chapter 42

When I awoke the next morning, John and the kids brought me breakfast in bed and shouted, "Happy birthday, Mom!"

"Thank you," I said, kissing each of them. After I finished eating Ronnie and John ran out of the room and came back in with presents for me. The kids were excited and said, "Open them, Mommy! Come on, open them!"

Lauren opened their present to me first; it was a black Gucci suit. I looked at the kids and said, "I love it! Thank you so much!"

John unwrapped his gift to me and opened the box. Inside there was a beautiful pair of diamond and ruby earrings. "They're gorgeous," I said. "I will cherish them forever."

"When I saw them I had to get them for you." He leaned down and we kissed.

"Boy," I said, "this is starting out to be a great day!"

John replied, "I'm going to take the kids outside to play, so your nurse can get you ready."

Two hours later I came into the kitchen wearing my new Gucci suit, with my hair curled and makeup done. Lauren said to me "Mommy, you look so nice!"

"Thank you, honey," I replied.

Our friends Randi and Steve came over and spent the afternoon with us. Steve was a chiropractor and Randi, his wife, loved to talk. We had met them through Donna and Harvey, and they'd become close friends of ours.

We went to Maxwell's to celebrate my birthday. Donna and Harvey, Steve and Randi, all the nurses, and the children were there. Everyone had a wonderful time. On our way out, John had the pianist play "Let's Stay Together" by Al Greene. We both sang along, but I was sad because John and I could not dance.

The next morning everyone packed and got ready to go to the airport. As the plane took off, I was upset. The week had flown by too fast and I did not want to leave Florida. When we arrived home the children were tired. John ordered pizza and we all went to bed early. When I woke up all I wanted to do was unpack and relax. John drove the children to school; they were excited to see their friends after the vacation. We dedicated the rest of the month to eating healthy and getting fit. We had enjoyed way too much wine and heavy foods while away.

After a few days of rest, I began my exercise routine again. My nurse and I would drive to the Challenge Center for my therapy. While I was there, John would go to his personal trainer at the gym in La Jolla. The month flew by and the children were already getting out of school for summer.

Over the next three months, John and I hung out with the kids at the boardwalk, the beach, the ball park, the zoo, and amusement parks. Jeannie and I signed Ronnie and Zach up for little league baseball. When the season began, we would all go to the games to watch our boys.

One night John said to me, "I think we should start looking at homes in La Jolla to purchase."

"What about our home in Florida?" I replied. "I love it there."

"I love it too," John said, "but it brings back bad memories for me. Besides, La Jolla is beautiful, and we've made a lot of friends here."

We agreed to look at homes and John contacted a realtor. We looked in La Jolla but everything was too small. We looked into purchasing property to build a home, but there were no suitable lots on which to buy and build a large home. After three months of looking, we became frustrated that we could not find a suitable home.

The kids started school again in September. Ronnie was in fifth grade and the twins started third grade. When I picked them up on the first day they were excited to tell me about their teachers, and they couldn't stop talking about their friends. Bud and Beverly flew in that weekend for a visit. We went to Ruth's Chris steakhouse for dinner. While we were eating, John told Bud we were having a hard time finding a house. Bud said, "Is there anything I can do to help?"

"Not really," John replied.

"Why don't you look for a home in Scottsdale, Arizona?" Beverly suggested. "After all, your father and I are there six months a year. We'd love to have you and the children close to us."

"That might be a good idea," John said. "It would be perfect for Heather because it's always warm and with her spinal cord injury, she can't regulate her temperature and gets cold fast."

"That sounds like a pretty good idea," I agreed. "Aunt Gene and Uncle Harold live there, too."

On the way home we dropped off Bud and Beverly at their hotel. When we made it to the house, the children got into their pajamas and we kissed them good night. John took me to my room and lifted me from my wheelchair to my bed. We had a serious conversation about the possibility of moving to Arizona.

Chapter 43

John called Bud's realtor, Elli Shapiro, in Arizona. Mrs. Shapiro called back a few days later, with a few houses to show us. A week later, John flew into Arizona and spent two days there looking at different listings. When he returned home he was tired and grumpy. Out of all the homes he saw, there were only two that might work for our family. We sat with the kids and looked at videos of the homes that John had made to show me. After watching them John and I decided they would not do and we needed to look further.

A few weeks later he flew back to Arizona to meet with Sandra Wilkinson, a new realtor. When Aaron and I picked him up at the airport with the kids, John had a big grin on his face. He opened the door of the van, kissed me, and said, "I think I found the perfect home for us."

"Really?" I said.

"I'll tell you all about it at dinner," he replied.

John, the children, and I watched the video. After seeing it we all agreed the house was amazing. It was a 6,000-square-foot home in Paradise Valley, with four bedrooms, a large office, swimming pool, five-car garage, basketball court, and three fireplaces. John and I were elated. After the children went to bed, we watched the video a few more times.

The next day John called Sandra Wilkinson and told her we were willing to pay the asking price. John, Aaron, and I flew into Phoenix and met Sandra Wilkinson to see the house. The moment John took me inside, I said, "I love it! It's even better than I could have imagined." Within a few weeks, John and I owned our first home in Arizona.

I was excited to tell our family and friends about the move, but first we had to talk to our nursing staff. John and I approached both of my day nurses to tell them we would be moving at the end of December. We asked them if they would be willing to relocate to Arizona.

Chris said yes right away. Aaron said he would have to talk to his fiancée, Stacy, and get back to us. The next day Aaron told us both he and Stacy would be moving. Just knowing both of my day nurses were coming to Arizona alleviated a lot of stress. I felt safe with both Chris and Aaron, and I would only have to hire two night nurses.

The next evening we had dinner with Jeannie and Mike. At dinner we told them about our plans to move. They were happy for us, but sad to see us go. The next day our two families met at the Cabrillo National Monument at Point Loma. We explored the landmark while the boys gathered information for a school project. I was enjoying sightseeing when all of a sudden I felt a piercing headache.

"I don't feel well," I told Chris. "Can you look at my chest?" He unbuttoned my blouse and noticed red strawberry patches. He checked my leg bag and there was no urine. I said, "Chris, it's one o'clock in the afternoon. There should be urine. Could you take my blood pressure, please?" It read one eighty over one hundred. That was really high for me.

He said, "I think your catheter is clogged. If we don't change it your bladder will burst."

My paralysis was causing a condition known as dysreflexia, where my brain wasn't communicating with my body, putting me at risk of stroke or heart attack. "I'm scared Chris!" I cried. "I don't know what to do."

Chris told Lauren to get John. In a panic, John said, "Should we go to the hospital?"

"Where's the nearest hospital?" Chris said. "We're at the top of this hill and we might not make it. I'll change it here."

Chris quickly put me in the van and took out the supplies. I looked down and said, "My stomach looks like a watermelon. Please hurry, Chris." He changed my suprapubic catheter on the spot. Immediately after, my urine bag filled and he drained it. The red patches disappeared, my headache vanished, and I felt better.

Chris wiped the sweat from his forehead. "Thank God we carry the backpack with supplies!" he said. "It was a matter of life and death."

Chris opened the van door. John stepped in and said, "Is everything okay?"

"Yes," replied Chris.

John put his hand on Chris's shoulder and said, "Thank you."

We got out of the van and John handed Chris a cold bottle of water. He opened another, put a straw in it, and gave me a sip. Although we'd had a scare, we continued with our day. The kids finished gathering information for their project, and we drove back to La Jolla.

Chapter 44

The Christmas season flew by. This year we only put up a tree. We were busy packing, and our holidays were overshadowed by our move to Arizona. John flew to Arizona four days before us to wait for the movers and organize everything.

The moving truck arrived on December 26. They loaded up our boxes and clothes, and then stopped at Chris and Aaron's homes to pick up their things. We left California on December 28.

The flight was short and before I knew it we were landing in Arizona. As soon as we got off the jetway, John was waiting for us. He kissed me and said, "How was your flight?"

"It was fine," I replied.

John pushed my wheelchair and we all went to the baggage claim. When we gathered our things off the belt, my suitcase was gone. John and I went to file a report. "Don't worry, honey," John said. "You can just re-buy everything." Then he went to pull the van around to pick us up.

On our way to our new home, I looked at John and he was grinning from ear to ear. He was talking like crazy.

"You're excited aren't you?" I said.

"I can't wait to show you Scottsdale and the surrounding areas. I know you're going to love it here."

"I know I will," I said.

When we arrived at the house, the kids were excited and wanted to go in right away. As soon as we went in John offered everyone a soda. He had already stocked the fridge. We sat on the patio to take a load off and relax. The backyard was beautiful. There was a kidney-shaped pool with a rock waterfall. There were large king palms landscaped behind the pool. The entertaining area had a large stainless-steel grill and television. The lawn was green and plush, with flowerpots of petunias and impatiens around the pool and patio.

The phone rang and John went in the house to answer it. He came back out and said Beverly wanted to talk to me. He held the phone to my ear.

"Can I bring you guys dinner tonight?" Beverly asked. "I'm sure you're tired from the flight."

"Thank you," I said, "but John wants to take the kids to dinner."

"Bud and I want to see you. Can we take you out to dinner tomorrow?"

"That would be great," I said. "See you tomorrow."

After we unpacked our suitcases, Chris left to go to his apartment. We were all starving so we got ready for our first family dinner in Scottsdale. The kids chose California Pizza Kitchen. After we ate we were tired, but John insisted on driving us around the area. I tried to be enthusiastic, but I was done for the day.

The next morning it was cool. I put on my navy-blue cashmere sweater. I had thought when we got to Arizona, I would be able to wear my summer clothes. I guess not! John took us to Scottsdale Fashion Square, so I could replace what I had lost in my suitcase. We still hadn't heard anything from the airport. John took the kids to look around the mall, and they surprised me with stuffed animals they had made at Build-A-Bear.

That evening we went to Fleming's steakhouse for dinner. When we arrived, Bud and Beverly were already seated, so we joined them at the table. They hugged and kissed us all, and I appreciated how attentive they were to Ronnie, Lauren, and Joe. It was nice spending time with Bud and Beverly.

The following day, John and I were busy unpacking and organizing our new home. The master bedroom was spacious, with an all-glass fireplace centered between it and the attached sitting room. The bathroom had marble floors and granite countertops. It was large enough for me to maneuver easily around in my wheelchair. My closet was huge: all my clothes, shoes, and accessories fit with extra room to buy more. We were unable to finish putting everything in its place, because we were leaving for Las Vegas the next morning, to celebrate John's fiftieth birthday.

When we arrived in Las Vegas, we checked into the Bellagio Hotel. John and I had brought both Chris and Aaron along with us; the children had stayed behind with Ann, the babysitter. We dropped our bags off in the rooms and headed downstairs to the casino to play a few slots. Outside the streets were packed with people ready to celebrate the millennium.

On our way back we stopped to watch the fountain show in front of our hotel, as the water danced to an assortment of musical tunes. The crowd was so large that I kept getting bumped into, so John stood in front of my wheelchair to make a path, and we headed back into the hotel to get ready for the evening. Aaron changed me into my Donna Karen black tux with a white blouse, cufflinks, and a black bow tie. He touched up my makeup and re-curled my hair. When John came to get us he said, "You look amazing."

"Thank you," I said, "You do, too. I can't wait to see the concert. I've been looking forward to it."

We drove to the MGM Grand and ate at the Hollywood Brown Derby. After our steak dinner, we entered the concert hall to see Barbra Streisand. We sat in the fourth row.

I kissed John. "Happy birthday," I said. "I love you."

"Thank you," he said. "This is an amazing present."

I waited with enthusiasm for Barbra to start the show. I knew many of her songs, and I sang along with her throughout the concert. John and I both thought the concert was incredible, and she was funny and entertaining.

Back at the Bellagio, on the casino floor we toasted in the New Year with champagne. It was one thirty in the morning when we returned to our room and my nurse put me in bed. I was exhausted and, as I fell asleep, I thought "what a wonderful evening."

Arriving back in Arizona, I kissed the kids and asked them if they'd had a good time. They told me all the fun things they did with Ann. I wanted to talk more, but it was late and time for them to go to bed. I was happy to be home.

Chapter 45

Over the next week, John and I enrolled Ronnie, Lauren, and Joe in Kiva Elementary in Paradise Valley. Mrs. Holmes was Lauren and Joe's third-grade teacher, and Ronnie had Mrs. Ganz for fifth grade. John and I spent our time furniture shopping for the house and patio. Our backyard was picturesque, and we were looking forward to settling in and enjoying the warm Arizona weather.

A couple of weeks later, John came into my room while Chris was putting on my makeup. "Can you hurry it up?" he said. "My father just called and he wants us at his house for lunch."

When we arrived at Bud and Beverly's, Bud opened the garage door and greeted us. We followed him in and Beverly gave me a big kiss. Bud led us into the living room and introduced us to three men sitting at their dining-room table. "This is Juan Rodriguez, a diplomat from Mexico," he said. "And this Miguel Sanchez, a lawyer I hired from Mexico. And of course you know Tom Greene."

We greeted the gentlemen and joined them at the table. Bud asked Beverly to order lunch; I waited patiently for someone to tell me what was going on.

Tom Greene started the meeting by stating, "I have asked these gentlemen here to discuss Ron's present conditions in the Monterrey jail. Mr. Rodriguez has been monitoring Mr. Samuels. Please tell them what you know," he said, turning to Mr. Rodriguez.

Mr. Rodriguez said, "At first Mr. Samuels was having a difficult time when he arrived. The local criminals would fight with him, steal his pillows, and take his food. This continued for eight months until he began paying bribes for things he wanted. He has become more comfortable; he gets clothing, sheets, and conjugal visits. In 2000, his mother, Francis, and his brother, Mark, came to Monterrey to visit him and stayed for a month."

Mr. Sanchez then said, "The Mexican police know Mr. Samuels has money. As long as he continues to pay them, they will continue to help him."

"Do you think Ron would be able to pay his way out of jail?" John asked.

"I don't know but anything is possible," Mr. Sanchez responded.

Bud said, "We have to do something to keep my son and his wife safe!"

Just then Beverly brought in our lunch and we continued.

"I think our best bet," said Tom Greene, "would be to try to have him extradited back to the United States so that he is in jail in Florida."

At the end of the meeting it was decided that we would have attorney Miguel Sanchez file paperwork in Mexico asking for Ron's extradition for prosecution of crimes committed in the United States. If that didn't work, then Tom Greene would speak to Senator McCain and tell him about our situation. Senator McCain would then speak to the Mexican president, Vicente Fox, requesting Ron's extradition to the U.S.

John and I thanked the gentlemen for their help. When we left Bud and Beverly's house, I was hopeful that Ron would be brought back to the U.S. so he could be charged for what he had done to us.

In April, Bud and Beverly had a birthday party at Fleming's steakhouse for Uncle Harold and Ronnie. Ronnie had invited his best friend, Zach, to spend the weekend with him.

Uncle Harold had been diagnosed with Parkinson's a year before. When John asked how he was doing, he responded, "I feel good."

"I'm glad to see you're doing so well," John said.

"I've been going to the Barrow's Institute," replied Uncle Harold, "and it has been very beneficial to my health."

"I have heard so many wonderful things about Barrow's," I said. "My doctor, Candice Williams, is with them also."

On the way home I told John that I'd had a good time and it was nice to see Uncle Harold. I thought his color looked good, and I was glad he was in such good spirits.

The next morning John and I had a birthday party at Fiddlesticks for Ronnie, with Zach and twelve of Ronnie's friends from school. We played arcade games, rode in water boats, played miniature golf, and raced on the go kart raceway. His cake had a soccer ball on it that read, "Happy Birthday, Ronnie."

When the children were being picked up, John and I met Paul and Karen Arrot, Charlie's parents. They were a funny and friendly couple. We hit it off with them right away and made dinner plans for the following week. Charlie joined Ronnie and Zach at our house for a sleepover that night. In the morning we drove Zach to the airport and Charlie to his house.

A few days later, I met Janie Shapiro for lunch. Her father, Sydney, and Bud had been friends for a long time. Janie was five-foot-five, with mid-length dark-brown hair and an inviting personality. She asked many questions about John and me, and how we met. I told her about our life and asked her about her husband, Lola. By the time lunch was over, we had learned a great deal about each other.

Later we drove back to our house and John, Janie, and I had iced tea at the kitchen table. I got a kick out of listening to John and Janie reminisce about their families and childhood. When the kids came home from school, I introduced Janie to them. By the way her face lit up, I could tell she loved children. Janie turned to John and me and said, "My brother is coming into town with his two kids. Would you like to come to my house for dinner while they are here?"

"Yes," I answered. "That would be nice."

John and I walked Janie to the door. I thanked her for the lovely afternoon and we said good-bye.

Laura Keene had filed a petition with Judge Rasmussen for a name change for Ronnie, Lauren, and Joe. John wanted to adopt them. Their last name was still Samuels, but we had registered them at Kiva Elementary under the name Kaufman. We now wanted to change their name to Grossman. It took two weeks for Judge Rasmussen to sign the papers, but finally it was done.

The hardest part was going to the school and explaining the name change to the principal, Mr. Huminski. John and I told him our story and explained that we had been in witness protection. I presented him with the judge's paperwork showing the name change. We stayed in the office and waited for the school bell to ring. We loaded the kids in the van and drove to old town Scottsdale for ice cream. As we sat at the table and ordered our cones, John and I told the children about the name change.

"Remember when I talked to you about adopting you?" John asked.

The kids replied, "Yes."

"Well, your last name is going to be Grossman now."

The kids seemed agreeable. Ronnie looked at me and said, "Mom, can I change my first name to Zach? I don't want to be called Ron anymore."

"Ronnie, wait until you are an adult," I replied. "Then, if you still want to change your name, you can."

"Okay, Mom," he said.

We finished our ice cream and drove home so the children could start their homework. That evening we sat outside and had dinner. John grilled steaks and made fresh asparagus. The weather was perfect now, and at 7 p.m. it would get down to a comfortable seventy-five degrees.

Chapter 46

The morning of May 3, Aaron and I took ice cream sandwiches and cold water to Kiva Elementary to celebrate Lauren and Joe's ninth birthdays. We sat outside under a tree and talked while I visited with the teacher and met some of their friends.

I never wanted the children's friends or classmates to be scared of me, so I always made it a point to volunteer in class. I would read books to the students and allow them to ask me questions about my wheelchair and ventilator. Aaron would show them how he took my vitals and explain that he was with me all the time to keep me safe.

When recess was over, Aaron and I drove to the airport to pick up my girlfriend Terry. She was coming to celebrate Lauren and Joe's birthdays with us. When we arrived home, John and I gave Terry a tour of our home. Terry said, "It's perfect for you guys."

"It will be perfect when our addition is done," I said. "We're adding another thousand square feet. It is going to include a small exercise room for my bike, a nurses' room, a walk-in shower, a bathroom, and a bedroom."

"When are they going to be finished with that?" Terry asked.

"In another five to six months," I said.

John's cell phone rang. "Excuse me," he said. "I have to take this call in the office."

Twenty minutes later he came back. "I just got really bad news," he said. "Tom Greene called. They won't extradite Ron. He has to serve five years in the Mexican prison for his drug charges."

"That's ridiculous," I said. "Now we'll worry about our safety for five years."

"We'll have to keep monitoring him. Don't let it ruin your day, hon."

"You're right," I said. "His day will come."

When the children got home they were glad to see Terry. John grew irritated as they ran around and played. He started yelling so loudly I became embarrassed. I told the kids to calm down and come with me.

Terry helped me get the children ready for the night. While she curled Lauren's hair, she said, "John is acting like a child. Is everything all right?"

"I've seen some changes in him," I said. "He's very impatient with the children. He yells at them for absolutely nothing and has been swearing in front of them."

"What are you going to do?" Terry asked.

"I don't know. I asked him not to swear in front of them, but he continues to do it. I don't like the way he's been talking to the kids. I don't know what to do."

"If you need anything call me," Terry said.

"I will," I said.

We went to Ichiban's Japanese Restaurant at the Biltmore. After we ate, the children opened their gifts. They both got exactly what they asked for. That evening, Terry came to my room and we talked, had a glass of wine, and watched a movie. When everyone woke up the next morning, we had brunch and took the kids to the railroad park. John played football with them, and Terry and I sat and watched as they played and laughed. Terry looked at her watch and said, "We better go." "Come on kids," I said. "We have to take Terry to the airport."

Chapter 47

It was summer and the kids had just gotten out of school. It was already one hundred and eight degrees. I didn't want the kids to be bored at home, so I signed them up for summer camp. Monday through Friday they played sports, watched movies, swam, and made art. The kids enjoyed going to camp because they did something different every day. Bud and Beverly had gone back to Minnesota in May. They had only been gone a few weeks, but I already missed them.

Aaron and Stacy were getting married in San Diego that weekend. We loaded up my van and the Lexus with luggage. Chris drove and two night nurses, Kathy and Debbie, came along. John drove the Lexus and the kids rode with him. John had bought walkie-talkies so we could talk during our drive.

We drove through Yuma, Arizona, and shortly after crossed the California border. In San Diego were staying at the Hilton Bayfront Hotel. When we walked into the lobby you could feel the cool ocean breeze. The hotel sat right on the bay.

That night we took our nurses to one of our favorite Mexican restaurants, Casa De Reyes, in old town San Diego. We ordered our favorite Mexican dishes and drank margaritas. John started telling crass jokes and calling Chris a "pussy." I asked him to stop, and not to ruin the evening, but the more I asked the more he talked down to the nurses. After dinner we strolled around old town and shopped in different boutiques. We went back to the hotel and turned in early.

Sunday morning both Debbie and Kathy dressed me for the wedding. I wore white dress pants and a lavender Chanel sports jacket. Chris put me in my chair and continued getting me ready.

Ronnie and Joe were dressed in suits and ties. Lauren wore a pink dress with matching shoes. We went downstairs and met John in the lobby. We waited while Debbie and Kathy finished getting ready.

John said, "Let's go or we're going to be late."

Everyone got in the cars and we drove to the venue. The wedding was at the Marriot, in the courtyard. It was a lovely, quaint ceremony. The rows of white chairs had bouquets of yellow and pink flowers at the entrance. The day was perfect for an outdoor wedding. Aaron and Stacy said their personally written vows. The minister pronounced them husband and wife, and then Aaron kissed his bride. Aaron looked so happy.

The reception followed in the hotel banquet hall. They served lunch and afterward played music. John "danced" with me, placing his hands on mine and moving around. He knew I loved to dance. I smiled and laughed with him. Then he danced with Lauren. As we were leaving, we stopped to take a picture with Aaron and Stacy. Aaron kissed me on the cheek and said, "Thank you for everything." I could see the excitement and happiness in his eyes. "You're welcome," I said. "Have a great honeymoon."

It was five o'clock when we returned back to the hotel. That gave us plenty of time to take one last walk by the bay with the children. John and I met Kathy and Debbie by the pool, and the children went for their last swim. We sat, had appetizers, and watched the sunset. Finally, we said good night to Debbie and all went up to the room.

Kathy began my night care and John ordered room service for Ronnie, Lauren, and Joe. He came and sat with me, and everyone watched a movie together in my room. When the movie ended, I kissed the kids goodnight and they went to bed. John kissed me and reminded me we had to be up early in the morning for the drive home.

"I love you," he said.

"I love you, too," I replied.

Our drive back to Paradise Valley was uneventful. When we pulled into the driveway, I was relieved to be home. After dinner, I kissed the kids good night and they went to bed. It was nice to finally be alone with John, and we talked for a while. By the time my night nurse arrived, I was already asleep.

The kids started school the first week of August. Ronnie was in sixth grade, and the twins were entering fourth. The kids were excited to go back to school. Their teachers were excellent, and there was a lot of support and family involvement at the school.

John flew to Ft. Lauderdale to meet with Ken Hawkins. I was glad when he left because I could tell the nurses and children were driving him crazy. The nurses would have to tiptoe into the kitchen for my water and breakfast, because John did not want them in his kitchen. If the children made even the slightest mess making breakfast, he would scream at them so loudly I could hear it echo through the house.

Even though he was gone, I didn't get a break, however. He called me on my cell phone every thirty minutes to ask me where I was and what I was doing. I always made sure to answer the phone, because if I didn't he would get mad and scream at me. This made it difficult to drive anywhere, because my nurses would either have to hold the phone to my ear as they drove or pull off the road and hold the phone to my ear so I could talk to him. While I had previously brushed off his changed behavior as stress, I was now growing concerned about it.

I called Janie Shapiro and asked her to come over. When she arrived, Ronnie answered the door and brought her to my bedroom. I gave her a hug and thanked her for coming. I asked Kathy if we could have a little privacy.

"Janie," I said, "I'm worried about John's behavior. Something is not right. He's becoming very mean to the kids."

"I know," she replied. "When you came over for dinner, John was roughhousing with them too hard, almost like he was hurting them. And I didn't like the way he was speaking to you."

"He never had any therapy after the accident, and I think he needs some. What do you think? You're a psychologist."

"Of course he does," Janie said. "He has to be hurting, too."

"I think he's lying about things and I don't know whether I should ask him," I said. "I'm scared he might flip out on me."

"Have you ever been afraid to ask him about things before?"

"No, but he's been so short-tempered lately."

"Heather, you need to talk to him," she said.

My cell phone rang; Janie answered it and held it to my ear. "Hello," I said. On the other end John answered, "Hey baby." I spoke with him for a while. When he found out Janie was there, he became upset. I told him she had come to visit and we were going to watch a movie. That seemed to calm him down. "I love you," I said as I hung up the phone.

Aaron and I picked up John at the airport. John was in a good mood, and when we got home, he was happy to see the children. After I tucked the kids into bed, John called me into his office. He began the conversation by asking, "Why did you have Janie Shapiro over, and what did you talk about?"

"Because she's my friend," I said. "What is the big deal?"

"Well, nothing I guess."

"I don't understand why you had to go to Florida for five days. You could have just called Ken Hawkins on the phone."

"I was investigating things."

"What?"

"Things about Ron."

"That makes no sense," I said. "Everything is over. What were you really doing there?"

I never got an answer from him. By the time we were done talking, I was in tears. John pushed the button on the intercom and said, "Hey, pussy, come get Heather now!"

I looked at him and said, "John, what is wrong with you?"

Aaron opened the door. "Are you okay?" he asked. "I can see you've been crying."

"I'll be fine," I said. Aaron transferred me to my bed. Kathy looked at me and said, "Are you okay?" "Yes," I said. "I am."

The next day Chris started his three-day rotation. He was rushing to get me ready because John wanted to go to breakfast. Chris and I met John at Bagels N' Bialys. Later we drove to Fashion Square Mall, where we met up with John and went to BCBG. I found a pair of black capri dress pants and two sweaters to match.

"Let's get them," John said. "They would look great on you."

We paid for them and left. On our way out, John was driving my wheelchair and he noticed a man and a woman staring at me. The man stared so hard he bumped into another person walking the opposite way. John leaned over and said into my ear, "I don't know how you can take people looking at you like that."

"John, it's okay," I said. "I'm used to it by now. Usually when they stare at me I just smile back."

"I'm tired of this shit!" John replied.

Before I could say anything else, he turned my wheelchair around and raced up to the couple. "Here, take a good look," he said. "Would you like to get out your camera?" The couple looked stunned and just stood there, frozen.

"I'm sorry," I said, feeling embarrassed. "John, can we please just go?"

Chris looked down at me. "Heather, are you okay?" he asked.

"I'm fine!" I said. I looked up at John. "Why would you do that?"

"These fucking idiot people. I can't stand them."

"Calm down," I said. "It's not that big of a deal." As we continued through the mall, I tried to ease John's mind.

We stopped in front of Nordstrom at the coffee shop. Chris and I found a table while John ordered two Frappuccinos and one hot café mocha for me. While we were enjoying our drinks, John's cell phone rang. "Excuse me," he said. "It's Dad. I have to take this."

Chris said, "I am so confused, Heather. You tell me to do one thing and then John yells at me and tells me to do something different. I don't know what to do."

"Chris, you're the nurse," I said. "You need to make your decision based on what is best for me."

"Thank you for clarifying that," he said.

John came back looking irritated. "Is everything okay?" I asked.

"Yes, you know Bud," he said. "He's always on me about something." We left the mall and drove home before the bus dropped off the kids.

We had dinner at Bud and Beverly's that evening. When we walked into the living room, Beverly had invited many guests—Frank Greene, Uncle Harold and Aunt Gene, and Janie Shapiro and her parents, Sydney and Rose. The room was exquisitely decorated with orchids and flowerpots all around. Bud was serving drinks behind the bar and Dori, their housekeeper, passed appetizers on a tray to everyone.

It was a beautiful night and Beverly had opened all the windows in the back so we could walk onto the patio by the pool and look up at Camelback Mountain and the stars. The children loved coming with us to see Bud and Beverly and they were always well behaved. Dori came out and announced, "Dinner is served." We had grilled salmon, roasted baby potatoes, and fresh steamed asparagus. It was simple but delicious.

The kids, John, and I said good-bye to everyone and Chris loaded me into my van. When we arrived home the children took their baths, put on their pajamas, and then came to give me a kiss good night. I kissed them all and said, "I love you; sleep tight."

Chris changed me into my pajamas and took me into our master bedroom. He put me in bed with John so we could watch a movie together. We watched *The Green Mile* and shared popcorn. After the movie ended, John pushed the intercom and said, "Chris, can you come get Heather?" Chris came and transferred me into my wheelchair, and John and I said good night.

The next morning, John stormed into my room and started yelling, "I have been up since five thirty in the morning! Those fucking workers started working on the addition way too early!"

"Oh, calm down, John," I said. "They're closer to my room than they are to yours."

John said, "I'm going to give Jim Greager a piece of my mind." He walked out into the kitchen and all I could hear was him screaming at our builder. When John returned to my room he was laughing. "He'll never send them early again."

The day continued to get worse. When the children got home from school, John started throwing the boys over the leather sofa thinking it was funny. Then he grabbed Lauren and picked her up. "I'm scared," she said. "I don't want to do it." He didn't listen and threw her over the back of the sofa.

"John, stop it," I said.

"I'm just having a little fun," he replied. He continued to throw Ronnie and Joe over the leather sofa again. Lauren sat on the ground and said, "I am not doing that."

John said, "Yes, you are." He grabbed her by her hair and dragged her along the floor until she stood up. She started to cry and then I began to cry, too. I said in a firm voice, "John, I mean it. Knock it off."

He looked at me and laughed. Then Chris yelled, "Would you leave her kids alone? Can't you see Heather is upset?"

"Who the hell are you to talk to me that way?" John said.

"Why the hell does it matter who I am?" Chris said. "Why are you being an asshole?"

"Stop fighting," I said. "Please!"

John turned to Chris. "You're fired!"

"Come on, John," I said. "You don't mean that."

Chris spread his legs and pointed at his crotch. "Suck my dick, you asshole!"

"Get the hell out of my house!" John yelled.

Chris gathered his things and left. I was upset with John, but he was so mad I was afraid to say anything. Two hours later Aaron called and told John that Chris and Stacy had a fight at the apartment and Chris threw the phone and hit her in the forehead.

"That guy is an idiot," John said.

"John, he was probably upset because you fired him," I said. "Now we have to find another day nurse."

The next morning Aaron came into my room. "What the heck happened?" he asked.

"John just went crazy. He and Chris got into an argument, and before I knew it, John was firing him. I feel really bad."

"I'll put an ad in the newspaper and we'll interview people for the position," Aaron said. It took a few days, but we finally found a good registered nurse named Randy. Randy was six-foot-two with sandy-brown hair, neatly dressed, and quiet. Aaron trained him for a week and we felt confident that he was ready for the job.

Chapter 48

In mid-September I flew back to Craig Hospital for a routine reevaluation. We took my night nurses, Kathy and Debbie, and also my day nurses, Randy and Aaron. When we arrived at Craig, we checked into the reevaluation area. They handed me a schedule for five days. It covered everything from a wheelchair check to seeing every single one of my doctors. I waited for my appointment with Dr. Luke. When he came into the room, I was glad to see his smiling face. He was my favorite doctor at Craig.

"Hi, Dr. Luke," I said.

"Mrs. Kaufman, you look great! How have you been feeling?"

"I feel better than ever."

John said, "We're out of witness protection and her ex-husband is in jail in Mexico."

"That's good," Dr. Luke said. "I'm glad you guys are safe, but why Mexico?" John told him what had happened. "Unbelievable!" Dr. Luke responded.

"Our real last name is Grossman," I said.

"Well, nice to meet you, Mrs. Grossman. How are the children doing?"

"They're doing great and growing up fast. They love their school and friends in Arizona."

"My wife and I were just in Scottsdale, Arizona, visiting my oldest daughter," he said. "She teaches math at Saguaro High School."

"The next time you're in town we should go to dinner," John said.

"Sure," said Dr. Luke. "I'll give you a call."

Over the next forty-five minutes Dr. Luke did his assessment and asked me questions about my health. Afterward, we went downstairs to the wheelchair clinic. Two occupational therapists evaluated my chair and adjusted the arms and laterals. Next on our schedule was lunch. We only had an hour to eat so John suggested the hospital cafeteria. That was the last place I wanted to eat. But I didn't want to burst his bubble so I kept quiet. We had a boring lunch and then went to my next appointment in radiology. It was freezing in radiology. I had to have a kidney scan done that took an hour. On our way out, we stopped and said hello to many of the staff we knew.

John's son Ben worked for the Colorado Rapids soccer team in their marketing department. He had been working there for a year now and loved his job. We were excited to meet him for dinner at Gordon Biersch. When we arrived at the restaurant, Randy parked in the wrong area. When John figured out we had to go across the mall, he started screaming at Randy.

I intervened. "John, please it's not his fault."

We started to make our way to the restaurant and saw we had to go over cobblestone. Randy drove my chair slowly, so as not to jerk my neck and body. "Come on, we're going to be late." John said. "What is wrong with you, idiot?"

Randy continued to follow slowly behind John. John turned around, came back to me, and said, "Move out of the way! I don't have time for this."

John took my wheelchair and started driving it very fast. I thought my neck was going to break off and I began to cry. "What's wrong with you?" he said.

"You're driving too fast and it's hurting me."

"If you hadn't been shot, we wouldn't be late," he said. "So suck it up."

"Could you please just go meet your son and I'll take Heather," Randy said.

"No!" John said.

When we entered Gordon Biersch, Ben greeted us with hugs and introduced us to his new girlfriend, Joanna. John was good-humored through dinner in front of them. I tried hard to look happy, but every once in a while a tear would run down my cheek.

When dinner was finished, I asked Randy if he could please drive the car around front. John and I said good-bye to Ben and Joanna. On the drive home, I was quiet. John asked, "Are you feeling okay?"

"I'm tired and have a headache."

"I'm sorry you're not feeling well. We'll be at the hotel soon and you can lie down."

The next morning John and I met with my neurosurgeon, Dr. Scott Falci. Dr. Falci came in the room, sat down, and said, "Hello." He asked me questions about my neck.

I told him, "My neck is sore and the muscles are tight all the time."

"I have looked at your X-rays and they show that the titanium rod has healed well," he said.

"That's good news."

"For the tightness in her neck, could she have massages done?" John asked.

"Not really," Dr. Falci answered. "She has too many bullet fragments in her neck."

"I'm glad you told us that, because we were going to set some appointments for her," John said.

We left and went to our next appointment in radiology. My pulmonologist, Dr. Peterson, had scheduled a diaphragm test. While going through the test the radiologist came over and said, "I can see your diaphragm is completely paralyzed. How are you breathing without your vent?"

"I suck in air to breathe," I said.

"Oh yes, I can see your stomach moving and your traps. You're using your accessory muscles."

"I do what I have to do."

Randy put me back into my wheelchair and drove me to Dr. Peterson's office. At Craig Hospital he was considered the best pulmonologist. He was successful at weaning high quadriplegics off their ventilators.

Dr. Peterson began by saying, "You are an amazing woman. You are like a racehorse breathing in air every ten to fourteen seconds so you can speak and stay off the ventilator during the day. That has to be taxing on your body."

"It doesn't bother me at all," I said. "It just seems natural. I sleep really well because I'm always tired at the end of the day."

After the examination, Dr. Peterson said, "You're doing great. Keep up the good work." The day ended at three o'clock and we drove back to the hotel to relax. We were meeting Ben and Joanna at a seafood restaurant for dinner.

We all ordered steamed Maine lobster with baked potatoes and broccolini. This time I was able to talk to Joanna more, and I could tell that Ben and she had a lot in common. John was laughing, talking loudly, and interrupting me. I couldn't figure out why he was doing that. I decided to keep quiet and wait for somebody to ask me something.

Everyone had a nice evening and as we walked out Ben said, "Dad, let's come back here again. The food was amazing."

We drove back to the hotel, and Randy put me into bed and said good night. John went to his hotel room. Kathy started doing my night care. Three hours later, there was a knock at my door. Kathy went to the door and opened it; it was Aaron. He walked to my bedside and said, "We have a problem."

"What?"

"I found Randy in the bar at the Mexican restaurant across the street. He was so drunk I had to help him to the room and put him in bed."

"Maybe he just had a little too much fun," I said. "He doesn't work tomorrow."

"I just wanted to let you know."

"Thank you, Aaron," I said. "I will see you in the morning."

When he left Kathy said, "Don't let this bother your sleep. I am sure everything is fine."

In the morning, Aaron brought me coffee. "I talked to Randy," he said. "He told me that John is driving him to drink. He can't take the way John talks to you or treats you, and it's upsetting him a lot."

"I feel really bad," I said. "Should I talk to him?"

"That might help," said Aaron, "but Randy is an alcoholic and has been sober for five years. He hasn't had a sip of alcohol since he started AA."

"Well what do you expect?" Kathy said. "John treats everyone like crap!"

"I feel terrible for Randy," I said, "but John has been through a lot since this happened to me."

"I know you love him, but you have to stop making excuses for him," Kathy said.

"Don't worry about Randy," Aaron said. "He's off the next three days, and by that time we'll be home."

"Please let me know if anything else happens with him."

"I will, Heather."

Over the next few days, I had an appointment with my physical therapist, John Burchenal, and I saw my gynecologist, Mary Walters. I had two more radiology tests, a CAT scan, and a bone density test. On Friday, my last day, John and I met with Dr. Luke and my team of doctors. Each doctor discussed his or her evaluation and any necessary treatment.

Overall, my health was excellent and my doctors encouraged me to continue on my same healthcare plan. We thanked them and told them we'd see them next year.

We took the nurses to Fogo De Chao, a Brazilian steakhouse. It was one of Ben's favorite places. Everyone sat down and ordered their drinks. We started with their massive gourmet salad bar. Then the waiters began to bring out skewers. They had sixteen different prepared meats. It was a fun evening for everyone and my nurses enjoyed this new dining experience. John and I said good-bye to Ben and Joanna—we all knew we wouldn't be seeing each other for a while. They hugged us and thanked us for such a nice dinner.

The next morning we packed our bags and left for the airport. I slept through most of the flight. When I woke up the plane was landing and we were back in Phoenix.

When we got to the house, Aaron drove me in. The kids jumped and yelled. They were excited we were home. I spent time with the children for a while and talked to them about their weekend. Before bedtime I had Lauren come into the boys' room, and I read them a book and kissed them good night. This upset John. "Why do you have to do that? he asked. "Why can't you come to the office and talk to me?"

I said, "Because I haven't seen the children in a week and I need to spend time with them." After I finished with the children it was already nine o'clock. I said good night to John and kissed him. Aaron took me to my bedroom and transferred me to bed. "I feel like I'm being pulled in two different directions," I confided to Aaron and Kathy. "I need to spend time with my children, too, and it seems like everything I do upsets him. John wants my time but my children need me."

Kathy said, "You're doing the right thing, Heather."

I said, "I'm just trying to make everyone happy."

Chapter 49

I knew John was frustrated, so over the next month I tried my hardest to make him happy. We spent more time together and I was sympathetic toward him. I also got bad news about my night nurse, Debbie. She was leaving to take a day nursing job. Interviewing began and I hired Denise Foster. Kathy trained her for a week. On her first day of working on her own, she leaned toward me and said, "Your husband makes me nervous. I've had diarrhea all morning long."

"Don't worry," I said. "His bark is bigger than his bite. You're doing a great job, Denise."

Randy came in and Denise gave him a report. He transferred me to my wheelchair, washed my hair, and did my makeup. The rest of the day went smoothly. We went out to breakfast and then took the kids to Castle and Coasters. John rode all the rides with the kids, and when we returned home he grilled burgers for dinner. The kids helped clean up the kitchen and I told them to take their baths and get ready for bed.

Randy put my pajamas on me and took me into our master bedroom. He transferred me into bed and John helped with placing pillows behind me. Randy left and closed the door. John and I watched TV and talked. He began to kiss me softly and we got carried away. He became aroused and said, "I want you." He pulled my legs apart. While he was still kissing me he moved on top of me. He pulled down his briefs and entered me. To my disappointment I could not feel anything. "John stop," I said. "I can't feel you inside me." He continued to thrust inside me until he came. I lay there staring at the ceiling, wanting to cry.

John called Randy over the intercom and asked him to come get me. Randy transferred me to my chair and drove me to my room. When he put me in bed he said, "Heather are you okay? Your eyes are all puffy."

"I'll be fine," I said.

Kathy walked into my room and started my night care. She washed my face and checked my skin. When she lifted my legs, she said, "What the hell happened? You look mutilated."

I started to tear up and said, "I don't want to talk about it."

"Heather, I'm worried about you and the children," she said. "Is there anything I can do?"

"Kathy, you're so kind, but I don't think there's anything you can do."

The next morning Aaron came in early and the two of them talked. Kathy came to my bedside and said, "I need Bud and Beverly's number in Minnesota. They need to know what's going on."

"Are you serious?" I said.

"If you don't give it to me Aaron will," she replied. I gave her the number and she left, saying she'd see me that night.

The next day, Aaron got me out of bed. During my morning routine, I didn't feel well. He noticed something was wrong and asked if I was okay.

"I'm a little worried and I feel sick to my stomach."

"Don't worry," he said. "I'm sure everything will be fine."

We left to go to Fashion Square Mall. After a few hours of shopping, my cell phone rang. Aaron said it was Beverly and placed the phone to my ear.

"Hi, Heather," Beverly said. "Is everything okay? I just spoke to your nurse, Kathy. Bud and I are concerned."

"Things are not good here," I said. "I don't know what's going on with John, but I'm scared."

"I don't want you to worry. Bud and I will be there in a week."

"I'm glad you guys are coming. I really need your help."

"Call us if you need anything else, Heather," she said. "We'll see you soon."

I turned to Aaron. "Bud and Beverly are coming," I said. "Reinforcements are on the way."

I bought two outfits for Lauren and we left the mall. On our way home, we stopped at the school. I went to pick up Ronnie from his classroom. When he saw me he was excited. I talked to the teachers and asked how they were doing. I was pleased to hear Lauren and Joe were doing well. The kids hopped in the van and we went home.

While the children were doing their homework, John came in from the office. "Your Ergys bike arrived," he said.

"I'm so excited!" I replied.

"James, the owner of the company, will be back in an hour to go over the settings and train you on it."

Aaron and I spent two hours with James learning how to operate the bike. The next morning, Denise got me dressed in my bike pants and put ultrasound gel on the pads. Aaron transferred me onto my bike and I was up and riding, with the help of electric stimulation to my leg muscles. I rode my bike for thirty minutes, and it felt great. It was the first cardio exercise I had done in a long time.

Bud and Beverly came back to Scottsdale the first week in November. They invited the family out for dinner at Franco's. Ronnie, Lauren, and Joe were happy to see Bud and Beverly. John seemed loving and was on his best behavior in front of them.

Our house addition was finally done. Aaron and Randy moved my furniture into my room. When we were putting away my clothes, Randy approached me. "Heather," he said, "you know I love being your nurse, but I can't do it anymore."

"Randy, please don't leave."

"I have to. I can't take how John treats you and the children. Its making me sick. I even worry about you on my days off."

"I understand and I don't want to cause you any problems," I said, feeling upset. "You're a good nurse and I'm going to miss you."

"I'll stay on until you find a new nurse," he offered.

"I appreciate that," I said. His notice put a damper on the rest of the day. Aaron placed an ad in the paper for a new nurse and we started looking right away.

Fortunately, a few weeks later we were having dinner at Fleming's steakhouse, when we met Paul Anderson, our waiter. He was a new RN graduate. He overheard us talking and said he was looking for a nursing job. We took his number and called him the next day to set up an interview.

Aaron and I met with Paul. He had no experience, but he had a good attitude. He was professional, clean-cut, and physically fit. I hired him to start training the next day. Paul was thirty years old, stood about five-foot eleven with light-brown hair, and was smart. He caught on to everything quickly.

The holiday season was filled with joy. We spent it with family and friends. We went over to Janie and Lola's on the first night of Hanukkah. We lit the first candle on the menorah and sang the Hanukkah song. To follow Jewish tradition, Janie gave all the children chocolate gelt. As she handed out the gold coins, their eyes lit up with excitement. On our way out, I said to Janie and Lola, "Thank you for inviting us. This was the kids' first Hanukkah and we really had a nice time."

The next day we continued the celebration at Bud and Beverly's. She prepared a traditional dinner and lit the second candle. Over the next six days, the children lit candles and opened presents.

On Christmas day we met Bud and Beverly to watch *Cast Away*. By the time we bought our popcorn and drinks, we were rushing to get to our seats because the theater was full. When the movie was over we went to Jade Palace and had Chinese food for dinner. It was not the traditional Christmas I was used to, but the day was enjoyable.

We rang in the 2001 New Year at Bud and Beverly's. As soon as we walked up to the door, we could hear the music. We walked in and saw a man in a tuxedo playing the baby grand piano. Beautiful music filled the air. People were dancing and sipping on champagne. The room was filled with fifty guests.

When Beverly spotted us, she came up and kissed us. "Come with me," she said. "I want to introduce you to my friends from Minneapolis." She took me over to a group of her friends and said, "This is my daughter-in-law, Heather, that I was talking to you about."

She had her hands on my shoulder and continued, "I'm so proud of her, because even with her disability she does a lot. Not only is she a wonderful mother, but she also belongs to the PTA and volunteers at the elementary school." Her friends were intrigued by my story and wanted to know more.

When dinner was ready everyone found their place cards. Bud and Beverly made a toast to their friends and family, wishing us happiness and prosperity in the New Year. The party continued until after midnight. Everyone was singing Frank Sinatra's "New York, New York" by the end of the evening.

Shortly before one in morning, the music went down and Bud said, "It's time to go home, everyone! Thank you for coming!"

I looked at John, laughed, and said, "I can't believe your dad just did that."

Chapter 50

Janie and I went to get makeovers for date night with our husbands. The four of us were going to a fund-raiser for the Herberger Theater.

We arrived at the Hilton where the event was being held, and were surprised to see all the members who had arrived already. John and Lola ordered us glasses of wine and we walked and looked at the silent auction items. I bid a hundred dollars on an Elizabeth Arden spa package, and John bid on a weekend getaway at the Four Seasons Resort in North Scottsdale. John also joined Janie in bidding on a Diamondbacks suite for twelve people.

By this time John had had four glasses of wine and was becoming obnoxious. They closed the auction and announced the winners. Janie and John had won the Diamondbacks suite. While standing in line to pick up the tickets, John started hitting on an older, unattractive woman wearing a lot of makeup. He was hanging on her and saying disgusting things. I could hear Janie say, "Knock it off, John. You're drunk."

"No, I'm not," he said. He kept talking to the woman and she was laughing.

When they were done we walked over to Fleming's for dinner. On our way there Janie said, "Did you see him?"

"Yes," I answered. "I'm so embarrassed."

They sat us at our table and we ordered. John had a vodka martini. By the time our entrées arrived, John was telling dirty jokes and making fun of me in my wheelchair. Everyone at the table was quiet and was getting upset with him. Paul, my nurse, leaned over and asked, "Are you okay, Heather?"

"I'm trying to ignore him," I said. "He's drunk and being mean."

I was happy to see the check come. We said good-bye to our friends and Paul drove us home. John kept trying to talk to me and I wouldn't respond. John asked, "Are you mad at me?"

"Yes, I am," I said. "You hurt my feelings." I didn't speak to him the rest of the night.

A week later John asked me if I would like to go dinner at The Other Place. Aaron touched up my makeup and we got ready to leave. John, Aaron, and I sat at a table by the window. John said, "Aaron, could we have a little privacy?" He gave Aaron some money for a soda and he went and sat at the bar.

The waiter brought over our drinks and took our order. John started to talk, and I could tell he was agitated. "Is everything okay?" I asked.

"I had a huge fight with my father. I'm tired of him telling me what to do."

"I'm sorry you got in a fight with your dad," I said. "But he's understanding. I'm sure you can talk to him and patch things up. What was the fight about?"

"Don't be concerned about it," he said. "This is between my father and me."

By the time our food arrived, John had already had two drinks and he ordered another one. "Please don't have another drink," I said.

"I'll have as many as I want," he replied.

He cut my scallops and gave me a bite. "These are delicious," I said. "Would you like to try one?"

"No, I'm fine." It was obvious he was still angry.

We continued eating dinner, and I avoided asking him any more questions about his dad. All of a sudden he started yelling at me. "If you hadn't been shot," he said, "we wouldn't be living in Arizona. My dad is yelling at me all the time and it's your fault."

I started to cry. "What do you mean?" I said.

"I'm tired of all this shit. You ruined my life!"

I cried harder because what he said hurt.

"John, I love you. You don't mean that." I could feel my lungs fill up with secretions. He began feeding me at a rapid pace. I didn't have a chance to chew or swallow my food.

"You're feeding me too fast," I said. "I can't breathe."

He wouldn't stop. I pressed my lips together, and he took the fork and pried my mouth open, ripping my lip. I tasted blood. I continued to cry and John tried to comfort me. People were starting to stare. He raised his arm to gesture Aaron over. "She's upset," John said to Aaron when he reached the table. "I'm not sure what happened. Can you help me out here?"

John stood up and went to the restroom. Aaron took my napkin and wiped my lip. "What the hell happened?" he asked.

"John got mad and ripped my lip."

"Are you okay?" He gave me a sip of ice water and I swished it around in my mouth. I spit out blood.

John came back and sat down. "Are you okay?" he asked.

Aaron glared at him and said, "Heather, you hardly ate any of your food."

"Let's get it to go," I said. "I'm done eating."

When we returned home, Aaron transferred me to my bed. Kathy came into my room and looked at me. "What happened now?" she asked.

I started to cry. Aaron told her what had happened. Kathy put her hand on my forehead and pushed back my hair. "Oh honey," she said. "I'm sorry. Let me take a look."

I opened my mouth and she said, "There are cuts inside your lip and at the bottom of your gums. I can't believe this asshole did this to you. Does it hurt?"

She looked at Aaron. "How could you let this happen?"

"He sent me away. I was sitting at the bar."

"This is getting worse," Kathy said. "You have to talk to Bud and Beverly."

Aaron and Kathy left the room and talked outside. Kathy came back in and said, "Okay let's get you ready for bed."

I kept crying, and she wiped away my tears with a tissue. "Honey it's going to be okay," she said.

I told her, "I love John so much, and no matter what I do or say he gets upset with me." She tried to comfort me, but I was so distraught that I could not sleep at all.

The next morning my lip was hurting, and I asked Aaron to bring my mirror so I could see. He held the mirror and I looked at my lip. It was bruised and swollen. A tear ran down my cheek. Aaron helped me put on my earpiece and I called Bud and Beverly's home. When Bud answered, I said, "Hi, Bud, this is Heather. Is it okay if I come talk to you today?"

He said, "Yes if you can be here by eleven."

Aaron put me in the van. John came outside as soon as he saw us leaving. "Where are you going?" he asked.

"I'm having lunch with Beverly," I replied.

"Have fun," he said and we drove off.

I was nervous when we entered Bud and Beverly's home. Beverly came over and kissed me. "Bud's on a phone call," she said. "Would you like some iced tea, dear?"

"Yes, please."

Bud came in and said, "Hello, Heather. Let's talk in the office."

Aaron drove me to the office and sat beside me. Bud sat behind his desk and, in a formal manner, said, "How can I be of assistance?"

"I'm here to talk to you about John. His behavior has changed since I was shot."

"His behavior? How has it changed?"

"He's becoming physically abusive with me and the children. He dragged Lauren across the floor by her hair and he gets the boys in headlocks between his knees until they cry. He is always yelling at the kids for anything. As for me, it doesn't matter what I do or say; he always gets mad at me. He's been drinking too much, and when he gets drunk he becomes belligerent, mean, and abusive."

Bud asked Aaron, "Is this true?"

"Yes," Aaron said. "I've seen it with my own eyes, and I'm intimidated by him. He's even verbally abusive to the nurses."

"Last night John cut my lip open," I said. Bud stood up, walked toward me, and looked at my lip.

"I'm sorry this is happening," he said.

"I'd like your help convincing him to talk to someone."

He paced around and said, "Didn't you know who you married?"

I was shocked by his response. "Yes, I do!" I said. "I married a wonderful man who was kind and loving, but he's changed. I'm asking for your help because I don't know what to do."

He said, "I'm going to consult with the other Grossmans and I'll get back to you later."

Stunned by his response, I thanked him and Aaron and I left the room. Beverly asked us if we wanted to stay for lunch. "No, thank you," I said.

In the car driving home I asked Aaron, "What just happened? I'm so desperate for help and I feel like nothing was accomplished."

"At the very least," Aaron said, "Bud knows what's going on."

"I wish Beverly had sat in on our conversation. She's more supportive."

John called and asked me to meet him at Costco. I picked up the children from school and met him there. We shopped and loaded the cart with food and cleaning supplies. As the kids walked in front of the cart, John started ramming the back of Joe's legs.

"Ow," Joe cried out, "that hurts!"

I was looking at books with Aaron and Carrie, the nanny, came up to me and whispered, "Heather look at what John is doing." Aaron turned me around and I saw John shoving the cart into Joe's heels. I told Aaron to drive me up to them.

"John stop doing that to Joe."

"I'm just playing around."

"No, you're hurting him!"

He stopped pushing the cart and gave me an angry look. Joe walked up to me with sadness in his eyes. "Are you okay?" I asked him.

He said, "Yes, Mom." I had him turn around so I could look at the back of his legs. There were visible red marks where the cart had been hitting him. I said, "Joe, jump on my lap," and Aaron drove us to the checkout.

When we got home, John and Aaron unloaded everything from the van. I was outside when Carrie approached me. "Heather, I can't work for you anymore," she said. "I can't watch what's happening to the kids. What he's doing is evil."

"The children really like you and I don't want you to leave," I said. "Please stay."

"I'm sorry I can't," she replied. This was the fifth nanny we had lost since we moved to Arizona.

Later that evening I talked to John. "We've lost Carrie," I said.

"Why?"

"Because of what happened at Costco today. I think you're carrying a lot of anger because of what happened to me and how it's changed our lives. Maybe you should talk to somebody to help you through this."

"I'm perfectly fine. I don't need to talk to anyone."

"You are not fine. Please think about getting some therapy."

"I don't have time to discuss this right now," John said. He called Aaron on the intercom to come get me. For the rest of the evening, I was frustrated. John was in denial and didn't care about my thoughts or feelings.

Two weeks later I was still desperate for help and hadn't heard anything from Bud. Paul went to get me a glass of water in the kitchen. When he came back he said, "John has hired a home theater and audio company to put cameras in every room of the addition, even the shower. Did you know about this?"

"No," I said. "That is absolutely crazy."

When John brought the installers to my room, I asked, "Why are you doing this?"

"It's for your protection."

"That's ridiculous."

Paul leaned over and whispered, "He's going to be spying on us."

Shortly after, I had my first appointment with Nancy Repkey, a psychologist Janie Shapiro had recommended.

The first time I was in therapy was at Craig Hospital. My therapist, Lisa Payne, had helped me so much. I waited for Nancy in her office and was impressed by her degrees hanging on the wall. She walked into the room wearing a bright pink suit and black glasses. Even in flats she was nearly six feet tall. She towered over my wheelchair.

Our session started with a history of my background, starting from when I married Ron to present day. She asked me questions to fill in any blanks and finished the session by asking me what I would like to accomplish during therapy.

I said, "My life is hard as a quadriplegic and I have underlying stressors. I want to develop coping skills to help myself and my family."

I felt comfortable talking with Nancy and I was excited to tell John about my session. However, when I told him he became infuriated. "Damn you, Heather!" he yelled. "You need to talk to me before you make a decision like that."

"I'm sorry. I didn't think you'd mind. You didn't care about me getting therapy before."

"I don't care about then," he said. "This is now!"

John left the room. Afterward—as though nothing had happened—he came in the kitchen and cheerfully suggested, "Let's take the children to Tony Roma's for dinner."

At dinner the children were happily entertained by the paper placemats and crayons provided by the host. We ordered our ribs and John and I talked and laughed with the kids.

Halfway through our meal, something suddenly angered John. Before I knew it, he was up from his chair telling me, "I'm outta here!"

With a puzzled expression, Paul looked at me and asked, "What the heck just happened?"

"I have no idea." We waited for the children to finish their food and I asked for the check.

Later that evening, John came to my bedroom. "I'm so tired of having nurses around," he said. "It really ticks me off."

"You have to be patient," I replied. "Neither one of us *wants* nurses around all the time, but we do need them."

"I understand. I know you're right," he said. Then John kissed me and left the room.

After John left, I called Denise over and said, "Lean over my face." I whispered to her, "John has cameras installed in all the rooms in the back of the house, so he can see everything we're doing."

With a stunned look on her face she asked, "What? When did this happen?"

"Today. And do you see the knob on the wall over there? That's so he can hear us," I explained. "Now, please go turn it off."

Once Denise had the volume turned off, she asked, "What's wrong with him?"

"I don't know," I said. "But it's only getting worse." Denise continued with my night care, and I distracted myself with television until I fell asleep.

Chapter 51

In March, John's brother Andy and his wife, Lynn, came for a visit and stayed with Bud and Beverly. We were thrilled to see them and their two children, Alyssa and Jarrod, then three years and six months old, respectively. We bought gifts and Ronnie, Lauren, and Joe were excited to give them their presents. We had a nice lunch and a long visit, catching up on each other's lives and watching the children play together.

The following day, Beverly and I met to watch Lauren's recital with the string orchestra from Kiva Elementary. Lauren shined during her violin solo, and Beverly and I were both proud. Later, Beverly and I met Andy, Lynn, and their children at Einstein's. Unfortunately, we had to cut lunch short as Jarrod was crying and miserable with an earache.

When Paul and I returned home, John said he was upset that he couldn't make Lauren's recital due to a meeting that ran late. He made an offhanded remark that I was getting "pretty chummy" with his family, to which I replied, "I really like Andy and Lynn, so why should that be a problem?"

"Well, I just feel left out," John replied.

One morning, John and I ran into Bud at the bagel shop. We chatted for a moment, and before we left, Bud suggested to John, "Why don't you take your beautiful wife out to dinner tonight?"

"I think I'll do that," John said. Turning to me he asked, "How about Fleming's?"

"That sounds good," I said.

Bud put his hand on John's shoulder and said, "You better be good to her." Then he leaned down and kissed my cheek and told me to have a good day.

After John and I ran errands and picked up the kids, we all returned home. The kids did their homework while Paul transferred me to bed to change me into my suit for dinner. When I was done getting ready, John said, "You look great!"

When we arrived at Fleming's, the host sat John, Paul, and I by the wine room. Our evening got off to a pleasant start. John was being cordial and we were laughing and having a good time.

I said, "I think it would be a great idea if we got a dog for the kids. They're lovable while still teaching responsibility and they add so much to your life."

"No, it's not a good idea," John responded. "We already have too much on our plate."

Our waiter brought us our food and asked us if we'd like another cocktail. Paul placed a napkin on my lap and started feeding me a bite of salmon.

"I would hope you'd at least give it some thought before disregarding the idea altogether," I said.

John said, "I'm thinking of buying a condo in San Diego. I need a place to get away from the fucking nurses."

"What?" I said in surprise. "Can we even afford that? Are you going to be running back and forth between home and a condo in San Diego all the time?"

"So what if I am!" John replied. "What's your problem with that?"

"What about our family?" I asked as I saw the rage building in him, his face reddening and jaw tightening.

Before I could say anything else, John spit in my face. I was absolutely shocked and tears instantly began streaming down my cheeks.

"What? You're going to cry now?" he said and got up to go to the bathroom.

Paul took the napkin and cleaned my face. "Heather, I'm so sorry," he said. I was still crying when John returned and sat down at our table. Minutes later, the restaurant manager, Mike Hodges, came by and asked, "How are you folks doing tonight? Did you enjoy your meal?"

John said with a smile, "Everything tasted great!" Unable to finish my food, I asked for it to be boxed up as John asked for the check.

Upon returning home, I asked Paul to take me directly to my room and we waited for Kathy, the night nurse, to arrive for her shift. I told her what had happened. She was obviously upset and sympathetic as we talked. I asked the questions out loud: "What is happening to my life? Why is John so angry? Why is he so cruel?"

I loved John so much. I couldn't understand how everything was falling apart. Questioning and crying myself to sleep were becoming a regular occurrence in my life.

I told Kathy I wanted to call my mom, but I was worried John would find out and be furious. She shut off the lights in my bedroom, grabbed her cell phone, and said, "Honey, what's the number?" She dialed and held the phone to my ear. My mom answered. "Hi mom," I said. "It's Heather. Did I wake you?"

"Yes! But I don't care. Are you alright?"

"Yes, I am, and the kids are good, too. I miss you so much! I'm sorry I haven't called until now, but John still doesn't want me talking to you guys. I don't care. I just wanted to hear your voice."

"I understand, honey," she said. "I miss you, too. Is everything good with you and John?"

"I'm okay," I said. "I don't want you to worry. I better go, Mom, but remember I love you!" She said, "I love you, too."

Kathy hung up the phone. "I'm so glad you finally talked to your mom."

The next morning, John poked his head in the room and excitedly said, "I've been on the phone calling breeders from the classifieds, and I've found a German shepherd puppy for the children. When Aaron gets in, can you have him quickly get you dressed and ready to see the puppy?"

An hour and a half later we were in the van driving to Queen Creek. The kids' eyes lit up with joy upon meeting this black-and-brown little pup with enormous paws and long, floppy ears. We all fell in love with the little guy, and after John paid the breeder we loaded him into the van. On the way home, we stopped and bought everything this cuddly little pup could ever need or want. We got home and let little Raider run around the backyard with the kids until he tuckered out, curled up in Lauren's lap, and fell asleep.

Over the next couple of days Raider was the center of attention. We took him on long walks around the lake at Chaparral Park, and the kids learned how to care for their new dog—everything from brushing to using a pooper scooper. They were excited to bathe him for the first time. They brought Raider into the big marble shower next to my room, hosed him down and lathered him up. When they were done, they were as soapy and wet as the puppy.

Upon seeing Raider, Paul said, "Oh my goodness, that is the cutest puppy I have ever seen. When did you get him?"

"Over the weekend," I said.

"How did you change John's mind?" asked Paul. I told him I had no idea.

Paul made me a sandwich and we sat and ate at the kitchen table. He looked at me and said, "Heather, you are the sweetest person. It's because of you that I've tried to stick it out so long. But I'm going to have to leave, because I want to beat the crap out of your husband and I don't know how much longer I can hold back. He treats you like shit."

"Paul, please don't leave. You're a wonderful nurse."

"I have to leave," he said. "I'm afraid I'm going to act on my feelings and end up losing my nursing license."

By the following week, Paul was training his replacement. Phil, the new nurse, was tall and lanky with blond hair and glasses. He was attentive, but hardly spoke a word. Within days of starting, he witnessed John bullying us and pushing around the kids in a hurtful manner. There was a night at the Bamboo Club when John spit on me at dinner and Phil watched in quiet horror. Another night, while out with our friends Paul and Karen Arott, John referred to me as "My wife, the bitch." After just two weeks, Phil quit without giving notice.

At this point I was meeting with Nancy Repkey every week, and I shared with her what had been going on with John. I asked Kathy to meet me at her office for moral support. Halfway through the session, Kathy said, "Heather, stop sugar-coating John's behavior."

Dr. Repkey turned her attention to Kathy and asked, "What's your point of view on this?"

Kathy said, "There are nights I don't sleep because I'm worrying about the children and Heather. That man is a cruel, evil human being. He takes pride in intimidating everyone around him so that they're too afraid to disagree with him. He controls Heather by watching her every move on all the cameras he's set up in the back of the house, listening in on her phone calls, and reading her cell phone bills. If she crosses him in the slightest way he threatens to put her in a nursing home and the kids in foster care. It's absolutely disgusting what he does to this family. He's just a monster. She's living in this nightmare and feels like she has no way out."

"Heather, do you think what Kathy's saying is accurate?" Dr. Repkey asked.

I hesitated and then answered, "Yes. I love my husband, but I feel that his behavior is due to post-traumatic stress disorder from the shooting. He should have seen a psychologist after it happened, but he hasn't."

"Have you discussed this with him?"

"Yes, but he refuses to go to therapy. I've been trying to get his family to help me persuade him to see a psychologist, but nothing has come of it so far."

Dr. Repkey then asked, "Do you think one of John's family members would be willing to meet with us here?"

"I'm not sure," I said, "but I'll try." When the session was over, I thanked Kathy for coming and told her I would see her at the house.

When I returned home, the children were playing with Raider outside by the pool. Aaron brought me outside, and after saying a quick hello to everyone, I had him dial Beverly's number. When she answered we exchanged our hellos and I told her, "I was just at an appointment with my psychologist, Nancy Repkey. I was wondering if you would come with me to next week's session."

After a long pause, Beverly responded, "I'd like to, but I'll have to talk to Bud first. I'll call you back when I know something." I thanked Beverly and told her I'd look forward to hearing from her soon.

Before the weekend, Beverly called me and said, "Bud and I would like to celebrate all the children's birthdays together this year. I'd like to have it on Saturday at six o'clock and Ronnie, Lauren, and Joe can each invite a friend."

"Oh, that's so nice of you!" I replied. "The kids will be so excited. Thank you."

On the day of the party, we arrived at Bud and Beverly's with six energetic kids. The area around the pool was decorated with colorful streamers and balloons. The kids and their friends swam in the pool for an hour until John told them it was time to eat. The steaks and fries were a big hit with the kids and quickly disappeared as they talked and laughed with each other over dinner. We sang "Happy Birthday" and Ronnie, Joe, and Lauren blew out the candles in unison.

As we were leaving, Beverly took me aside and said, "I'm sorry, but I'm not going to be able to come with you to your session next week."

"Why?" I asked.

"Bud said no," Beverly responded. "He doesn't want us to get involved." I felt immediately discouraged and my heart sank.

The next morning Aaron drove me into my shower and backed me up to my hair bowl. He rinsed my hair with water. As he added shampoo, my tears started running down my cheek. "Don't cry, Heather," he said. "I can't take it. I'm going to cry, too."

"We aren't getting any help from Bud and Beverly," I said, "and I don't know what to do."

"I can't believe that. Do you know I've worked fifty-six days straight? Stacy's upset and on me all the time about working so many days."

"I'm sorry," I said. "I didn't realize it had been so long. We need to focus on finding another nurse."

After Aaron put on my makeup we all went out to lunch. It was movie day and on our way to the theater John was playing slug bug with the kids. Whoever saw a Volkswagen beetle first would punch the other players on the arm and say "no slug backs!"

At first I thought it was a cute game, but then I heard Ronnie yell, "Ow, John, that hurt!"

"What's going on back there?" I said.

"We're just playing around."

"Don't be rough, please."

When we got to the theater we were at the snack bar and I could see a dark red mark with bruising on Ronnie's arm. I was angry, but holding back my emotion I said to John, "Ronnie has a bruise on his arm. You're not going to play that game anymore."

"Okay," John said, "but I used to play with my boys."

When we arrived home, Lauren opened Raider's crate. The children put on their swimsuits and took him outside to play. As they swam, Raider ran around the pool and barked continuously at the kids, but was scared to get in with them. John, Aaron, and I laughed at little

Raider. When the children came inside we ordered pizza and watched another movie.

Chapter 52

We finally found another day nurse, and Aaron was able to stay married. Ray was a confident, straightforward person. On his first day of work he was kept busy watching over energetic children. Over Cinco de Mayo weekend, John and I had a birthday party for the twins. My girlfriends helped me decorate and prepare food. Forty of Lauren and Joe's friends enjoyed dunking each other in a dunk tank, having water balloon fights, and swimming in the pool.

John brought out the cake and we all sang "Happy Birthday." Lauren and Joe eagerly opened their presents and thanked their friends. As the kids said good-bye to everyone, John and I handed out party favor bags. John, Ray, and the kids cleaned up the backyard before Raider ate any more balloon pieces. I was surprised at how helpful and kind John was being and I thanked him.

The next morning, John and I stopped by Bud and Beverly's house to say good-bye to them before they went back to Minnesota. I was sad to see them go but knew they were only a phone call away. June came fast and before I knew it I was saying good-bye to Ronnie, Lauren, and Joe at the airport, as they left for sleepaway camp for a month. Camp Thunderbird was in Bemidji, Minnesota, on Lake Plantagenet. Kids came from all over the United States to experience the camp's horseback riding, archery, canoeing, waterskiing, rock climbing, and sailing, and to learn how to become independent, resilient, and confident. I was going to miss them terribly but I knew once they got there they would have a great time.

When I found out the kids had a two-hour layover in Minneapolis I called my mom and said, "The kids will be at the airport at one o'clock. Can you make it to see them?"

"It's so nice to hear your voice," she said. "What flight are they on?"

"US Airways flight number 725. You better leave now, Mom, if you want to see them."

She said, "I love you, Heather. Please call me again." I hung up feeling desperate and wanting to tell her everything that was going on. I hoped John wouldn't see my parents' number come up on the cell phone bill.

The next day John left for San Diego to look at condos. He asked me if I wanted to go but I said no. While he was gone I had dinner with Janie Shapiro at Busters. We talked about John and she asked how things were going. I told her, "Things are not getting any better and my nurses keep quitting." Just then the phone rang. "I'm sorry," I said. "I have to get this. It's John."

"Hello, hon, have you found anything you like?"

"Not yet," he said, "but I have plans to meet with a realtor in the morning. What are you doing?"

"I'm having dinner with Janie."

"Why her?"

"Why wouldn't I? She's a good friend. I really have to go now. Love you."

"I love you, too," he said.

We hung up and I looked at Janie. "That's the tenth time he's called me today. I thought I would have peace and quiet while he was gone, but he's driving me crazy."

He called me three times during dinner. The last time he called, Janie looked at me and said, "What the hell? Don't answer it!"

"I have to or he'll get mad." I answered the call and said, "Yes, John?"

"I just walked by this Greek restaurant that I want to take you to next time we're in town."

"That's nice, John. I'm still at dinner. Can I call you when I get home?"

"Yes," he said. "When do you think that will be?"

"I don't know, but it won't be long."

When we were done Janie and I walked out together. I apologized for all the interruptions, and Ray and I drove back to the house.

John found a three-bedroom condo in downtown San Diego, near the gas lamp district. It was a new gated community with panoramic views of the city. Within a matter of days John furnished the whole condo and was on his way back to Arizona.

Every three days I would mail Ronnie, Lauren, and Joe a letter at camp so they wouldn't feel homesick. One morning I received a call from Camp Thunderbird's office. It was the children asking for more blankets and warm pajamas because they were freezing in the morning. Right away I bought long underwear, thermal pajamas, and two more blankets for each of them.

Over the next couple of weeks things were quiet around the house. John, Aaron, and I went to see *Chicago* at the Orpheum Theater. We also went to visit Uncle Harold and Aunt Gene. His Parkinson's was getting worse. When we arrived there was a caregiver helping him into the living room. We sat with them and had cocktails and hors d'oeuvres.

"How are you doing, Uncle Harold?" I asked.

"Oh, I'm fine but I can't stand these people being around me."

"Who?"

"You know them!" he said. "The nurses! Do you like your nurses?"

"Yes I do, I said, "but it took me a while to get used to having them around. It will get better."

Aunt Gene left to pick up dinner. When she returned we all sat in the kitchen to eat, me with my nurse, Aaron, and Uncle Harold with his caregiver, Carol. I admired Aunt Gene's teapot collection from around the world. After dinner we said good-bye and went home.

Summer camp was finally over and the kids were coming home. I could hardly wait to see them. We went to the airport gate to meet the kids. When Ronnie, Lauren, and Joe saw us they came running up and kissed us both. They looked rough around the edges and tired.

"I'm so glad you're home," I said. "Did you have a good time?"

"Yes, Mom," they said. "We did but we missed you guys."

Lauren asked, "Where's Raider?"

"He's at home. You'll see him soon," John said.

Everyone was in a great mood and happy to be together again. Lauren said, "It was nice seeing Grandma and Grandpa at the airport." I froze and wanted to crawl under the table.

In a loud voice John said, "What! You saw your grandparents at the airport?"

"Yes," Lauren said, "and Tiffany, too."

"Heather, you know I don't want the kids to have any contact with them."

"John, they haven't seen them in a long time and they are their grandparents."

John was quiet during the rest of the lunch and read the paper. On our way home the kids were anxious to tell me their camp stories. John grumbled the whole way.

When we got home, John went straight to his office and slammed the door.

The kids were happy to see Raider. He ran up to them and jumped and licked them all over. They took him outside to run around and play fetch. I asked Ray if he could pour us a couple of iced teas and help me unpack the kids' trunks. Their clothes were full of sand, grass, and bugs. Suddenly John stepped out of the office, waved his arm, and said "Heather, come here."

Ray drove me into the office and then he stepped out. I sat there waiting for John to speak. He said, "What the fuck were you thinking, when you called your parents?"

"It was the perfect opportunity for them to see the children. Why are you so upset?"

"They're a bad influence on you and the kids, and I don't want you to have any contact with them again."

I started to cry. "You know that's not true," I said. "You used to get along so well with my parents."

"They embarrassed me while you were in the hospital by telling the doctors I was being too rough with the children!"

"I think you're rough with them now."

"How dare you!" John said. "We're just playing around!"

"But they're crying, John."

John paused for a second and said, "I don't care. I don't want you talking to your parents anymore."

"Could you please call Ray?" I said. "I just want to leave."

Ray came and took me from the room. My eyes were puffy. "Are you okay?" he asked.

"No," I said. "I just got in trouble for calling my parents."

After dinner the children and I put in the video *Monsters, Inc.* The kids were excited to see it. As they watched they laughed and pointed at their favorite character. In the middle of the movie, John came over and stood beside me. "Do you want to watch with us?" I asked. "It's really funny."

"No," he said. "The kids have not done their chores yet. They need to pick up the dog poop."

"I'll have them do it as soon as the movie is over," I replied.

John walked away. The kids and I continued to watch and laugh at the movie. John came back a little while later holding a paper towel filled with dog poop, and smeared it all over my clothes. The children and Ray were in shock and just stared at John.

"What is wrong with you?" I said.

"Maybe next time you'll have the kids do their chores on time."

"Mommy, are you okay?" Lauren asked.

"Yes," I said. "I'll be fine."

Ray said, "Let's take you to the bedroom and get you cleaned up."

Ray took a washcloth, wiped the poop off my blouse, and changed my top. I started to tear up and Ray said, "Heather, don't cry! That guy is an asshole!"

"I don't understand!" I said. "We were so in love. Now he's changed and I don't know how to deal with it. Can you take me to the kids? I want to make sure they're fine."

I tucked them in bed and kissed them good night. Later that evening, I cried and told Denise what had happened. She was appalled. John did not come to my room to say good night. He called over the intercom and said, "Good night, Heather. I love you."

The next day John woke up as if nothing had happened. "Let's take the kids to San Diego," he said. "It's perfect there now and we can get out of this 118-degree weather."

I hesitated for a moment and said, "That sounds like a good idea." We packed our bags and were on our way to San Diego. We brought Denise and Aaron. When we arrived at the condo, John was excited to show us around. John was cheerful and relaxed, not anything like the previous day.

We didn't spend much time at the condo because everyone was hungry. We walked along the streets in the gas lamp district, until we found a restaurant we all could agree on. When we were finished with dinner we walked back to the condo. While the kids put on their pajamas Aaron transferred me into bed. Denise was right on time, and Aaron answered the door for her. "Wow!" Denise said. "This is going to be a mess. I'm going to have to rearrange things for your care." Aaron gave her a report and left.

The children were tired from the trip and went straight to bed. John came in the room and we talked for a while. When it was time for me to go to bed he kissed me and said good night.

In the middle of the night, I woke up with my teeth chattering. I yelled, "Can you come here, Denise?" She came to my room, felt my arms, and said, "You're freezing." I asked her to check the thermostat. She said "It's set to sixty-nine degrees. You'll be an ice cube by the morning if I don't get you warmed up." She left the room and came back with towels that she had heated in the microwave. "Thank you," I said. "They feel so warm."

I woke up to the kids saying, "Mom, hurry up! We're going to go have breakfast." We drove to Elijah's Deli for breakfast. John looked tired and I said, "Did you sleep okay?"

"Hell, no!" he said. "Every time Denise suctioned you it sounded like a jackhammer coming through my wall. I tried everything, even covering my ears with pillows, but I still heard the sound."

"I'm so sorry, John."

He yawned and said, "Well, those damn walls are paper thin. I don't know what I am going to do tonight."

"Maybe we could buy you some ear plugs today," I said.

John thought about it for a minute and said, "That's probably a good idea."

That night in the condo, I was cold again. John abruptly woke me up and said, "Tell your fucking nurse to leave the thermostat alone."

"What?"

"She moved it to seventy-six degrees and I can't sleep."

"I'm sorry!" I said.

John left the room and I could feel the air come on again. Denise tiptoed in and whispered, "Do you want me to turn the thermostat back up?"

"Absolutely not!" I said. "John will flip out. Just heat me some warm towels and I'll be fine."

When I woke up Aaron got me ready for the day. John took us to a local breakfast joint by the condo. John had three cups of coffee. It was obvious the ear plugs hadn't worked and he hadn't slept a wink.

When we finished eating, John said, "Aaron, why don't you take the day off and spend it with your mom?"

"I don't think that's a good idea," I said. "It's too hard for you to take care of me and the kids."

"I'll be okay. Don't you remember the kids are going to Jeannie and Mike's for the day?"

"Oh yeah," I said. "That's right." Aaron left for the day and Jeanie and Mike picked up the kids so they could spend the afternoon with Zach and Alexis.

John and I went around Seaport Village and enjoyed the variety of shops and art galleries. We stopped for something to drink and shared an Italian ice. It was the perfect day to be outdoors. John pushed my wheelchair along the boardwalk as we talked. With the breeze coming off the water, my long hair kept blowing in my face and I asked John to stop and put it behind my ears. After about four times of this he became irritated. "I'm tired of your hair," he said. "Why don't you just cut it off?"

"No, I like my hair. Why can't you have a little patience? It's not my fault. If I could put it back myself, I would."

On our way back to the condo we took a shortcut behind the Embassy Suites hotel. John brought up Denise and "the fucking nurses." He said, "I'm so tired of them being in our life."

"I understand where you're coming from," I said, "but they're all nice people and they help me live my life."

John said, "Ron Samuels and you ruined my life."

"Don't you even put me in the same category as that monster," I said. I stuck up for myself and we kept arguing.

"Here," he said, "let's see how you feel now, when you have nobody." He pushed the sip-and-puff straw I used to drive my wheelchair away from me and left me sitting in the middle of the road.

I desperately yelled, "John, come back here, please! Don't do this to me!" He kept walking and didn't look back.

Panicked, I tried to control my emotions, but I didn't know what to do. I couldn't drive my wheelchair by myself because my sip-and-puff straw was unreachable. I was stuck sitting in the road. I started to cry and kept looking for John, but he was nowhere in sight. I hoped a car would come down the road and see me, but there was no one in sight.

After about twenty minutes, I was hot and sobbing. I was too embarrassed to yell for help. Ten minutes later a man and two women came up behind me and said, "Are you okay? Can we help you?"

"Can you please help me get to the curb?" I said. I explained to them how to drive my wheelchair and they walked me to the side.

"Who did this to you?" they asked. "We're going to call the police."

"No, please, don't do that. Can you just stay here with me?"

John came walking toward us. "Did you leave her out here?" the man asked, upset. "You're an asshole! She could have been hit and killed!"

"Don't talk to me that way!" John said.

"We'll see. I'm going to call the police."

"There is no need to do that. I'm her husband."

I tried to calm things down by saying, "I really appreciate your help, but I will be fine with my husband."

On the way back to the condo, John pushed me very fast. "See the problems you cause me!" he said.

"You scared me!" I said. "I can't believe you would do that!"

When we went upstairs, my face, neck, and arms were badly sunburned. I started to feel feverish and my head was pounding. When Jeannie and Mike brought the kids back, John wanted to take everyone to dinner. I didn't feel like going, but I had to because I had no nurse. The next morning we drove back to Arizona. I was happy John was driving separately in his Mercedes and I was in my van with Aaron and the children.

Chapter 53

After we returned from San Diego, John started German shepherd training classes with Raider. The classes were held at Chaparral Park. Lauren was attached to Raider and always ended up going along.

Even though John and I shared many happy moments, things between us seemed to be getting worse. We had several dinner dates with Paul and Karen Arrot, and Nancy and Tom Killian. Each time we went out, John did something inappropriate and rude toward me and I'd end up upset and crying. No matter how hard I tried to keep him happy, he always found something wrong.

One July afternoon I took the kids shopping for some things they needed. When we returned home, the kids and I waited for John to get home so we could go out to dinner. When John came in the kitchen he said, "Did you guys have a good time shopping today?"

"Yes, we did," I said. I told him his new haircut looked really good.

All of a sudden, John looked down at Lauren, who was sharing a Popsicle with Raider. He walked toward her and pulled her off the ground by her hair. He screamed, "I told you not to feed anything to Raider but dog food."

Lauren started to cry. "John, stop it," I said. "You're hurting her!"

"Shut up! She has to know the rules!"

"Don't yell at Mom!" Lauren said.

John turned to her and said, "I'm gonna kill you, you little shit!"

He began chasing her around the kitchen, trying to catch her. Lauren picked a tomato off the counter and threw it at him. It hit him and splattered all over his silk shirt, which made him even madder. He caught her and pulled her by her wrist to the front door. He pushed her out and locked the door.

I turned to Aaron and said, "Drive me over there!"

I looked at John and said, "What is wrong with you?"

Right then Lauren started throwing rocks at the front door and cracked one of the glass panels. John screamed, "That little bitch, I'm going to kill her!"

"You're crazy! She's only ten years old and you're scaring her."

"I'm crazy!" he said, looking at me. "All of you get out of my house. I'm not going to pay for your nursing anymore!"

"Fine," I said. "Aaron, get my purse." I told Ronnie and Joe, "We are leaving."

Aaron put me in the van and the kids got in the back. I called Janie and said, "John just kicked us out of the house and I don't know what to do."

She said, "Why don't you drive over to Village Tavern and meet Lola and me? We can talk."

When we arrived at the restaurant Janie and Lola were already there and they sat us on the patio. We ordered dinner and we sat and talked about what had happened. I was desperate for some answers, and asked Janie what she thought. Janie said, "I can't believe he's acting like this. His behavior is irrational. He can't treat you or the children like this. He's becoming dangerous."

"I know," I said. "At times I'm scared of him."

"Does Bud know what's going on?"

"Yes, I tried to tell him."

"Maybe I should talk to my father," she said, "and tell him what's going on. But that could put him in a bad position, because he values Bud's friendship so much."

"I can understand that," I said. "I'll leave it up to you to decide."

My cell phone rang; it was John. "Where are you?" he said. "Are you coming home?"

"I don't know. Am I allowed back in?"

"Yes," he said.

After dinner was over, Janie and Lola hugged the kids. I thanked them for everything.

Aaron drove into the garage. Before we got out, I called John's father in Minnesota. When Bud answered the phone I said, "John and I had a fight tonight and he threatened me by saying he was not going to pay for the nurses."

"That's nonsense," Bud said. "I'm the one who pays for your nurses. He should have never said that."

"I'm so sorry to bother you this late, but I wanted to make sure I didn't have to worry."

"You don't have anything to worry about," he said. "You can call anytime."

When we entered the house, I told the kids to get ready for bed. That night John came to my bedroom while Kathy was doing my night care. "I will call Jim McGregor," he said, "and have him fix the panels on the front door."

"That sounds good."

John leaned over the bed, kissed me, and said, "Good night."

Lauren came back into my room. "Mom, I'm scared to sleep on the other side of the house with John," she said.

"It's okay, honey," I said. "You can sleep back here with me." Kathy made her a bed of blankets and pillows on the floor next to mine.

The children went back to school in August. The twins were in fifth grade, and Ronnie started seventh grade at Mohave Elementary School. Joe was excited to start Little League baseball this year. because he was on the same team as his good friend Jake. Their coach was Jake's dad, Ted Schuman. When we couldn't get Joe to practice, I could always rely on his coach to pick him up. That was always a big help for me.

One evening, before one of Joe's baseball games, John, Ray, Ronnie and I had dinner at Un Bacio, an Italian restaurant we frequented. Before we ordered our food, Sam, the manager, came by and asked, "How are you doing tonight, Mr. and Mrs. Grossman?"

"We're doing great," John replied. "Which one of the specials would you recommend?"

Sam answered, "The seafood risotto is one of my favorites."

When we started to eat John said, "Jim gave me an estimate on the door. It's going to cost a lot of money to replace the glass panels. It pisses me off that Lauren did that."

"She's just a little girl and you provoked her," I said. "She has never acted like that before."

John became enraged. "You dumb bitch!" he said. "How can you take her side on this?" He then spit in my face and I started to cry. I looked over at Ronnie. He looked terrified and said, "Mommy, don't cry."

"Why would you do that?" I said. "What is wrong with you?"

"I can fucking do whatever I want and I'm tired of your shit."

All of a sudden a man sitting with his wife at the next table said, "Hey, asshole, don't talk to your wife that way! What is wrong with you?"

John immediately stopped talking and turned around. "Mind your own business," he said.

He then turned back toward me and began eating again. Our conversation was much lighter. The waiter brought us a piece tiramisu for dessert, and we heard, "You fucking asshole!" We all looked up and saw the six-foot-three man and his wife standing by the door. He pointed at John and said, "I'm talking to you. Why don't you come outside and try to pick on somebody your own size?"

John stood up. "Are you kidding me?" I said. "John, please don't go!"

"I'm going to take care of this smart ass!" he said.

John walked toward the door and followed the man outside. So did five waiters, anticipating a brawl. I said, "Ray, go out there and stop him, please."

Ray left the table and went outside. I tried to look through the window to see what was happening, but all I could see were people standing around. Ten minutes later John, Ray, and Sam, the manager, walked back in the restaurant. I said to John, "Thank God you came to your senses."

"Can you believe that asshole?" he said. "I really wanted to punch him, but Sam held me back. Can you believe people these days?" I didn't say a word.

Totally embarrassed, we left the restaurant and drove to Chaparral Park for Joe's baseball game, and to meet Lauren and her friend Natalie. We said hello to the parents in the stand and sat down to watch the game. Joe was catcher and he played well, throwing out two guys at second base. When the game was over Joe's team had won. We went home, and Joe went with his coach and the other players for ice cream after the game.

The next day, when Aaron was working his shift he received a call from Ray. Ray told Aaron that he was quitting, and he left without giving notice. Aaron put in another ad to find a nurse. We hired John Cervantes; he was Hispanic, stood five-foot-eleven with dark hair, and was quiet. One morning, about two weeks later, I was lying in bed with my exercise clothes on, all gelled up to ride the bike. My phone rang and Kathy held it to my ear. It was John Cervantes. "I'm in New Mexico and I have a flat tire," he said. "I will have to call you when I get back in town." We never heard from him again.

Aaron put out another ad and we hired Steve Jarrett. He was not a nurse but had just graduated school as a naturopathic doctor. He worked for me while he built his client base. Steve was neat with short, dark-brown hair and handsome. His only flaw was he had been in a horrible paint gun accident and was missing his index finger, which freaked out the children. Steve fit in almost immediately. He changed my vitamin regimen and I felt like I had more energy.

At the end of August, John came to me and said, "I have a job opportunity with Sony Records in their Latin American division. I'm going to fly to Florida to find out more about it."

"How long will you be gone?" I asked.

"A few days," he answered.

I knew John was lying but I didn't want to cause a fight. While he was gone the kids and I went out to dinner, went shopping, and watched movies. It would have been enjoyable if John hadn't been calling me fifteen times a day. Janie came over to have dinner with us. Talking about John, I said, "John was in Vietnam and was involved in a helicopter crash; he saved a man's life and was awarded the Purple Star."

"Heather, that's not true," she said. "Bud would never allow one of his boys to go to war."

"Are you sure?"

"Yes, I've known him most of my life."

"John told me his hair was on fire in the accident."

"Boy, are you gullible," she said. "His brother, Dick, is balding, too. He didn't say his hair got burned in the war."

I wondered why he would lie to me about that. Janie and I finished our wine and said good night.

John came home the next day. After he finished unpacking, he came in the kitchen and said, "I need to talk to you in the office."

Steve brought me in there, shut the door, and left. "How did your meeting go with Sony?" I asked.

"It was very informative, but I'm not going to take the job," he said. "It would involve too much traveling and I would miss you too much." I smiled and stayed quiet, but thought "yeah, right."

"I met with Ken Hawkins, the private investigator, while I was there," he continued. "We talked about Ron and the possibility of him escaping from jail. I decided to buy a gun in Florida. Do you want to see it?" He opened his desk drawer and pulled out an all-black pistol.

"You know how I feel about guns," I said. "I don't want it in this house."

"I'll lock it in the safe."

"I still don't feel comfortable having it in the house."

"Just you wait!" he said. "When that bastard Ron Samuels comes here I'm going to blow his head off. I'm going to shoot him in the knees, and watch him bleed to death."

"I know you have a lot of built-up anger," I said, "but what you just said scares me. I'm worried about you!"

"Don't worry, honey," he said. "I have it all under control."

That evening when Kathy came into work, Steve and I were waiting for her in the exercise room out of view of the cameras. I told them that John had bought a gun. They both looked at each other and said, "What! When did he do that?"

"He brought it back from Florida," I said.

I continued to tell them what he'd said, word for word. They both looked scared and so was I. Steve said, "What if he gets mad and starts shooting us?"

I said I honestly didn't think that would happen, but I wanted them to know there was a gun in the house.

Chapter 54

The first week of September I felt like my life was closing in on me. I was at the point where I was scared to be alone with John. One morning Kathy shocked me by saying, "Heather, I called and reported John to Child Protective Services. I called them two months ago and told them what was going on, but I didn't hear anything back. I called them again, and they told me they're going to interview the children at school tomorrow."

"Kathy," I said, "I know you're worried about the children, but John is going to be furious if he finds out."

"I'm just trying to help," she said. "He has to stop."

When Aaron came in my room we both stopped talking. "Is everything all right?" he asked.

"Yes," I replied. "Everything is fine." I started my day with butterflies in my stomach. When the kids came home from school I asked them how their day was, and they said fine. They didn't mention anything about being interviewed, so I didn't ask them anything.

Later that night, John came into my room and asked Kathy to leave so he could speak to me. He said, "Right before dinner I received a call from CPS. They want to speak to us in a couple of days."

"Why would they want to talk to us?"

"They're accusing me of abusing Ronnie, Lauren, and Joe."

"See," I said, "I told you, you were abusive to them."

John became enraged. He came to the side of the bed, placed his hand over my mouth, leaned down, and whispered in my ear, "If anything comes out, you'll end up in a nursing home and I will send your kids to foster care."

I could not remove his hand from my mouth. I began to cry. "Do you understand?" he said.

I nodded my head and he left the room.

I yelled for Kathy. When she walked in I said, "CPS wants to interview John, Aaron, and me. John is going crazy. He just threatened to put me in a nursing home and put the kids in foster care."

"Oh my God," Kathy said. "I am so sorry! I just wanted to get John help."

"I know," I said. "It's not your fault. I just feel trapped. Bud pays for my medical expenses and my family is in Minnesota. I just don't know what to do."

The next day, there was a knock at our door. John went to answer it and said, "Heather, can you come here?"

Aaron drove my wheelchair to the foyer. There were two gentlemen standing in the doorway. The first one said, "I'm Detective Fanning from the Paradise Valley Police Department." The second man said, "I'm Detective Cole."

John came and stood beside me and placed his hand on my shoulder. Detective Fanning said, "The police department has received some complaints and we need to ask you some questions, Mrs. Grossman."

"Yes," I said, "how can I help you?"

Detective Fanning continued. "Do you feel safe in your home?"

"Yes, I do."

"Has your husband ever hit you?"

John pressed down on my shoulder and I answered, "No, he never has."

Detective Fanning then asked, "Has your husband ever spit on you?"

"No," I said, "he has not."

As I sat there, terrified and lying, I thought, "Why would you ask me these questions in front of John? If I tell the truth, he'll hurt me."

Detective Fanning thanked me for answering his questions. Detective Cole placed his card on top of my hand and said, "Here's my card. If you ever need to reach us, you can call anytime."

"Thank you," I said.

They then left. John asked Aaron to leave and then drove me to the office. He started screaming "What the hell is going on? Who is talking to the police? Do you know?"

"I have no idea."

"We need to replace the night nurses."

"Oh, no you're not! They're both very good and I like them."

"I don't care," he said. "I am not going to change my mind."

Things were tense around the house until we spoke with Child Protective Services. I have no idea what John and Aaron said to them, but I was nonchalant and would not give them a straight answer. That night when Kathy came to work, she said, "The police have advised me that it's not safe to work with you anymore, in case John finds out I'm the one who reported him."

"No, Kathy!" I said. "You can't leave me."

"Oh, honey! I love you and you know I would take care of you forever if I could."

"Please don't go!"

"I've even talked with my friend, Jan," she said, "and she also feels I need to leave."

I started to cry and Kathy gave me a hug. The next morning, when Kathy finished her shift, she and I said good-bye to each other and cried. I didn't know how I was going to get through everything without her.

After Kathy left, John was suspicious of everyone in the house. His personality took a 180-degree turn and he became loving and concerned for me.

Aaron and I immediately started looking for a new night nurse. I hired Ceal Anderson, who had just moved here from Seattle, Washington, with her husband Swede. She was five-foot-five with short, grey hair and a beautiful tan. When Denise trained Ceal, I could see she was bright and caught on quickly.

We were also in the process of hiring a new nanny after our previous one quit. John and I interviewed several people, and we were impressed with Cassie Malone. She had worked for the owner of the Home Depot until she moved to Arizona from Atlanta, Georgia. She was an amazing Southern cook, who always had a smile on her face and was a pleasure to be around.

One morning, John came running into my room. "Quick," he said, "turn on the TV!"

A plane had hit the World Trade Center. In shock, I wondered what was going on. We continued to watch the news coverage together. I did not send the children to school. That day we went to lunch together and explained to the kids what had happened. We continued to watch the news and felt sad for all the people involved and their friends and families.

Over the next few weeks we enjoyed Cassie's cooking and didn't eat out as much. Ronnie, Lauren, and Joe absolutely loved her and I trusted her with them. Cassie was polite but I could see she was tough; she had no problem dealing with John's personality.

It didn't take long before John was back to his old self. He asked me if I wanted to go to San Diego with him for the weekend. I said, "No, I don't feel like going."

"What do you mean you're not going?"

"I want to spend time with the kids. Why don't you just go?"

He looked at me with anger in his eyes and said, "That's fucking bullshit!"

He marched into the kitchen and yelled at Cassie. "Throw the steaks and asparagus in the garbage," he said. "No one is eating dinner tonight."

"Why?" Cassie said. "I don't understand."

"Just do what you're told," John said.

Cassie threw all the food in the trash while John watched with his arms crossed in front of his chest. I couldn't believe it. When Aaron transferred me to bed, we called Denise. I asked her if she could bring sandwiches for the kids because they hadn't eaten dinner. She offered to pick up some hamburgers at McDonald's.

When Denise arrived I told her what had happened, and she sneaked into the kids' bedrooms with their burgers. I went to bed hungry and sick to my stomach, but felt a little better knowing my kids ate that night.

John came into my room early the next morning to tell me he was leaving for San Diego. He kissed me and said, "I'll call you on the way there. I love you."

"I love you, too," I said. After he left I immediately asked Denise if she would call my mom from her cell phone. When my mom answered, I said, "I miss you so much. Will you buy a ticket and come to Arizona this weekend? John is out of town."

"Yes," she said. "I'll fly out today."

Cassie picked her up from the airport that evening and brought her to the house.

I was so happy to see her. We stayed up for hours and talked. My mom said, "Heather, I didn't want to say anything while you were trying to recover, but I think you should know John was mean to me. He treated me like I was inferior to him and as if I were his servant. I couldn't even get away to get a haircut. One of the security guards felt sorry for me and took me on his own time. He treated his security guards like they were his servants, too, and they would talk about him behind his back. Nobody liked him. He wouldn't allow me to take the children to church. John only let me see you in the ICU a few times; he always told me I had to stay and take care of the kids. When Tiffany came down from Minnesota, she wasn't allowed to see you either. I don't know what happened to him, but he was absolutely evil."

"Mom, I'm so sorry you had to go through that," I said. "It had to be so hard on you. I had no idea he would act that way with my family."

"Don't worry. I got through it." She kissed me on the forehead and said good night.

The next morning I didn't ride my bike. I was up early drinking coffee and having breakfast on the patio with my mom. "Make sure to finish your eggs," she said. "You look like a cadaver. You've lost a lot of weight, Heather."

Aaron said, "She weighs ninety-three pounds."

"A lot of times I end up crying and not finishing my food," I explained.

"Honey, you have to eat or you'll get sick and waste away."

"I know, Mom. It's just hard sometimes."

The phone rang; it was John. "I tried to call you last night," he said, "but you didn't answer."

"I'm sorry," I said. "I went to bed early."

"What are you doing today?"

"I have to buy groceries. Can I call you when I get back?"

"Okay," he said. "I'll call you later."

We spent the rest of our day enjoying each other's company. We went to the grocery store to pick up things for dinner. We were interrupted by another phone call from John.

When Ronnie, Lauren, and Joe came home from school, they asked Grandma to come outside and watch them swim. We sat outside and watched them dive and swim races while Cassie grilled burgers. The kids took their baths and my mom tucked them into bed.

Aaron took me to my bedroom and put me in bed. Ceal came in and I said, "Hello!"

"You're in a good mood," she said.

"My mom is here visiting—and FYI, John doesn't know." We both laughed. My mom came back to the bedroom holding a bowl of popcorn in one hand and *Bridget Jones's Diary* in the other. We laughed throughout the whole movie.

Saturday morning my mother made French toast and scrambled eggs for everyone. She always made the kids breakfast in Minnesota. I could tell they missed it and were happy to eat Grandma's cooking again.

We drove to the mall and shopped the rest of the afternoon. John called me for the sixth time that day. I was brief on the phone and said I would call him back. That day was my mom's last day here. I was sad she was leaving and I could tell she was worried about me. I cried while I watched her pack her bags and told her I didn't want her to go. We went to lunch at Houston's, and then took her to the airport.

I knew John's flight was arriving that afternoon, but I didn't know what time. We were driving on Forty-Fourth Street, heading south toward the airport. I looked over and saw John in his silver Porsche driving toward us. "Quick," I yelled. "Duck down! John's going to see you." My mom lay down on the back seat.

"That was close!" Aaron said. "He would be pissed if he knew you were in town." We pulled up to the terminal, and my mom opened the passenger door and kissed me. I told her I loved her and would call her soon. Tears rolled down our cheeks as we said our good-byes. Even the kids were sad, saying, "Grandma, don't go!"

The minute we walked in the door, John asked, "Where were you?"

"Running errands. When did you get back?"

"Thirty minutes ago," he said. He came over, kissed me, and said, "I missed you."

At dinner, everyone gathered around the table, prayed, and enjoyed the meal Cassie had prepared. The children helped Cassie clear off the table. Ronnie put on *Men in Black* and Lauren and Joe sat and watched it with him.

John said, "Why don't we watch TV in the master bedroom?" When he drove my wheelchair into the room, John closed the blinds and lit the fireplace so that I wouldn't be cold. Instead of watching television, John started questioning me.

"What were you up to this weekend? Every time I called you, either you didn't have time to talk or you were short with me and hung up."

"I'm so sorry," I said. "I had a busy weekend."

He took his finger and pushed it into my chest. "That's no excuse," he said. Again he pushed his finger into my chest and said, "When I'm out of town, we usually talk eight times a day or more."

"I'm sorry."

John punched me in the chest right below my trach and said, "What's going on with you?"

I started to cry. "Why are you doing this? You're hurting me."

"Don't talk back to me," he said and punched me in the chest again.

I cried harder. "Please stop."

The secretions built up from my crying and I had a hard time saying, "Please, John, can you suction me?"

He looked at me with anger in his eyes. "No," he said, "go ahead and choke for all I care. You used to talk to me for hours on the phone. Now you don't care about me!"

I couldn't answer him. Panicked and unable to breathe, I started clicking with my tongue. As I turned blue, John yelled for Aaron. "Heather's not breathing," he said. "I don't know what happened. Can you suction her?" Aaron quickly pulled out the portable suction machine at the bottom of my chair and started to suction me. I felt relief immediately and said, "I'm so glad you came. I couldn't breathe at all."

Aaron drove me to my room and could tell I was upset. When he transferred me to bed, he asked, "What happened to your chest? It's all bruised up."

"It must be from John," I answered. "He was hitting and poking me because I didn't talk to him enough this weekend."

At that moment Denise entered the room. "Heather," she said, "what happened to your chest? Did John give you these bruises?"

"Yes, he did."

She turned to Aaron and said, "How could you let this happen to her?"

"They were alone in the bedroom," he said. "There was nothing I could do. Heather, I have to go home now; I'll see you in the morning."

Denise came to the side of the bed. She leaned over me and whispered, "You have to call the police and report this."

"I'm afraid to," I whispered back. "What if John's dad gets upset and stops paying for my nurses?"

"Heather, you have to do something. This is a dangerous situation."

"I know," I said, "but I don't know what to do." I spent the rest of the night crying and talking to Denise.

Chapter 55

Thank goodness it was fall and cool outside; I wore sweaters for the next week to cover the bruises on my chest. Every time John called me I answered my phone immediately. Bud and Beverly moved back to Scottsdale in November. A week later Beverly asked us to dinner at their home; it was nice to see them again and the kids all hugged Grandma and Grandpa. Bud grilled steaks for dinner while Beverly prepared a salad and baked potatoes. It was nice to feel the warmth of family and share a meal together.

On the morning of Thanksgiving, we went to Eddie Matney's restaurant. We had signed up to help serve food to the homeless. Eddie always had a bus waiting to drive people from Phoenix Rescue Mission to his restaurant on Thanksgiving Day. While John helped serve in the food line, I watched Ronnie, Lauren, and Joe serve coffee and dessert and clear tables. I was proud of them for jumping in and being so willing to help.

We drove to Norman and Cathy Ross's house. They had invited us over for Thanksgiving dinner. I was excited to meet some of John's family from his mother's side. Cathy prepared dinner for everyone and I enjoyed hearing stories about John's mother, Alene. I was surprised to see how friendly and easygoing the Ross family was compared to the Grossmans. They made us all feel at home.

John and I had lunch with Bud and Beverly at a new restaurant in town called Bloom. We were enjoying each other's company until my lips turned blue and I felt like I was going to faint. Bud quickly said, "Heather, are you okay?"

"I think I'm cold," I said. "I just need to recline my wheelchair back."

Steve reclined my chair for a few minutes and everyone waited for me to feel better. When I came back up I apologized for the interruption. "That's okay, dear," Beverly said. "We're just glad you're feeling better."

After lunch, Beverly and I explored the new boutiques in the Shops at Gainey Village. Beverly asked, "How are things going with John?"

"For the last few weeks, things have been pretty good," I said. "Sometimes he gets so mad it scares me. And, Beverly, he has a gun in the house now and that terrifies me."

"He has a gun? I'm going to have to tell Bud about this."

"I love him, but I don't know what to do."

"I know you do, and you both have been through so much. How has he been with the children?"

"He's been about the same," I answered. "Sometimes he can be very loving, and other times he can be downright mean to them."

"Well, that is too bad," she said. "I was hoping things would get better."

We stopped at the salon so Beverly could make an appointment for her nails and then shopped a little more before saying good-bye. Steve and I picked up the kids from school and went home. After dinner, John and Lauren took Raider to his training session together. Lauren and Raider had developed a strong bond; he was her best friend and protector.

Mrs. Curtain and Mrs. Ganz organized an international holiday luncheon for the twins' classes. With Steve's help, I baked a traditional beef brisket to take to the party. I enjoyed seeing the parents of Lauren and Joe's friends. Joe introduced me to Tyler's mom, Jill Brenenstuhl, and we ultimately became good friends. When the party was over, Lauren and Joe went home with their friends.

It was a good thing Steve and I returned home after the party. As we drove up to the house we could see Ronnie sitting outside the door. John was not home and Ronnie was locked out. When Ronnie finished his homework, we took Raider for a walk around the lake at Chaparral Park. During our walk John called and asked, "Where are you?"

"We're at the park walking around."

He was upset. "Why didn't you wait for me?"

"I didn't know you were going to be home."

"I want to go to Houston's for dinner."

"Okay," I said, "we'll be home shortly."

We went to dinner and as soon as John had finished his second drink, I could tell it was not going to be a good night. He asked Steve to sit by the bar. The conversation became heated. "Did you and Steve have fun making brisket?" he said. "I'm really tired of these fucking nurses."

"Please don't swear in front of Ronnie. I asked you to help me make the brisket, but you said no. So what was I supposed to do?"

"I don't want to see the nurses in my kitchen anymore."

"That's ridiculous!" I said. "They need to get me water for my medication and make me breakfast."

I looked over at Ronnie. I could tell he was uncomfortable about us arguing. "Ronnie," I said, "don't worry. Everything is okay. We're just talking about the nurses."

I looked at John and said, "We can talk about this when we get home." Then I turned back to Ronnie. "I'm so proud of you for getting straight A's."

"It was easy, Mom. Can I show Grandma and Grandpa Grossman my report card?"

"Sure you can," I said. "We can fax it to them tonight."

When we got back to the house John helped Ronnie fax his report card to Bud and Beverly while Steve took me to my bedroom and got me ready for bed.

At seven in the morning, John's voice echoed through the intercom system, "Keep your fucking nurses out of my kitchen!" The following night Ceal went to get me water and the door from the addition into the main house was locked. She came back to my room and said, "Heather, what am I supposed to do? John locked the door and I can't get you water, and I won't be able to make you breakfast. But my main concern is I won't be able to check on the children. I'm worried because they are on the other side of the house with him."

"Ceal, I don't know what to do. I've talked to him about this, but he won't listen to me."

"Heather, this is bullshit!" Ceal replied. "It has to be so hard on you. You and the kids have to walk on eggshells all the time."

We welcomed in 2002 at Bud and Beverly's again. My New Year's resolution was to bring my family closer together and get my husband help. I had my yearly checkup with Dr. Candice Williams, and while I was there I told her John was becoming abusive to me. She asked, "Are you seeing a psychologist?"

"I was seeing Cathy Repkey until John stopped me. I've asked his family for help but they don't want to get involved. I'm desperate and don't know what to do."

"I want you to see Dr. Kevin O'Brian," she said. "He is a neuropsychologist. I'm very concerned about you, Heather. How are you feeling?"

"At times I feel fine, but I'm stressed and worried about my situation."

"Do you think an antidepressant would help?"

"I don't want to take one now," I said, "but I will call you if things get worse."

Dr. Williams hugged me and said good-bye.

When Aaron and I got home the children were sitting at the kitchen table with Cassie doing their homework. John seemed to be in a good mood—an even better one when Matt called and said, "I am driving a friend to NAU. We'll be at the house in a couple of hours."

When Matt walked into the house the kids were so excited they ran right up to him and pulled him into the kitchen. Lauren said, "This is Raider, our dog."

Matt bent down and pet Raider on the head. He gave his father a hug and then came over and kissed me on the cheek. Matt turned and introduced us to his friend. They were both college students and loved to be outdoors. John and I took everyone to Eddie Matney's for dinner. It was a perfect restaurant for Matt, who was a vegetarian, because the menu had a lot of dishes he could choose from. Matt and his friend stayed up late talking to John and spent the night at the house. The next morning, after the kids left for school, John and I took the boys out for breakfast. I wished Matt could have stayed longer, but they left that afternoon for Flagstaff.

One morning, Aaron took the day off for a doctor's appointment, and Denise worked the day shift. By the time we met John for lunch and were finished eating, he was yelling at Denise and saying, "Hurry up, you're taking too long. Why can't you load her in the van?"

Denise was frazzled. "You have to be patient," I said to John. "She's never worked days before."

"She is an idiot!" John said. "Steve should have worked!"

It only got worse when we went to the mall. John was walking fast and Denise was having trouble driving the wheelchair. "Come on!" he yelled at her. "What the hell is wrong with you?"

Denise said, "I'm only trying to be careful."

John looked like an enraged bull. He came at me and took control of my wheelchair, and Denise followed behind us. "You're being an asshole!" I said. "She's only trying to help us out." John and I got into a huge fight and he left me in front of Williams-Sonoma and walked off. Denise came running and asked, "What happened? Are you okay?'

"John is upset with me," I said. "Can you drive me to the tables outside of Nordstrom and I will call him?"

It took John an hour to cool down. As we were drinking coffee, I saw him walking toward us. I said, "Are you ready to go?"

"Yes."

Denise and I were quiet on the drive home. Cassie had prepared lasagna for dinner and we sat down and ate. I was embarrassed when John criticized the way Denise was feeding me.

After the kids were done bathing I kissed them all and they went to bed. Denise brought me to the bedroom and John transferred me into bed. When Ceal arrived Denise said, "Be careful. John has been livid all day. I don't know what he might do tonight."

I said good-bye to Denise and apologized for John's behavior. Halfway through my night care, Ceal called her husband and said, "If things get out of control here, I will call you and I want you to call the Paradise Valley Police Department. Don't forget to tell them that John has a gun." And she hung up.

I waited for John to come back and kiss me, but I knew he was still mad when I heard him say over the intercom, "Pick up the phone." When John called Ceal held it to my ear. "I'm tired," he said, "and I don't want to deal with the nurse. I love you. Good night." He then hung up.

The next night, after I had told John about Dr. O'Brian, he came back to my bedroom and asked Ceal to leave and turn off the intercom—but she left it on. John yelled at me about seeing Dr. O'Brian and started pushing his finger in my chest. I started to cry. "Please stop!" I said. "That's hurting me."

Ceal came in and said, "What is going on?"

John looked at the intercom and realized she had not turned it off. He grabbed the knob in a fit of rage and pulled it out of the wall. He looked at Ceal and said, "Get out of the way" and left the room.

"Oh my gosh!" Ceal said. "Heather, your chest is all red and blotchy; I hope you don't bruise like you did last time."

"I'll be okay," I said. "But I'm worried about the kids. Could you check on them?"

"Sure, I'll be right back," she said. Within a few seconds, Ceal returned and said, "John has locked me out of the main part of the house."

"Could you walk outside and peek in the windows?"

"Yes, I'll be right back." When she came back she said, "They are asleep and everything looks fine."

"That's a relief," I said. "Thank you for checking on them."

I went to my appointment with Dr. O'Brian the next day. I knew I needed help and I was not going to let John stop me from seeing him. When I went into his office, I asked Aaron to sit in the waiting room. Dr. O'Brian was soft spoken, had light-brown hair, and was casually dressed. I was impressed with his knowledge about spinal cord injuries. I did not disclose my problems with John, but when I left my appointment I knew I could trust him.

When Aaron and I returned home, John was playing football in the backyard with the kids and Raider. When the kids realized I was home they stopped playing and came in to kiss me. Raider followed them, drank his water, and slobbered all over the floor. John came in and said "Joe, clean that up."

After dinner, Cassie and I were talking in the kitchen and I heard John yelling at Joe. I told Aaron to bring me to Joe's bedroom to find out what was going on. Joe was crying and John was calling him stupid and an idiot and telling him to clean up his room.

"John," I said, "leave him alone."

John turned around and said, "I want his room cleaned up." He walked away.

A few moments later I was with Lauren in her room when Aaron came in and told me that Joe was still crying and trying to find change in his room to pay for his tutor. John must have made him feel really bad.

I went to talk to Joe in his room. "Don't worry about it, Joe. You're smart and a lot of kids use tutors." Joe wiped his tears away and gave me a hug. I lovingly kissed him on his cheek.

I went to the office to confront John about how he'd treated Joe. "Why are you treating Joe this way?" I said. "He is such a sweet kid, and you're always hurting his feelings and picking on him."

John was defensive. "You always used to listen to me and support my decisions."

I knew that John was being abusive and a bully, but I didn't feel like I could say these things to him without making matters worse. "I still support you," I said. "But please be more patient with the kids."

"I will," he said.

When John and I came out of the office, Lauren was in her pajamas, running around the kitchen and throwing the ball to Raider. Raider was barking loudly and Lauren was laughing. John said, "Don't throw the ball in the house."

Lauren was having so much fun she didn't hear him. John walked over to her, grabbed her wrists, and yelled, "Stop it!" Raider growled at him. John yelled at Raider and he cowered down.

"Don't be mean to Raider," Lauren said.

John picked her up by her hair. "Don't you talk back to me," he said.

Lauren started crying. "John, please stop!" I screamed. "Leave her alone." He pulled her across the marble floor and I started to cry, yelling, "John, stop!" John let go of her and she ran into her room. I told Aaron to bring me to Lauren. As I passed John I said, "This is exactly what I was talking about. What is wrong with you?"

Lauren was crying in her room. "Honey, are you okay?" I asked. "I wish I could hold you. Come sit on my lap."

"Mom, I'm scared," she said. "My head hurts."

"Lauren, I'm so sorry," I said. I sat with her until my night nurse arrived.

Later I told Denise what had happened and asked her to check on Lauren. Denise came back and said, "I looked through the window and she had a chair wedged to block the door." John had not locked the door to the main house yet, so I told Denise to go get her.

While Denise was taking care of me, Lauren grabbed her sleeping bag and laid it beside my bed. Lauren asked me, "Mom, do you ever wish you weren't paralyzed?" I said, "No, I'm okay with being paralyzed. I just wish I could put my arms around you. I love you."

Denise woke me up around six o'clock the next morning. "John was back here," she whispered, "and he put these pictures around Lauren on the floor." She showed me a picture and on it was written: "You're a Samuels."

"Denise," I said, "that's a picture of Ron."

"Why would he do something like that?"

"I don't know," I said. "But please pick up the pictures before Lauren wakes up." When Lauren woke up I kissed her, said good morning, and told her to go get ready for school.

After talking to Beverly on the phone and telling her what had happened with Lauren, all three of us met for lunch at Bloom's. Beverly had a carefree and sunny disposition and always made Lauren feel special. After we finished eating, Beverly and I took Lauren shopping. Beverly bought all the outfits Lauren liked, and Lauren could hardly wait to show them off at school. Lauren seemed in better spirits, but I couldn't stop replaying what had happened. And I was scared of what might happen next.

Chapter 56

It had been a week since I had seen Dr. O'Brian. With my emotions running high, it took less than ten minutes before everything started spilling out. I told Dr. O'Brian everything that had been happening and how desperate and helpless I felt. I felt defeated because John and I had been so much in love. It felt like Ron was winning, even while in jail. Dr. O'Brian looked more and more shocked as I continued to tell him what had been happening to me.

"I can't believe you've been dealing with all this," he said. "But do you honestly think Ron is responsible for John's behavior?"

"Yes," I said. "Everything was fine before I was shot. Now there is so much torment in our relationship. Being shot affected everyone close to me."

"The course of your life has changed, Heather," Dr. O'Brian said. "But John is still responsible for his own behavior."

When I left his office I felt relieved to have somebody to talk to. But I also realized my life was a mess.

At the end of February, John wanted me to go to San Diego with him. When I told him I didn't want to go, he said, "If you don't go with me I'll stay here this weekend and take it out on the kids." I immediately changed my mind, and John, Aaron, Denise, and I were on our way to San Diego.

Cassie spent the weekend at the house and took care of the children. On the way to San Diego, Denise was driving and it was stormy and windy. Going through the mountains, Denise slowed down. John began screaming over the walkie-talkie. "Hurry up!" he said. "Can't you keep up with me? What is taking you so long? Denise is such an idiot."

Denise pushed down the button and said, "Hold on. I'm doing the best I can. The wind is blowing the van all over the road and it's dangerous."

"I don't care," John said. "Just catch up!"

"Denise, I'm sorry," I said. "Just drive however you're comfortable."

"He's such an asshole, Heather," she said. "I've never met anybody like him."

When we arrived, to make things more comfortable, I stayed at the Embassy Suites with Denise and Aaron while John stayed at the condo. John was in good spirits and happy to have me with him. The first day we had plans to meet my old night nurse, Debbie Cason, and her girlfriend, Angela, for cocktails at a downtown bar in the gas lamp district. It was nice to see Debbie again and when she introduced me to Angela, I could tell they were very much in love.

We laughed and enjoyed each other's company for a couple of hours, until everyone was hungry and ready to eat. We walked along the sidewalk and ended up at the Hard Rock Café. It was loud and busy, but after everyone had a couple more drinks we fit right in, yelling over the crowd to one another. We had fun with Debbie and Angela, and by ten o'clock we were partied out and headed back to the hotel. It was the best time John and I had had together in a long time.

The next day it was cool and brisk. Aaron put extra blankets on top of me while the three of us walked along the boardwalk by the water. John was loving and attentive and stopped to kiss me and wrap my scarf around my neck after the wind had blown it off. He was in a good mood because that night we were meeting Matt for dinner. Matt had been living in San Diego for two years now, and we were meeting him at one of his favorite Mexican restaurants, Miguel's Cocina on Coronado Island.

When we arrived Matt was waiting for us at the hostess desk. He gave John a big hug and kissed me on the cheek. We then went to our table. Matt liked to drag his feet when it came to school, so the topic of conversation was getting him to finish college. When we finished, we said our good-byes to Matt and drove back to the condo.

The following morning we had breakfast and were on our way back to Arizona. When we arrived at the house, John let Aaron go home early. I wanted to tell Aaron to stay, because I was scared and did not want to be alone with John and the kids. But before I had the chance, he was headed out the front door.

I talked to Cassie and asked her how the weekend had gone. Cassie told me everything had gone well, except for when she caught Joe running naked down the lane because Ronnie had dared him to. John and I were both tired, so he ordered pizza for dinner and we all went to bed early.

Chapter 57

In March, Beverly was busy planning a birthday party for Bud. He was turning eighty-three years old on April 5. She was reserving rooms at the Phoenician Hotel for the whole family, planning dinners at two different venues, and organizing a large private party at the house. I asked her if I could help with anything. Her only request was for every family member to write a letter to John's father and give it to her. As a gift she was going to make him a memory book full of the letters everyone had written.

Meanwhile, John and I were busy helping Lauren and Joe with their projects for the school science fair. Joe's project involved Cosmo the mouse and a maze. Joe would put a piece of food at one end and the mouse at the other, and then time the mouse to see if the food influenced his speed through the maze.

Lauren's project was an alarm to keep her brothers out of her room. She tested it by placing it on the other side of her doorknob. When the boys came in her room, it would make noise and alert her. Joe's project wasn't working out too well. Cosmo was eating too much cheese and getting so fat, it was hard for him to maneuver around the maze's corners.

One afternoon, while I was getting a facial with Robyn at her salon, there was a knock at the door. Aaron peeked his head in and said, "John is on the phone and has to talk to you." Aaron held the phone to my ear and all I could hear was John yelling, "The fucking mouse is out of the cage! I told you not to get that damn thing."

"I'm sorry, John," I said, "but I'm getting a facial. I will be home in a little bit."

"It's all your fault. I need you home now to help me find that rodent."

"Okay," I said. "I'll be home as soon as I can."

Aaron hung up the phone and left the room. I was embarrassed and wondered if Robyn had heard John yelling at me. Before I could say anything, Robyn said, "That was a heated conversation. He was yelling so loudly I could hear everything through the phone."

"I'm sorry for the interruption," I said.

"I'm sorry you had to go through that."

When I arrived home, I saw Joe crying and John yelling at him about the mouse. When John realized I was home he started yelling at me, saying, "You better find that mouse. I don't want babies around this house, and they carry diseases. I'm sick of this shit. You should have listened to me."

"John, please don't yell at me," I said. "I will find the mouse."

Cassie, Aaron, all three children, and I searched the house from room to room, but could not find Cosmo. I was scared to tell John, but I knew I had to. That evening I told Connie about Cosmo getting out. She said, "If I find him tonight, Heather, I will try to catch him for Joe." John came back to my room and resumed yelling at me about the mouse. "Please, John," I said, "leave me alone." He kissed me on the cheek and said good night.

The following morning I was awoken by the intercom and John saying, "Keep the fucking nurses out of my kitchen!"

I knew John had seen Connie getting me yogurt for breakfast. When Connie came back, she started feeding me and said, "I have good news and bad news. I caught Cosmo last night, so I put him in a jar with holes on top and this morning he was dead. Is Joe going to be upset?"

"Maybe a little," I said. "But don't worry, at least you found him."

When John came to my room he was happy the mouse was dead. "What are you going to do now?" he asked.

"I'm going to buy another mouse so he can finish his experiment."

"Why not just give up?"

"Because that is not what a good parent would do," I said. The new mouse that Joe and I picked out was skinnier, faster, and obviously smarter than Cosmo. She ran through the maze like a champ. Both Lauren and Joe won awards at the science fair and John and I were proud of them.

After my next appointment with Dr. O'Brian, I came home feeling relieved and less stressed. John had been pleasant for the last week and I was feeling content. When I came in the house Cassie was preparing dinner, Lauren was playing with Raider, and the boys were in the TV room playing video games. John came into the kitchen, leaned over, and gave me a kiss. "How was your day, honey?" he asked.

"It was fine and the weather is just beautiful today."

"I agree," he said. "Would you like to sit outside and have a glass of wine together before dinner?"

"That sounds great," I said. John and I sat alone outside and talked about the big weekend coming up.

When dinner was ready, Cassie told us it was time to eat and had the children wash up. We sat down as a family and said our prayers. Halfway through dinner, John reached up, slapped Joe across the face, and said, "Get your elbows off the table."

Everyone stopped eating and looked at John in shock. "Joseph," I said, "are you okay, honey?"

With a sad little face and tears running down his cheeks, Joe came and stood by my side. I looked at him and saw blood on his ear. Enraged I said, "Oh my God, John, what is wrong with you? You are crazy."

John threw up his arms. "Joe has to learn some table manners!"

"Maybe you should tell him instead of abusing him."

"That's it," John said. "I am done eating!" He stood up, grabbed his dishes and threw them in the sink, breaking a plate.

As soon as John left the room, I had Joe sit on my lap and I kissed his cheek. Steve checked Joe's ear. "Heather, I think it will be fine," he said. "If it starts to bother him or starts bleeding any more, I would take him to the pediatrician."

Later that evening, when Denise arrived, she found Joe, Ronnie, Lauren, and Raider all in my room watching TV. "What's going on?" she asked. Steve and I told her what had happened, and Denise went over and hugged Joe. "I am so sorry, Joe," she said. "Are you okay?"

Joe replied, "I'm scared of John."

After Denise finished my night care, I kissed Lauren and Ronnie and told them to go to bed. Denise tucked Joe into a sleeping bag beside my bed and he fell right to sleep. Denise leaned over my bed to block the cameras and whispered, "I swear, Heather, if that man was sick and needed help, I would drag him into the shower and let him die. John is too evil to live!"

"I feel terrible!" I said. "I can't even protect my children. If I were able-bodied I would walk right out and never look back."

"I know how you feel, Heather, but you have to be strong."

"Denise, I know you're right, but what would I do if I lost my nurses and medical care?"

"I don't know," she said. "But you have to figure out what to do."

Right then, John called. Denise held the receiver to my ear and John started yelling. "After I get done at the doctor's tomorrow, I'm coming after you," he said. "There's no amount of time or money I won't spend to emotionally kill you."

I started to cry. "What did I do wrong now?" I asked.

"I'm tired of you," he said. "You've ruined the last eight years of my life." I didn't know what to say, so I told Denise to hang up the phone.

The next day, Aaron and I drove by Kiva Elementary on the way home from shopping with Beverly for an outfit for Bud's party. Aaron took me out of the van and drove me to Lauren and Joe's classrooms, so I could speak to Mrs. Ganz and Mrs. Curtain, their teachers. When the bell rang, I said hello to Mrs. Ganz. "Hello, Heather," she said. "Hold on while I get Sharon also." When they came back into the room, we talked about Lauren and Joe's book projects. I was pleased to hear they were doing well and staying on track.

Mrs. Ganz said, "Sharon and I have noticed that when John picks up the children after school, Lauren and Joe seem scared of him. Is there anything we should know or be concerned about?"

Taken aback I said, "I know John can be strict at times, but I have been addressing it with him. He's gone through a lot since the shooting and sometimes loses his temper."

"I know that your family has been through a lot," Mrs. Curtain said. "Is there anything we can do to help?"

"We just love Lauren and Joe and want to make sure they're happy," added Mrs. Ganz.

"I really appreciate that," I said. "Thank you for your concern." I said good-bye to both teachers and found Lauren and Joe waiting outside.

On Friday, John and I arrived at Bud and Beverly's right on time. John ordered us two glasses of wine and we mingled with the other guests. When it was time to eat dinner everyone walked over to their tennis court. The tables were covered with white linen tablecloths, and fresh flower petals surrounded candles floating in water centerpieces. The band played while the guests enjoyed a catered four-course meal.

When dinner was almost finished, John walked to the front of the room and spoke about his father. He started out by saying his father was the only eighty-three-year-old who refused to take a cart and walked the golf course at Gainey Country Club. He talked about his father's positive influence in his life and his generosity to the community. Then John turned the topic to Beverly and sang her praises. At the end, Bud and Beverly joined John and everyone clapped for them. Aaron and I looked at each other. "He did a really good job," I said.

After dinner, couples danced under the stars. We had a wonderful time and stayed until the end. We thanked Bud and Beverly and said good-bye. By the time we returned home, Denise had been waiting for a couple of hours. While everyone was laughing, Aaron transferred me to the bed and said good night. I could not get John to go to sleep. He'd had a little too much to drink and was slurring his words, saying over and over what a great job he had done with his speech.

The next weekend, all the Grossmans and their families came to Arizona. Ben and Joanna checked into the Phoenician Hotel and then drove to the house to see us all. John was excited to see them both. He gave Ben a hug and we stood and talked in the family room for a while. The children were also excited to see Ben and wanted to meet Joanna. After fifteen minutes, John started playing around with the kids and torpedoing them over the couch. "John, stop that," I said. "Someone is going to get hurt."

"Hey, I'm just playing around," he said.

Joanna looked over at me. "Heather, they could break their necks."

"I know." I then yelled loudly and said, "Stop it!"

The tone of my voice made John turn around and stop. When he left the room, Ben took me aside and said, "Tomorrow all the Grossmans are meeting with Bud to discuss my dad's behavior." With hope I said, "Oh good, I've been trying to get him help."

"I'll let you know tomorrow what happens," Ben said.

John left early the next day to meet with the Grossman men at the Phoenician. After the children dressed in their swimsuits, we met everyone there too. I found John with Ben, Matt, and Joanna, and we all had lunch outside by the pool. Afterward I sat with Lisa, Jane, and Lynn, and we watched the children swim and play on the slide.

When we arrived back at the house, I told the children to shower and change into their outfits for the party. While Aaron was putting on my makeup, I heard Ronnie say, "Mommy, I don't feel well." I turned my head and he threw up all over the floor.

"Oh, honey," I said, "you must be sick. Aaron, can you see if he has a fever?"

"He looks flushed and feels a little hot," Aaron said. He cleaned up the floor and drove me into the nurses' station and Ronnie followed us. John suddenly appeared and said, "What is taking so long?"

"Ronnie is sick and just threw up," I said.

"Oh, that is just great. What are we going to do with him?"

"I'll call Cassie and see if she can stay with him."

"Now our family picture is going to be ruined," he said.

"John, calm down," I said. "It's only a picture." He shook his head and stormed off to the other side of the house. At five thirty everyone was dressed and ready to go. Cassie stayed with Ronnie.

Beverly hosted the party at Mary Elaine's in the Phoenician hotel. We walked into the elegant restaurant and all the family members were enjoying appetizers and cocktails. Lauren and Joe seemed shy, but once they saw Ben, Matt, and Joanna they ran over and began talking with enthusiasm. Most of the Grossman grandchildren were already adults and had graduated from college, except for the children of Joe, John's younger brother, whose kids were sixteen and fourteen.

Beverly gathered everyone together for a group family portrait. Then the photographers took individual pictures of each family. After the photos, everyone found their places at their tables. John and I sat with the adults and Lauren and Joe sat by the older grandkids. When they served dessert, Beverly stood up and made a birthday toast to Bud, presenting him with the memory book. Bud stood up and said, "This is the perfect gift." He thanked Beverly and kissed her. We had a nice time but had to leave at ten thirty because Lauren and Joe were both tired.

By the time Aaron and I were finished getting ready the next morning, John had already left to have breakfast with his family. I was waiting for a call from John to see what the plans would be that afternoon. Four hours later, John came in the house. I took one look at him and could tell he was livid. "I need to talk to you in the bedroom, now!" he said.

"Hello to you, too," I answered. "Why are you so upset?"

"Just come here," he said. Aaron drove me to the bedroom and shut the door behind us. John said, "I found out from Joe that my dad called all my brothers together for a private meeting today." He started yelling, "It was about me and the way I treat you!"

"John," I said, "I'm sure people notice how you treat me."

He pressed his hand over my mouth and said, "Have you been talking to them?"

I couldn't speak so I shook my head. John pressed his hand harder on my mouth. I couldn't breathe and I started to panic and cry. John kept screaming at me, but I was so scared I couldn't focus. Just before I was about to pass out, he removed his hand. Crying, I gasped for air.

When I caught my breath, I noticed John's face was bright red. I was afraid to say anything else. John walked into the master bathroom and washed his hands. When he came back I was still crying. "You and your kids can stay home," he said. "You're not coming with me to our family dinner. I'll tell everyone you can't make it because you're sick." He called Aaron on the intercom and told him to come get me and stormed out the front door.

"What happened now?" Aaron asked. "Did he hurt you?"

"Yes," I replied. "He could have killed me and he scared the crap out of me."

Aaron was speechless. He walked over to my bedside table, grabbed a tissue, and wiped my eyes. "Here, let's wash your face. I'll redo your makeup for dinner tonight."

As Aaron started my makeup, I told him the children and I were no longer invited and I started to tear up again. "Heather, you have to work with me here," he said. "Take a deep breath and stop crying, or I'll never get your makeup done. You need to call Beverly and talk to her."

I called Beverly and told her John didn't want me and the kids coming to dinner. "Why on earth would he say something like that?" she asked. "Bud will be very disappointed if you don't show up."

"I don't want John to become angrier with me," I said.

"Don't worry," she replied. "I will handle it."

"I guess I'll see you there," I said. Part of me wanted John to go alone because I was so mad at him, but I didn't want to upset Bud.

Aaron, the children, and I arrived at Veneto Trattoria for dinner. All the Grossman families were seated at a long table outside on the patio. Bud stood up and opened the gate for us to enter. Beverly came over, gave me a kiss, and sat me and the children next to her. I could tell John was surprised that I showed up, but he came over and kissed me. "What took you so long to get here?" he asked. I looked at John but had no response for him.

Everyone at the table was in a great mood, laughing and talking about the weekend's festivities. While everybody ate and had a good time, I was having a hard time getting my food down. I said to Beverly, "You look so happy and at peace. I wish I could have one moment of that feeling."

"Oh, honey," she replied. "I've just been fortunate that both men I married were good to me."

"You are a lucky one!" I said.

When the evening was over I said good-bye to everyone. John seemed to be in a better mood and walked us to the van. Aaron, not paying attention, pushed the remote to open the ramp on my van. "Aaron you idiot," John yelled, "the ramp is going to hit that Mercedes!"

"John, don't talk to him that way," I said. That response angered John and he walked off, got into his Porsche, and slammed the door. The kids and I got into the van and drove home separately. Later that night, when everyone was in bed, I told Denise what had happened and how terrified I was. She said, "Heather, I'm scared for you, too."

The next morning began the final day of the family get-together. The family members who were still in town met at Bud and Beverly's for a barbeque. John was in a foul mood when we arrived and I could see him arguing with his brother Andy out of the corner of my eye. I could also tell Bud was upset. I felt uncomfortable because the tension in the room seemed to be caused from the meeting that had taken place the prior day.

When dinner was ready, everyone filled their plates with barbequed hot dogs, hamburgers, or ribs and sat down outside to eat. John and I were seated next to each other at a table and Bud and Beverly sat down next to us. I took a bite of my food and said, "Mmm!"

"I can't stand when you do that," John said. "What is wrong with you?"

"I'm sorry, John. Everything tastes really good." The next bite Beverly put in her mouth, she loudly exclaimed "Mmm!" I felt a whole lot better. After we enjoyed our dessert, everyone left early to relax after the busy weekend.

Over the next two weeks, John's behavior stayed the same. I continued to see Dr. O'Brian on a weekly basis to talk about my problems. When I described John suffocating me, Dr. O'Brian said, "I am afraid that due to this information and because of my responsibility as your psychologist, I'm going to have to report this to Adult Protective Services."

"Oh, no, please don't, Dr. O'Brian," I said. "If they were to come to the house I don't know what John would do to me."

"I don't have any other choice," he said.

That was the first time I left his office feeling anxious and worried. When the children got home from school, we took them to dinner at Houston's. John and I did not argue and we enjoyed a pleasant evening.

When we got back to the house, Ronnie started laughing. "Oh, Mom," he said, "Raider got into the garbage."

John and I looked down and Raider had pulled the bag out of the can and onto the floor. He was neck-deep in garbage, chewing on a banana peel. We all laughed, except for John.

"Raider, get out of there!" he yelled, grabbing the hair on the back of Raider's neck and throwing him outside. He turned around and said, "It's not funny. It reeks in here. Someone forgot to shut the garbage." He pointed to the kids and said, "Was it one of you?"

Ronnie, Lauren, and Joe all said no.

John began walking toward them. "John, please," I said. "It was an accident. Anyone could have left it open."

Enraged, he gathered the bag of garbage, picked it up, and walked toward my bedroom. "Don't worry. It's just garbage," he said when he returned, walking past us and into his office. I looked at Steve and said, "Please drive me to the back." The kids followed us.

In the bedroom we could see that John had spread the garbage all over my medical bed; it was wet and smelled disgusting. Steve and I looked at each other in disbelief. "I can't believe he did this," I said.

I started to cry. "Heather, it will be okay," he said. "Please don't cry." He opened up the window, turned on the fan, and went to get a broom and garbage bag. Steve and the children cleaned up the mess. Steve took sanitizer and washed my entire mattress. "I'm sorry you had to clean that up," I told him, "but thank you for doing it."

"Don't worry about it, Heather," he said. "Everything is fine now."

It was two days before the smell of garbage was completely gone from my room and three days before Steve gave his notice. When he told me I cried and asked him to stay. He said, "Heather, I have been trying to stick it out because I care about you and the children, but I just can't anymore. I can't sleep because I worry about you on my days off; and I want to beat the shit out of John."

Aaron put an ad in the paper and we hired Damon. Steve trained him for a week. Damon was married and stood five-foot-nine with sandy-brown hair. While he was average looking, he thought he was really hot stuff. He had a portfolio and wanted to become a professional model. He spent most of his days at work checking out his pecks and smiling in the mirrors.

Beverly called me one morning and invited me to lunch at her house. I told her I would be there by noon. When Damon and I arrived at Beverly's, she was busy packing to go back to Minnesota. Suddenly my heart sank knowing Bud and Beverly were leaving again.

Beverly and I sat and talked while we ate a chicken salad she had prepared for us. She asked me how things were going with John. "They're not getting any better," I said, "only worse."

"I'm sorry," she said. "I thought things would get better after Bud's party."

"He doesn't even want to pay to send Lauren to Camp Thunderbird this year. She wants to go so badly, and it would be good for her to get away."

"I can't believe he won't pay for it. Lauren loved camp last year. By the way, isn't it about time for a new van? I would like to buy you one again."

"It's three years old now," I said. "I'm sure I can keep it for another year but thank you." We chatted for half an hour longer, and then Bud and Beverly walked me outside to my van. We all said good-bye to each other. Bud kissed me on the forehead and Beverly kissed me on my cheek. All of a sudden tears started running down my face and I could not stop crying.

"Are you okay?" Bud and Beverly asked.

I caught my breath. "I will be fine," I said. "I am just going to miss you."

Damon pulled me onto my ramp and loaded me into the van. Bud and Beverly waved good-bye and I kept crying. "Heather, are you going to be okay?" Damon asked. "Please stop crying."

When we pulled up in front of the house, I was crying so hard I started to hyperventilate. It took thirty minutes for me to calm down and finally say, "I don't know what I'm going to do. I am desperate for someone's help."

Damon wiped away my tears gave me a hug. "Heather, you are a strong person," he said. "I don't know how you deal with it either."

When we entered the front door, John heard me come in and yelled, "honey, can you come to the office?"

Damon drove me into the office, said hello to John, and left the room. "How was your day?" John asked. "Did you have a nice time with Beverly?"

"Yes, I did," I said. "She is so nice and I'm going to miss her."

"My father called and yelled at me about not sending Lauren to camp. Why would you say anything to them?"

"I'm sorry, John. I didn't know Beverly would tell Bud."

"Well, it makes me look like a jackass."

"No, it doesn't," I said. "Lauren just really wants to go."

"All right," he said, "I will call Camp Thunderbird and send a check tomorrow."

"Thank you so much," I said. "She will be so happy."

This was the first year that Lauren and Joe wanted separate birthday parties. We celebrated Joe's birthday on Friday. John and I, along with Aaron, took twenty of his friends to Harkins Theater for the premiere of the new *Spiderman* movie. When the movie was over, the kids couldn't stop talking about it. John and I were surprised we enjoyed it, too. It took three vehicles to bring all the boys to the house for a slumber party. Right away it was like a zoo. The boys were swimming, jumping on the trampoline, making forts out of sheets, and running to pick out where they were going to sleep. When they settled down, I ordered pizza and the boys watched a movie. John looked at me and said, "Have fun. I'm going to go relax and watch TV."

The next morning John came to my bedroom in a grumpy mood. "The boys woke me up at two thirty in the morning," he said. "They were running around the backyard and making all kinds of noise."

"I'm sorry," I said, "but that usually happens at a slumber party. Are Denise and Ken here yet?"

"Yes, they already started making blueberry pancakes, eggs, sausage, and bacon. My kitchen is a huge mess. I want that shit cleaned up when they are done."

"They'll clean it up," I said.

Damon arrived and took me into the kitchen to have breakfast with the boys. Ken, Denise, Damon, and I sat out on the patio and enjoyed our food while John walked back and forth holding his arms across his chest, yelling at the kids to pick up and bitching about the mess. Damon leaned over to Denise and said, "Why don't we just drown John in the pool and put him out of his misery?"

"Okay guys," I said, "knock it off. You know he's a neat freak."

When all the boys went home, John said, "Thank God they are gone," and went to his room. Damon, Denise, the kids, and I cleaned up the mess.

On Sunday, Cassie, John, and I drove twenty girls to GameWorks. Lauren and her friends spent two hours playing arcade games, pinball, air hockey, and racing cars. Then the girls cashed in their tickets, picked out their prizes, and went upstairs to have lunch. They served pizza and wings and the girls talked more than they ate. Lauren blew out the candles on her birthday cake. We dropped off all the girls at their houses except for Natalie, Paige, and Jill, who were sleeping over with Lauren.

The following Friday, John came to my bathroom while Aaron was putting on my makeup. "I am going to San Diego and I want you to come," he said.

"Oh, John, I really wanted to relax this weekend. Why don't you go by yourself?"

"No, I want you to come."

"No, I will stay here with the children."

He obviously did not like my response because he spit all over my face. This time I did not cry. "Why would I ever go to San Diego with a mean person like you?" I said.

"Well, I am packing!" John said and left the room. Aaron wiped the spit off my face and said, "He's getting bold. He even spit on you in front me."

"It's so humiliating," I said.

"I know, Heather. I don't know why he treats you like that."

Aaron fixed my makeup and drove me into the family room with the kids. John came out of his bedroom with his bag packed. "Ronnie," he said, "would you like to go to San Diego with me? We can see Mike and Zach while we're there." Ronnie hesitated and said yes. I did not want him to go with John, but it was too late to say anything. I helped Ronnie pack his suitcase and the two of them were on their way to San Diego.

Aaron and I took Lauren, Joe, and a couple of their friends to dinner. As soon as they brought our food to the table, John called and told me they were having dinner with Mike and Zach in the gas lamp district. I asked John if everything was going well and he replied, "The boys are having a great time together." When we returned home, Lauren and Joe got ready for bed while I talked to John. For over an hour he gave me a play-by-play of the day.

The next morning I dropped Lauren and Joe at their friends' houses. Aaron and I were alone for the day, so we drove to the mall to shop at Neiman Marcus. I was interrupted by a call from Ronnie. He told me John was being mean to him. "Are you okay?" I asked.

"No. I want to come home."

"Put John on the phone," I said.

John answered and said, "Yes?"

"It's me. What is going on with Ronnie?"

"He's not listening."

"Please be nice to him."

"If you would have come with me," he said, "you wouldn't be worried about this right now."

"Stop being a jerk and please be nice to him," I said. "Please put Ronnie back on the phone." Ronnie got on the phone and said, "Yeah, Mom?"

"Don't worry, Ronnie," I said. "You will be home soon."

On the way home, I stopped at Rolf's salon to buy a gift certificate for my friend Karen Arrot's birthday. At six o'clock, Aaron and I met Janie, Karen, and eight of her other friends at Mai Lee's Thai restaurant. All the girls ordered a glass of wine and gossiped and giggled throughout the evening. When everyone was finished eating, Karen opened her gifts. She kissed me on the cheek and said, "Thank you for the massages. I will use them well."

When Aaron and I returned home, Cassie was standing by the front door getting ready to leave for the day. When she saw us she said, "Heather, John has been trying to reach you on your cell phone. He called the house three times already but I told him you weren't home yet. Can you call him, please?" "Yes, I will," I said. "Have a nice weekend."

Aaron drove me to the kitchen and I asked him to get my cell phone out of my purse. There were seven missed calls, all from John. I asked if I could listen to the messages. He held the phone to my ear. The first message said, "Why aren't you answering your phone? I need to talk to you." The second message said, "What the hell is wrong with you? Pick up the phone." The third message said, "Are you trying to piss me off?" The fourth message said, in a screaming voice, "This is an emergency! Why is your phone off?' The next two messages were followed by the "f" word and more "f" words. The last message said, "Ronnie was in a car accident. He's at the hospital.

I immediately called John back but there was no answer. So I left a message saying, "Please let me know what is going on with Ronnie. Is he hurt? My phone was in my purse and I didn't hear any of your calls." Aaron looked at me and said, "Heather, stop grinding your teeth. I know you're worried, but there is nothing we can do until we hear how Ronnie is doing."

"Why hasn't John called back yet?" I asked. "There must be something seriously wrong." Aaron brought me to my room and made me a hot cup of tea, and we waited together for John's call. After an hour of Aaron pacing back and forth, he said, "Call John again." John did not answer.

In a panicked voice I said, "Please, John, call me back. I am worried." Aaron stayed past his shift and when Denise arrived, we all waited for John's call. Just before midnight, my cell phone rang. Aaron grabbed it and held it to my ear. John said, "How does it feel not being able to reach somebody?"

"What is wrong with you?" I said. "How is Ronnie? Is he hurt?"

"He's right next to me."

"What happened to him? Is he hurt?"

"Nothing happened to him," John said. "I just wanted to teach you a lesson. Maybe next time you'll answer your phone."

"You're sick!" I said. "I've been worried all night about Ronnie." I hung up the phone. I told Aaron and Denise what John had said and they were as furious as I was.

Chapter 58

Sunday morning, Lauren and Joe asked me to take them to Lox Stock and Bagel for breakfast. When we returned home, to my surprise, John and Ronnie were sitting on the couch. Ronnie came running toward me and gave me a big kiss. I said, "I missed you. Did you have a nice time?"

"Yes, Mom."

John bent down and wrapped his arms around me tightly. "I really missed you," he said. "I wish you would have come with us."

"Maybe next time," I said, although I was still upset with him.

John said, "Let's take the kids to the movies this afternoon." He looked at a paper on the counter and said, "How about *The Lord of the Rings*?" "Great," I said, "let's all get ready to go." On the way to the movie, John sat in the back of the van, laughing and joking around with the children. I was glad he was in a good mood and hoped he would stay that way. When we bought our tickets at Harkins Theater, the place was packed. We skipped buying refreshments while John and Ronnie went ahead to look for seats.

When I walked up, I could hear John arguing with people. "You're sitting in handicapped seats and you're not handicapped," he said. "My wife is. Get out of them." The older gentleman said, "Calm down. Just give us a chance to move." When they moved, we sat down in the handicapped seats. John was still upset. "Please calm down," I said. "The movie is starting." John placed his hand on mine and said, "Sure."

The next morning I was awakened by John's voice on the intercom saying, "I told you to keep the fucking nurses out of the kitchen." Startled, I saw Denise and she said, "I'm sorry, Heather. Lauren spilled cereal in the kitchen and I was helping her clean it up. When I saw John, I panicked and ran out of there."

"That's okay, Denise," I said. "Thank you for helping Lauren." Denise and I heard knocking coming from the sliding-glass door. Denise said, "Heather, it's Lauren. I'm going to let her in." Lauren walked to my bed and said, "John locked me out of the house because I spilled my cereal. I'm sorry, Mom, for making him mad."

"Lauren," I said, "it was an accident. What John did by locking you out was wrong." Denise turned on the TV so Lauren could watch it. She turned to me and said, "Heather, that guy's nuts!" Ronnie came to say good morning and see where Lauren was. I kissed Ronnie and told both of them to go to the other side of the house and get dressed for school. Lauren looked at me and said, "What if John's there?"

"Honey, don't worry. If he says anything to you, come and get Denise." She said she would.

Aaron arrived and washed my hair and quickly put on my makeup. I was determined to see Janie Shapiro. When I called her, she could not meet with me until four o'clock that afternoon. Aaron drove me to the kitchen and made me a cup of coffee. As I sipped my coffee with my straw, John came into the kitchen. "How many times do I have to tell you to keep the nurses out of here?" he said.

"John, you're being unreasonable," I replied. "My bottled water is here in the kitchen and they need it to give me my pills. If I want to have breakfast, I should be allowed to eat. Honestly, what is happening to you? You never acted this way when we first moved here."

"I'm tired of having all these people around me," he said. "I've had it up to here. I'm hungry; meet me at Chompie's for breakfast."

Not wanting to upset him, I said, "Aaron and I are ready to go. I just have to grab my purse, suction machine, and black bag."

When Aaron and I arrived at Chompie's, John was waiting at the table for us. We had a quick breakfast; John went to get his hair cut and

Aaron and I returned home. Pulling into the driveway, a car followed us and parked behind my van. When Aaron brought me down off the ramp, a gentleman stood in front of us. He said, "Hello, my name is Norman Wells."

Aaron said, "Could you please move to the side, sir, so I can move Heather toward you?"

"Mrs. Grossman," the man continued, "I am with Adult Protective Services and I am investigating a report my office received last week about your husband. Dr. Kevin O'Brian was the one who contacted our office. He went into detail about the abuse you have experienced from John Grossman."

"What did Dr. O'Brian tell you?" I asked.

"He told us John spits on you, he has suffocated you to the point where you could not breathe, and he sends your nurses away so he can abuse you. Are these things true?"

"Yes, they are," I said. "But you have to leave. John could drive up any moment and if he saw you here and found out who you were, there's no telling what he would do to me."

"Please calm down, Mrs. Grossman," he said. "I'm only here to help. Here is my card. Please contact me when you can come to my office and talk."

"Thank you for understanding," I said as he left.

Aaron looked at me. "Holy crap!" he said. "What are you going to do, Heather?"

"Aaron, I don't know. But I definitely have to do something."

I left the children with Cassie and at four o'clock met Janie Shapiro and her girlfriend, Kris, at Gainey Suites Hotel. We sat in the bar, ordered wine, and shared appetizers.

I told Janie things were getting worse with John. I said, "The abuse is escalating and I think John could hurt one of the kids or me."

"Heather, I am so sorry you're going through this."

"I know you are," I said, "and I appreciate you meeting with me. I need to find a divorce lawyer—the sooner the better."

"That is why Kris is here," she said. "She was divorced last year and she interviewed several attorneys." Kris gave me the names of three different lawyers and advised me to meet with each to determine which one I liked best. I thanked Janie and Kris for their advice.

The next day I had my appointment with Dr. O'Brian. With his help we called each one of the lawyers and set up times to meet with them. It was difficult meeting with the attorneys, because John wanted to know where I was and what I was doing at all times. I felt terrible lying to him, but I had no choice. After meeting with Bob Schwartz, I knew he was the attorney I wanted to hire.

Chapter 59

At the end of May, John asked me to go to San Diego with him. I said no. Soon after he left, I called my parents and told them what was going on. My parents were surprised that I wanted them to come right away, but they knew it was serious. My mom and dad dropped everything and flew into Phoenix the next day to meet with my attorney and me. When my father saw me for the first time since being at Craig Hospital, he hugged me and said, "Heather, you look like skin and bones." I replied, "Gee, thanks, Dad!"

During our drive to the attorney's office, John called me twice. I tried to get off the phone without being rude or upsetting him. Even as I entered my attorney's office, he was still talking. Finally, I said, "John, I have to go." I hung up the phone. I introduced my parents to Mr. Schwartz, paid him a $25,000 retainer, and discussed our strategy. I was going to file for a restraining order and, after I obtained it, the Paradise Valley Police Department would remove John from our home.

Mr. Schwartz asked Aaron to step into the office. When we told him what we were discussing, Aaron looked worried and said, "What if he flips out when he gets the papers?"

Mr. Schwartz said, "I need you to get Heather and the children out of the house when the police arrive."

When the meeting was over, my parents and I thanked Mr. Schwartz and his associate for all their help. On the way out, I received another call from John on my cell phone but I did not answer it.

That evening my parents took me and the children to dinner. Early the next morning, Aaron picked up my parents at their hotel and drove them to the airport. Their trip was short, but they had to leave town before John returned.

On Sunday, when John came back from San Diego, he was not only tired but also in a foul mood. He very strongly let me know that not answering my cell phone was not to his liking. I told John I was sorry and explained that the kids had kept me busy most of the weekend.

Over the next few days, everything went as planned. At night, when the lights were down and the cameras could not see, my nurses helped me prepare my financial statement for the lawyers.

On Thursday evening, the kids stayed home with Cassie while John and I grabbed a quick bite to eat at Houston's. As soon as we were seated, John asked Aaron to sit at the bar. "I'll be feeding Heather tonight," he said. Aaron placed my napkins on my lap, stood up, and walked to the bar.

John ordered his martini and I ordered a glass of Chardonnay. In a stern voice, John asked, "Why did you refuse to come to San Diego with me? These last three days I was there I missed you terribly and did not have a good time."

"It's hard for me to leave the children."

"You know we can always bring them with us. And I don't like it when I can't get a hold of you!"

Just then the waiter arrived and placed John's steak and my halibut on the table. I said, "You know, you can't expect me to answer my phone every time you call. Sometimes I'm busy."

"I don't give a shit if you're busy. I expect to talk to you whenever I call."

"I think I know that by now," I said. "I'm not dumb."

While bringing a piece of fish to my mouth, John said, "You used to love to be with me. You've changed so much. Ever since you were shot, you've become such a chore. You're no fun anymore." I started to cry while John put more and more food in my mouth. He said, "Being shot ruined you."

I cried even more; it was difficult to breathe. "Stop, I can't breathe!" I said. "I have too much food in my mouth! And the secretions are making me gag." John put down the fork and said, "The truth hurts, doesn't it?"

I waited a moment and said, "The truth is you're an abuser and that's why I don't want to go to San Diego with you!"

Immediately after those words, he spit in my face. Our waiter rushed over, glared at John, and asked me if I was okay. Still tearing, I said, "I'll be fine. Could I please get this food to go?" John gestured Aaron over and went to the bathroom.

"Are you okay, Heather?" Aaron asked.

"I just want to get out of here." Aaron grabbed my to-go box and we left before John came back.

When Aaron drove me home in the van I was still crying. "Please stop, Heather!" he said. "Soon all of this will be over."

When we arrived home, John's car pulled into the driveway behind us. Aaron took me back to my bedroom and we heard John follow us. He slammed the two doors to the house addition and locked them. I looked at Aaron and said, "Boy, he is pissed off this time."

Aaron transferred me to bed and put on my pajamas as we waited for my night nurse to arrive. When Denise arrived, Aaron gave her a report and left for the evening. Denise asked, "Heather, what are we going to do? I need to get your pills."

I told her to dial John on the intercom and hold the phone to my ear. "John," I said, "Denise needs to get my medication. Can you please open the door?"

"Hold on," he said. "I will bring them to the door for her."

Denise left me and walked to the door. John gave her a cup with my pills in it. "John," she said, "I need water to give these to Heather."

John slammed the door and locked it once again. A couple of minutes later, he returned with a five-gallon bottle and shoved it into the room. Denise said, "I've had enough of your shit. I am calling 911." John ran and shoved her away from the phone, but Denise was able to dial 911.

As I lay in my bed, I heard them screaming back and forth at each other. Ten minutes later, the doorbell rang and John went to get it. The chief from the Paradise Valley Police Department walked into my room and asked me, "Mrs. Grossman, are you okay?"

I responded, "Yes I am."

The officer said, "I need to speak with your nurse on duty, but I will be back to talk to you when I am finished."

By now my anxiety was at an all-time high, as I wondered what John was doing and what Denise was telling the police. When the officer returned, he walked to the side of my bed, leaned over, and whispered, "I would like to keep things as planned. We're going to remove your husband from the house on Monday. Will you be safe tonight?"

"If I have a problem with him, I will call 911 again," I replied. He placed his hand on mine and said, "Good evening, Mrs. Grossman. Call anytime."

He left my room and Denise came to me. "The police are talking to John now," she said. She gave me my medications. I did not hear or see John again that evening.

I woke up at four thirty the following morning and called for Denise. "It's the first of June," I said. "John's going to deposit money into my account for the month. What if he sees the $25,000 missing?"

"He'll be furious when he finds out," Denise responded. "The moment I'm done with work, I'm going to drive to your attorney's office and tell him what happened last night."

When Aaron arrived, Denise told him what had happened and left in a hurry. John came back to my bedroom, stood at the end of the bed, and in a stern voice said, "I'm firing that bitch! The minute we have somebody to replace her, she's gone." I did not respond because I wanted to avoid a confrontation. "The nerve of her," he continued. "Who the hell does she think she is? Why aren't you saying anything?"

"What do you want me to say?" I replied.

John stomped out of the room. Aaron got me out of bed and put on my makeup. My cell phone rang. Aaron answered it and held it to my ear. It was Bob Schwartz. "We just talked to Denise," he said, "and after everything she has told us, we want John out of the house today. We have to move quickly. I need you to meet me as soon as you can at the courthouse in downtown Phoenix on Jefferson and First Avenue."

"I'll be there within the hour," I said. "I will call you when we arrive."

I told Aaron what we had to do. He gathered my suction, purse, and black bag together, and drove me to the front door. John said, "Where are you going so early?"

"I have a lot of errands to run."

"Wait, let me go with you."

"That's okay," I said. "I'm in a hurry. I will call you and maybe we can meet up later."

Aaron and I drove to the courthouse and met up with Bob Schwartz outside the courtroom. We went in front of the judge on June 2, 2002, and I testified to John's abuse. The judge granted me a restraining order. "This is only a piece of paper," he warned. "It doesn't mean that he will stay away from you. Call the police immediately if you see him."

"Thank you, Your Honor," I said and we all left the courtroom.

"Please answer your phone when I call," my attorney said. "As soon as I get to my office, I will fax the restraining order to the police department." I must have looked terrified because he leaned over, put his hand on my shoulder, and said, "Don't worry, Heather. You are doing the right thing."

When Aaron and I returned to the parking lot, there were two missed calls on my cell phone from John. Aaron put me in my van and I asked him to please call John back. "Where have you been?" John said. "I have been trying to reach you."

"I have one more stop," I replied. "I have to go to the grocery store."

"Okay, I'll see you when you get back."

When Aaron hung up the phone, I felt sick to my stomach and wondered if I was doing the right thing. I felt sorry for John; after everything we had been through, I still loved him. Aaron and I quickly bought groceries so that I wouldn't come home empty-handed.

When we arrived home, Aaron put away the groceries and John came from his office, gave me a big kiss, and said, "I missed you today. I want to take the kids to Rustler's Roost for dinner. The kids have fun there and they like going down the slide."

"That's a great idea," I said. "I will call them at their friends' houses and have them home by six. I'm going to touch up my makeup before dinner. It will only take a few minutes."

Aaron brought me into the bathroom. "Aaron, I feel so awful telling him we're going to dinner, when I know what's going to happen," I said.

"This is the right decision," he reassured me. "Don't let your heart get in the way."

Shortly after, Bob Schwartz called and explained, "The police don't want you to be alone. I've called your parents at the show in Las Vegas; they're on their way right now and will be at the house tonight."

Surprised, I said, "Thank you for calling them. I really appreciate it."

"You are welcome. Is everyone out of the house now?"

"Not yet," I said. "I will call the police when we are."

Ronnie and Joe were both with friends at the time, so they were taken care of. I was waiting for Lauren to finish her piano lesson across the street at Carla Lukic's house.

The Paradise Valley police called me and asked if I had left yet. "No," I told them, "but I will tell you after we leave." By this time I was stressed. I called Lauren and told her to come home right away and go straight to my bedroom. When she came home, Aaron, Lauren, and I went out the back door and hurried into the van. As we pulled out of Mockingbird Lane, Lauren asked, "What are those four cop cars doing sitting across the road?"

"I don't know," I responded and Aaron kept driving.

With Aaron's help, I called the chief of police and told him that everyone was out of the house. We drove to McDonald's, ordered three sodas, and waited for a call.

"Mom, what's going on?" Lauren asked.

"Honey, the police are taking John out of the house."

"I don't understand."

"Living with him is dangerous," I replied. "I can't risk him hurting any of us."

Lauren started crying uncontrollably. "That's my dad," she said. "How can you do this?"

I started to tear up. "Lauren, I know you don't understand now, but you will."

She kept crying and I asked Aaron to give her a hug. A few minutes later, Lauren had calmed down and I received a call from the police chief. "John is out of the house," he said. "It's safe to go home now. Mrs. Grossman, please call us if anything happens tonight."

"I will," I said. "Thank you for your help."

When we arrived at the house, I called both boys and asked them to come home. I ordered pizza for dinner and told the boys about John. They seemed confused. But when I told them that Grandma and Grandpa would be there in the morning, they were excited and smiled from ear to ear.

When it was time for my nursing change, Aaron brought me back to my bedroom and transferred me into bed. When Denise arrived, the first words out of her mouth were, "Is John gone? Tell me what happened."

Aaron and I filled her in. When we were done, she said, "Good riddance to him."

Aaron said good-bye to both of us. I asked him, "Why are you holding a baseball bat?"

"It's for protection," he replied. "What if John is outside waiting for me?" He then left the house.

An hour later Lauren and Carla came back to my room with fresh-baked cookies they had made, and Lauren had a sign that she taped to the wall so I could see it. The sign had a big heart and said, "I love you, Mom!" I gave Lauren a big kiss. "I love you too," I said while we had cookies and milk as a treat.

When I woke up the next morning my nurse Damon was working. I was exhausted and felt like I was in a daze. Damon noticed I was not quite myself and asked, "Are you okay, Heather?"

"I'm not really sure. The police removed John from the house last night. I'm still trying to take it all in."

"That's crazy, Heather," Damon said, in shock. "That just happened within the last three days? Boy, John must have been pissed."

"I don't really know," I said. "I wasn't here when the police took him out of the house."

Damon drove my wheelchair into the kitchen and I introduced him to my mother and father. The smell of fried eggs and bacon filled the room and Ronnie, Lauren, and Joe were running around in their pajamas, playing with Raider and waiting to eat.

When Cassie came into work, she was stunned to hear about John. Cassie was happy for me and glad John was gone. "Heather," she said, "it was a nightmare for me every day coming to work, because I never knew what I was going to walk into. I felt so sorry for you and Ronnie, Lauren, and Joe. I almost quit but I'm glad I hung in there."

I gave her a kiss and said, "I'm so glad you didn't leave." Cassie went back to work and helped my mom clean up after breakfast.

My attorney, Mr. Schwartz, called. I took a deep breath and said, "Hello."

"How are you doing Heather?" he asked.

"I am fine. My parents made it in last night at midnight."

"I just got off the phone with John's father, Mr. Grossman," he said. "He was furious and I had to calm him down. I told him that it has been wonderful of him to take care of your medical expenses all these years, but due to the circumstances you had no choice but to file for divorce. When I told him that he seemed to be more reasonable."

"I never wanted to upset Bud or Beverly," I said. "I have always cared so much for them."

"I am sure they understand that. Heather. Now we just have to wait for a lawyer to take John's case."

I thanked him for his help and hung up the phone. I told Damon to drive me over by the big screen TV in the living room. I asked him to grab the tape out of the recorder on top of the entertainment center. "There's no tape here," he said.

"John must have taken it out, knowing it showed him acting crazy and fighting with Denise. I wish I would have thought of it sooner."

"You have entirely too much going on to remember that as well," Damon said.

The following day, as my parents and I sat watching TV, suddenly the house went dead silent as the electricity turned off. When I called the company to report the outage, I was informed that my husband had had it disconnected. I explained that I was ventilator dependent and needed to charge my suction machine and wheelchair, and that my name was also on the electric bill, and the power needed to be turned back on immediately.

An hour later Cassie said, "There is no water coming out of the sink. I think John shut that off, too."

"Oh my God!" I said. "Even with him out of the house that jackass is still trying to get to me." I called the water company and they reinstated my service.

Over the next few days, with the help of my parents, we filled the cupboards and fridge with a month's worth of food. My parents could not understand how there was no food in the house. I explained that Cassie and I would grocery shop on a day-to-day basis because we never knew if we were going to eat out or not, all depending on John's mood.

The first two friends I contacted and told about my filing for divorce were Janie Shapiro and Karen Arrot. Both of them were supportive and happy for me.

Chapter 60

It took two weeks for John to find a lawyer to defend him. After our two attorneys spoke, my attorney, Bob Schwartz, called and asked me to come down to his office. My father and mother came with me to the meeting.

When we arrived at the office, Margo, Mr. Schwartz's assistant, walked us to their conference room. I was nervous while I waited for Mr. Schwartz to arrive. When he came into the conference room, he was nonchalant and said, "I have good news. The Grossmans want to settle. They know you have hired one of the best lawyers and they don't really stand a chance."

"That's great," I said. "What happens next?"

"I want to depose Cassie, your cook and nanny."

"Why do you have to depose her if they are going to settle?"

"We have to move on with the case as if they were not going to."

"Okay," I said. "I will talk to Cassie and have her contact you."

As we walked out the door, Mr. Schwartz said, "John's attorney told me John would like to talk to you, but to call him only if the nurse is not listening in."

I looked at my mom. "Do you think I should call him?" I asked.

"Well, that is up to you, honey." she said.

By the time we got home, I had decided not to call John. Cassie gave me a message from Detective Cole of the Paradise Valley Police Department; he wanted me to call him back. When I returned his call he wanted to set up an appointment to meet with me.

Two days later I met with Detective Cole and Detective Fanning. They questioned me for four hours about John's abuse. After the questioning, I was shocked to find out that they had been compiling a case against John for more than a year, and that they had already interviewed ten of my previous nurses and six nannies, along with numerous restaurant managers and their employees. Detective Fanning asked me if there were any other employees I thought they should talk to. As I left I told him, "Let me think about it and I'll get back to you."

When Aaron and I returned home, I talked with my parents and told them about the case the police department was putting together. My mom and dad were confident in the police department's ability to perform the investigation.

A few minutes later I received a strange call from my girlfriend Jeannie Kushner in San Diego. She said, "John came to the house and he is absolutely traumatized over the police removing him from your home. Heather, he is sad and wants to talk to you. What is going on?"

"Jeannie, you have no idea what the kids and I have been going through," I said. "John is abusive to us. I had to file for a divorce before he seriously injured someone."

"I can hardly believe that! You two loved each other so much. Can't you just talk to him?"

"No, I can't," I said. "I feel bad enough as it is. I can't let my guard down. After everything we have been through, I still love him."

After Cassie finished her deposition, I received a call from Mr. Schwartz. "My God!" he said. "John sounds like a lunatic! I haven't heard anything from the Grossman side yet, but I am going to set up a court date for an alimony hearing."

"Thank you," I said. "Let me know when the hearing is."

On the Fourth of July, Janie and Lola Shapiro invited my parents, the children, and me to a party at the Gainey Country Club. We enjoyed a traditional Fourth of July barbecue with hamburgers, hot dogs, potato salad, and corn on the cob. Afterward, we all sat together and watched the fireworks over the golf course. It was the first time I went out with friends without John, and I had a really nice time.

The next week my parents flew back to Minnesota to pack up some of their things and drive back another vehicle. During the time my mom and dad were gone, the Paradise Valley police continued to ask me questions about my case. Detective Cole came to my house and requested my chart book with all the nursing notes in it. He wanted to use the nurses' notes to corroborate their statements. I could not believe how quickly the police department was working to build their case against John.

My parents and I met with Mr. Schwartz. John had been allowed to postpone two scheduled spousal support hearings. He had not paid my health insurance, utility bills, or any other bills for two months. I was frustrated and could not afford to pay them myself. For someone who had said he wanted to settle out of court, he was not being very cooperative.

I said to Mr. Schwartz, "I don't understand what is taking so long." He did not have an answer for me, but he wanted to know why I had spoken to the Paradise Valley Police Department.

"The police called me in to question me," I said. "What did you expect me to do? They have seven hundred pages of documented statements and testimonies from past employees. You have no idea the things I had to go through."

"Mr. Grossman is not going to be happy about this," he said.

"Whose lawyer are you anyway?" I said. "I refuse to be quiet any longer. John cannot manipulate me anymore." It is fair to say that meeting did not go well. I began to question whether I had chosen the right lawyer.

In September, four months after John had been removed from the house, we finally had a hearing for spousal support. We met Bob Schwartz outside the courtroom. When I saw John with his lawyer, I felt sick to my stomach and terrified to go inside. I waited with my lawyer for Judge Trebesch to enter the courtroom. When he entered he immediately called both lawyers into his chambers. When Mr. Schwartz returned, he said, "The judge does not want to hear any testimony. He wants us to come to an agreement on the spousal support."

"I can't believe that!" I said. "Why would I not testify to the restraining order and the reason for it?"

"The judge doesn't want to hear about the abuse."

"This is ridiculous! It has taken me four months to get here. John has cut off my electricity and water and has not paid any of the bills! He has to be held accountable!"

"Don't worry, Heather," he said. "We will get it all figured out now."

When Mr. Schwartz returned to the room, he said, "John is only willing to pay you $2,000 a month and he won't pay for Cassie. He's going to fire her. He also wants the $350,000 of the kids' child support to come to him."

"Absolutely not, to all of it!" I said. "You must think I'm stupid! First of all, $2,000 is not enough money for us to survive. Second of all, John does not pay for Cassie. Bud pays for Cassie. How am I supposed to clean a 6,000-square-foot home, paralyzed like I am? And third of all, that child support belongs to my children. That is an accumulation of eight years of back child support. Our lawyers found some of Ron's money in the Grand Cayman Islands. The Florida Judge awarded it to *me*."

"Well, Heather," Mr. Schwartz said, "that is all John will do."

"This is bullshit! I want to see the judge."

"You can't see the judge. Don't worry. Just agree to this, because John wants to settle out of court."

"I will agree to the $2,000 and getting rid of Cassie right now," I said, "but there is no way he's taking my children's child support."

When I left with Aaron, I was in tears and I cried all the way home. When I told my parents what had happened they could hardly believe it. My father said, "John's lawyer is trying to keep out any testimony regarding the abuse. I'm sure Bud does not want that to get out."

"This isn't fair!" I said. "I wish I could call Bud and Beverly, but they've cut me off completely. I have tried to call Janie Shapiro numerous times and she won't call me back."

I started to cry. "It hurts me to see you go through this," my mom said, "but the Grossmans are showing their true colors."

"I told them everything that was going on. All I wanted them to do was support me in getting John help."

"They obviously wanted to keep what was going on a secret."

Cassie had become a good friend and the kids just loved her. Two days later, dreading having to tell her, I talked to Cassie about what had happened in court. Thankfully, she took it well. She had been dating a pastor's son for the previous five months and he lived in Houston. He was the love of her life, and after going to the Grand Canyon with him, he proposed. She and her daughter were moving to Houston to be closer to him. Even though I was going to lose a good friend, I was glad that everything was working out for her.

Chapter 61

Over the next few months, it was a constant fight to get John to pay my health insurance and household bills. I was constantly faxing over past due notices to his lawyer's office. It was becoming a hassle.

My father was an avid tennis player and joined the Scottsdale Tennis Club by the house. For entertainment, my mother, the kids, my nurse, and I would have dinner on the patio at the club and watch my dad and three other sixty-year-old players warm up with calisthenics before playing their doubles matches. On the weekends, we would join their wine dinners and invite my friends Paul and Karen Arrot.

Lauren and Joe were in sixth grade at Kiva Elementary and Ronnie was in eighth grade at Mohave Elementary School. All three were doing exceptionally well in their classes. They woke up happy every morning, and their days were no longer filled with yelling and constant degradation

One night at dinner, Joe spilled his glass of milk on the table. He looked absolutely terrified and said, "Oh, Mom, I'm so sorry."

"That's okay, Joe," I said. "It was just an accident." Seeing his response reminded me how much John's behavior had affected the children.

For Thanksgiving, my mother and I invited Stacy, Aaron's wife, to join us for dinner. I couldn't wait to congratulate her on her pregnancy. This was their first child and Aaron and Stacy were overjoyed. The weather was a perfect seventy-five degrees, and instead of having our traditional meal, my father grilled the turkey. Aaron had never tried grilled turkey before; he enjoyed it so much my mother sent some home with them.

Two days later my parents and Lauren took a trip to Yuma, Arizona. While they were gone I spent quality time with Ronnie and Joe. When they returned home, Lauren walked up to me with a box and said, "Look, Mom, I saved this kitten. It was abandoned by the railroad tracks. The vet at the show gave it its shots and Grandma and I brought it home."

"I knew something was up," I said. "Every time I talked to you, you were giggling and laughing. He's cute, Lauren."

He was a seven-week-old, black-and-white tuxedo kitten. We named him Lucas. The minute Raider saw Lucas, he began licking him until he was sopping wet and carrying him around. In the afternoon, the two would lie together on the carpet in front of the window, soaking up the warmth of the sun.

In early December, I received a call from Bob Schwartz. "John's lawyer called," he told me, "and John wants to do a walk-through of the house to make sure you're not taking or selling his belongings."

I laughed and said, "You have to be kidding me. Do I have to agree to this?"

"Yes, you should," he replied, "so that John doesn't get upset and settles the divorce amicably."

"You can schedule a time to have him come. Just let me know so that I can be out of the house."

"Thank you," he said. "I will let you know."

On the day that John came to the house, the kids were at school and my parents, Raider, and I spent the afternoon at Karen Arrot's. While we were at Karen's house I received a call from Mr. Schwartz. "John wants the dog," he said. "He saw the kitten in the kitchen and believes you bought the kitten to terrorize Raider."

"John and I purchased Raider for Ronnie, Lauren, and Joe," I said. "He's just doing this to hurt the kids. The children will be heartbroken. You have to do something!"

"I'll see what I can do," he said. When I hung up with him, I told my parents and Karen what he had said. I was upset but glad I had brought Raider with me.

As the case with John progressed, it was time for my deposition at his lawyer's office. The thought of sitting across from John made me sick to my stomach, and I could not eat breakfast.

When Aaron brought me into the conference room, John and his lawyer were already sitting at the table. John had a cocky smile on his face and it was hard for me to look at him. The deposition began and although the questions were not difficult to answer, I found myself being attacked for the shooting and everything that followed. John's lawyer tried to portray Bud Grossman as a savior for paying my medical costs. I was thankful for everything that Bud had done for me; however, it sounded like I was a huge burden and should have been thankful John stayed by my side after the shooting. They had me so upset I began to hyperventilate and spasm in my chair. Throughout the questioning, the attorneys did not ask one thing about the abuse. When the deposition was over Aaron came in and wiped my eyes with a tissue. John shook hands with Aaron and said, "Congratulations on the pregnancy." I thought to myself, "How did he know about that"?

Aaron and I quickly left the office and drove to Mohave Elementary School for Ronnie's basketball game. We found my parents by the bleachers and only missed part of the first quarter. The Mohave team won and the parents and players screamed in excitement. When we returned home we had pepperoni and black olive pizza, Ronnie's favorite. After dinner I told my mother and father about the deposition. They were upset I was going through all this and didn't think Mr. Schwartz was doing a good job.

On the morning of John's deposition, when we were about to leave, I received a call from Mr. Schwartz. He told me the deposition was canceled because John's lawyer had the flu; I suspected otherwise. Mr. Schwartz also informed me that the Paradise Valley Police Department had called John in for questioning that morning. I was surprised to hear the process was moving forward so quickly.

A month later, John finally had his deposition in my lawyer's office. Mr. Schwartz asked him every possible question regarding his finances but not one question about the abuse. Following the deposition I asked Mr. Schwartz, "Why didn't you question him about all the abuse"?

"This was just about finances," he said.

"No!" I replied. "This was your opportunity to question him and uncover the abuse!"

"Don't worry," he said. "They're going to settle with you, anyway." I left the office feeling upset and confused.

I was informed by Detective Cole that John had hired two criminal defense lawyers to investigate the abuse charges the Paradise Valley Police Department had brought forth at the county attorney's office. I had no idea this would go so far, but they had been compiling nurse and employee documentation for over a year. The fact that John had hired lawyers meant he was scared.

A few days later, my parents and Denise were served with a lawsuit. John was suing them for slander. It was a tactical move, as John knew my parents and Denise did not have enough money to defend themselves. The Grossmans were using their money to intimidate us. I felt I had to protect them and started looking for a civil lawyer.

The holidays approached and I had a Christmas party for my friends and family. Steve, the nurse who had worked with me previously, returned to work now that John was gone. Many friends were in attendance, including parents and kids from Kiva Elementary, my father's friends from the tennis club, and many of my past nurses and their spouses. It was nice spending the Christmas season with my family once again.

On Christmas morning, my sister, Tiffany, and her fiancé, Dale, pulled into my driveway. It was a huge surprise and the kids and I could not wait to spend time with her. Dale was from Coon Rapids, Minnesota. After spending time with him, I found him to be funny, likeable, and easygoing. I could tell the two of them were very much in love.

As we sat and talked in the family room, I could see tears running down my sister's cheek. This was the first time we had seen each other since the shooting. "Tiffany, don't cry," I said. "I'm healthy and I'm making the best of my situation."

"I know," she said and gave me a hug.

"You can hug me a little harder," I replied. "I won't break."

Over the next few days my parents and I showed Tiffany and Dale around Scottsdale. On New Year's Eve, my father took everyone, kids included, to dinner at the Scottsdale Tennis Club. My family had a four-course dinner, listened to music, and danced. Two days later, Tiffany and Dale left. Everyone was sad to see them go.

Chapter 62

The following month, my parents, Denise, and I met with Brian Murphy at the house. Brian, a civil lawyer, was soft spoken. He wore glasses, had light-brown hair, and was dressed in a suit. When I asked Aaron to leave the room, I noticed he walked by my desk. After he was gone, I asked my mom to check the intercom on the phone. She said, "Heather, it's on."

"Turn it off," I said. "I think Aaron is trying to listen in on our conversation."

We started our meeting. I told Brian about the case and Denise opened her two calendar books that documented instances of abuse between 2000 to 2002. Mr. Murphy took notes and listened intently, raising his eyebrows while Denise and I recounted all the children and I had endured.

When the meeting was over, Mr. Murphy said, "I'll contact you if I have any more questions before I serve John with the lawsuit." We all thanked him and my parents walked him to the door. I called Aaron to the front and asked him to empty my leg bag. When he walked toward me, he had a child-like look of guilt on his face and asked, "Are you finished?"

"Yes we are," I said.

When Aaron walked away, I turned to Denise and said, "I think we found our spy!"

"Are you sure it's him?"

"It's hard to believe, but I think it could be," I said.

Later that night, when Denise came back for her shift, she brought both black calendar books with her. "I want you to give these to your mother and father to put away for safekeeping," she said. "They are too important to your case."

"Thank you," I said. "I'm so glad you wrote separate notes when John told the nurses not to write anything nonmedical in the charting book."

I was still seeing Doctor O'Brian once a week. I looked forward to talking with him because my stress level was at an all-time high. I kept hoping John would settle the divorce, but instead he turned confrontational and seemed to be on a quest to hurt me. Dr. O'Brian summed it up by saying, "Heather, he could have killed you. He's not the person you thought he was."

"I know," I said. "But I always try to see the good in people. John did have many good qualities."

"I know you feel conflicted, but the important thing is that you and your family are safe."

"You're right," I said. "But if he turns nasty, I could lose my medical care along with my nurses."

A week later we had a hearing with Judge Trebesch. My parents, Aaron, Mr. Schwartz, and I attended along with John and his lawyer. Mr. Schwartz had filed a petition for more spousal support in an attempt to bring the abuse to light. The hearing did not go well. We waited anxiously for Mr. Schwartz to show up. He was late to court and Judge Trebesch commented on his tardiness, and then made a snide remark regarding his expensive suit.

Of course when John testified it was a joke. He told the judge that Raider was a highly trained show dog he had bought for himself. I could not believe the outright lie he told. Raider could not possibly be a show dog because he was missing one testicle! Every time Mr. Schwartz tried to bring up the abuse charges, he was shut down by both the judge and the opposing lawyer. John was not sympathetic at all, and he came across as uncaring and indifferent.

When I was called to the stand, I explained that Raider had been purchased for Ronnie, Lauren, and Joe and that he was my children's pet. I almost started crying but kept my composure. I was not allowed to talk about the abuse despite that being the reason I was there that day. John's lawyer kept emphasizing how wonderful Bud and Beverly Grossman had been for covering my medical costs.

When we left the courtroom, I felt like I had wasted my time. Judge Trebesch seemed like he already had his mind made up and hadn't even listened to my testimony. As I rode down the elevator with Mr. Schwartz, he asked me, "Does your husband have any friends? He's a real asshole."

I giggled and said, "If he always acts like this, I wouldn't be surprised if he didn't."

The following week, I received a call from Mr. Schwartz. "Judge Trebesch has given his ruling," he said. "He is going to increase your spousal support by $500 dollars and he is giving Raider to John. You are to be out of the house by October 14."

I started to cry. "That's horrible!" I said. "How could he give Raider to John? The children will be heartbroken!" I continued, "How can he ask me to be out of the house with my disability before the final divorce hearing on October 28?"

"I don't know, but you have to make arrangements to be out by then," he said.

"That's so unfair!"

"There's nothing more I can do," Mr. Schwartz responded. "And I'm dropping you as a client."

"What do you mean?" I asked, shocked.

"You will have to find another lawyer," he replied and hung up.

Not knowing what to do, and in a total panic, I found my parents in the house and told them what had just happened. My father responded,

"He really didn't do a good job. He was probably bought off by the Grossmans."

"You're probably right, but what do I do now?" I said. "I need a lawyer."

While I told the children and nurses about John getting Raider, my mother frantically called lawyers to look for representation for me. Betty Adelman's law firm took my case and met with me and my parents the next day. Mrs. Adelman told us she had too many cases, but her associate could handle our case.

We shook hands with Mrs. Lisa Maggiore-Connor and sat down in her office. I almost fell out of my wheelchair when I heard her say, "I tried to find information on your case but it has been sealed."

"What? I never agreed to seal the case."

"It was sealed by permission of Mr. Schwartz."

"Isn't that illegal? Under no circumstance would I ever let them do something like that!"

"Well, it's sealed and there's nothing we can do about that now," she said. "I have to get up to date on your case and take care of the Raider situation." She immediately filed a petition containing 680 pages of documented abuse from the Paradise Valley Police Department along with twelve letters from family and friends pleading with the judge to overturn his decision about Raider. We knew it was a long shot, but we wanted to try everything we could to keep Raider for the kids.

Two weeks later, Judge Trebesch ruled in John's favor and we were instructed to give Raider to John's lawyer on Monday, April 20, at one o'clock. It was hard for me to look into my children's crying faces when the inevitable was about to happen. Both Denise and Aaron tried to talk me into letting Raider out in the backyard the night before John's lawyer came to get him. One of them would take Raider and keep him safe, and I would not know where he was. It sounded like a good idea, but I didn't want to be in contempt of court and end up incarcerated.

On Monday morning, Ronnie, Lauren, and Joe stayed home from school to spend their last moments with Raider. Lauren cried the whole morning and cut a piece of Raider's hair off to keep in her scrapbook. When John's lawyer showed up my father and Lauren walked Raider out to the front driveway and gave him the dog. My father turned around but Lauren didn't. As Raider left, she started screaming, "Don't take my best friend!" and "Raider, I love you!" while running after the car all the way down the street. We never saw Raider again.

Chapter 63

Everything was going wrong; I was so frustrated, I didn't know what to do. My friends suggested I tell my story to shed some light on the truth. I did two interviews: one with the *New Times* magazine, the other with the *Arizona Republic*. Both stories were well written, but when John and the Grossmans found out, all hell broke loose. They were upset that their little secret about John was out. Bud Grossman never wanted his family's name tarnished. I found out through many sources that John was the black sheep of the family; I was just the last person to know. After the interviews, there was no chance for a settlement with John.

My parents and I met Helen Pugh one weekend while looking for a home to buy. She was sixty-six years old and had a polished and professional demeanor. Not only did Helen become our Realtor, but she also became a close family friend.

Whenever we had spare time, Helen showed us hundreds of homes to find a house that would accommodate us all. This wasn't an easy task considering we had such little time and limited resources. It was the middle of the summer and viewing the houses was no small feat. My parents would first jump out of the car and go in to see if the house was accessible. If it was, I would then go in to see if I liked it. Then we would move on to the next one.

One time Steve and I were stuck in the van in 115-degree heat. The ramp broke and did not allow me to exit to see the home. We waited for a mechanic for an hour and a half. By that time I said, "Screw the house! I'll come back later," and we returned home to cool off.

One morning, Aaron came to work with a dazed look on his face. He was an exceptional nurse, but today he was clumsy and could not concentrate on my care. "What's wrong, Aaron?" I asked. "You seem distracted."

"I have to tell you something, and you're not going to be happy."

"What?"

"Yesterday, I was approached by John's private investigator and he wanted me to give a deposition on John's behalf. So I went to his office and they talked to me."

"Aaron, why would you do that?" I said. "It's going to hurt my divorce case. What did you say?"

"I don't know," he said. "They asked me nursing questions and questions about the abuse."

I started to cry and said, "I can't believe you would hurt me like this." Still crying, I asked him to bring me to the kitchen. When I saw my parents, I told them what Aaron had done.

"Please stop crying, Heather," my dad said. "We won't know what Aaron told them until we get a copy of the deposition."

"I feel betrayed!" I said.

After all this, I met with Helen for more house hunting. At last we found one I really liked. We scheduled another time to come back and see it with my parents. Aaron and I spent the rest of the day in uneasy tension. When Denise came in for her shift, she took one look at me and said, "Why have you been crying?"

"Aaron talked to John's lawyers," I said.

"What the hell is wrong with him? I bet John is paying him to spy on you."

"Maybe he is," I said, "but I feel so hurt."

A week after the previous incident, Brian Murphy obtained Aaron's deposition and faxed it to the house. After my parents and I reviewed it, we were all disgusted. Aaron had lied and John's lawyer had manipulated the questions to make it look like anybody could have hurt me.

For example, one of the questions was: "Could a nurse bruise Heather?" Aaron had answered, "I suppose they could when they did CPT (chest percussion)."

Another question asked, "Could Heather spit on herself?" Aaron had replied, "I guess she could."

A third question asked, "Could a nurse have cut Heather's lip?" Aaron had answered, "I suppose they could when they were feeding her."

The icing on the cake came when Aaron said, "John would never hurt the children; he is so loving to them." I was so upset, I felt sick to my stomach. I wanted to confront him but my father said, "Calm down. Getting angry at him will not change anything."

"Why would he lie like that?" I said.

"He told you he's an atheist and does not believe in God," my father said. "What kind of morals do you think he has?"

"At least we have his black notebook in which he wrote about the abuse," I said.

My mother asked, "Do you think you'll be okay working with Aaron for the rest of the day?"

"I guess so," I said. "I really have no choice."

The following day Steve and I met with Ceal, Denise, and Kathy for lunch. I showed them the deposition and they couldn't believe what Aaron had said. After considering my options, I decided not to fire Aaron at the moment. I was under too much stress and training a new nurse was not possible with everything else going on. Before I knew it, we were looking for a rental home to live in. In one week we found a five-bedroom home in Paradise Valley that would meet our needs for the time being. Thank goodness I had my parents to pay the deposit and rent, or we would have been out on the street. My parents, nurses, and I packed up the children's and my belongings in preparation for the move.

Everyone was up early when the moving truck arrived. My mother and I made a final walk-through of the house, making sure we had my things. I loved my home on Mockingbird Lane and it saddened me to leave it. When everything was loaded and it was time to go, I put my key on the countertop, took one last look around, and left.

Our rental home was not perfect but we managed as well as we could. My parents set up their office in the dining room, the boys shared a bedroom, and Lauren squeezed her things into an even smaller room. The house was centrally located between Ronnie's school, Notre Dame Preparatory Academy, and the twins' school, Mohave Elementary School. That made it easy to take the kids back and forth to school and to their sporting activities.

My friends and nurses helped unpack our boxes and organize the kitchen. There was only one problem: John's lawyer sent a letter requesting my personal items, which John claimed as his own. I left all the furniture, electronics, and sentimental items we had gathered during the marriage. I had no use for them anymore.

Chapter 64

When the divorce was final, Bud Grossman paid for one year of my nursing and medical care. John and I had to see a mediator to divide our marital assets. My civil case against John was still pending. I cried for five full days and was in a state of depression.

The first time I met with the mediator nothing was accomplished. John wanted everything. The night before the second meeting with the mediator, feeling defeated, I told my mother and Steve to box everything John wanted.

When I woke up the next morning, Steve and I drove in early to the mediator's office to avoid interacting with John. Steve asked me, "Heather, are you sure you want to do this?"

"Yes," I said. "I have lost my dignity. I can't fight John and all his money. I don't want to sit across from him at the table and have him laugh at me."

When I entered the mediator's room, I sat in front of him and said, "I've brought all the items that Mr. Grossman has requested. He can have everything in the house."

"Are you sure about this, Mrs. Grossman?" he asked.

"Yes," I said. "I can't take it anymore. I'm tired of fighting."

Steve brought in the boxes and we left his office as quickly as we could. Steve loaded me in the van and said, "Heather, John doesn't care about any of those things. Maybe we should come back in thirty minutes and see if he threw them in the dumpster."

"No, my heart is already broken," I said. "I just want to go home."

On the ride home I thought to myself, "I was married to a multimillionaire with a $6 million Roth IRA. We paid $1.6 million for our home in Paradise Valley. In the garage there was a Lexus 470 SUV and a Porsche Carrera. John still had my $350,000 child-support check, but despite that, I ended up with only one year of nursing care paid by his father, and nothing else to show for it."

Months later, my father and I, along with Aaron, went to a mediation hearing for my civil case against John. My mother could not attend because she was working at the Mesa Market. I felt sick to my stomach. The last thing I wanted was to see John.

The moment we turned the corner, there he was sitting next to his lawyer with a smug look on his face. He was whispering to him while holding his Tumi briefcase. The two of us had not spoken a word since the day he was removed from the house.

When we entered the courtroom, there was no sight of John. He and his lawyers were in an adjacent room. My father, Mr. Murphy, and I sat in the main courtroom. The judge walked over and introduced himself. He had a big smile on his face as he shook our hands and said, "We are going to start the mediation now. I'm going to speak with John and his attorneys first. Then I will be back to talk to you."

We waited for about an hour and the judge returned. We told him our side of the case and that we were not interested in settling unless we could come to a fair agreement. The judge went back and forth between the parties for two hours; we then took an hour break for lunch.

We walked down the street and found a restaurant close by. I ordered a salad but was so distraught I only took three bites. My father and I did not talk about the case in front of Aaron. We were unsure we could trust him, and I think he knew that.

When we returned after lunch, the whole atmosphere had changed. The judge and John's lawyers started browbeating me. I started crying and told the judge, "All I'm trying to do is get back my medical care so that I don't end up in a nursing home and die. My parents cannot afford to take care of me. I need your help!"

Every time the judge came back he and Brian Murphy, my lawyer, were trying to force me into settling.

I asked my father what I should do. My dad was quiet and said, "It's your decision, Heather."

Mr. Murphy said, "Aren't you tired of all this fighting? If you settle you can put this all behind you and move on with your life."

I felt sick to my stomach and was crying so hard I could not breathe. My father went to get Aaron, who was outside the courtroom, to come in and suction me.

Before I knew it, I was settling with them. The judge walked in with a big grin on his face. As I sat there crying, he touched my hand and said, "I'm glad we could get things settled here today. I have a dinner reservation at seven. The lawyers can write everything up."

My father and I waited for an hour. By this time I was sobbing and hyperventilating. All I could think was, "Get me out of here!"

I cried all the way home. I had no dinner and went straight to bed. Denise was finally able to calm me down at four in the morning. I slept for two hours and was up by six. Aaron came in at nine and I started my day. I was emotionally exhausted. Aaron washed my hair and put on my makeup. I started crying again. "You have to stop, Heather," he said, "or you're going to make yourself sick."

"I'm sorry, but I can't."

"What are you going to do when the money runs out and you can't pay the nurses?" he asked.

Upset, I said, "If you weren't such a liar, I wouldn't be going through this."

Aaron looked a little shocked but had no response. It took everything in me not to fire Aaron.

Unfortunately, Steve had moved to Prescott, Arizona, to take over an older doctor's naturopathic practice. He was happy; he lived in cooler weather and he loved to go camping.

The nurse who took his place was Kendall. He was an R.N. who had graduated from Brigham Young University. It only took a couple of months to figure out he was not the sharpest tool in the shed. He meant well but the other nurses couldn't read his nursing notes. He couldn't remember things and drove the kids and me around like he didn't have a license. He would run red lights and drive through four-way stops. After consulting my doctors and talking with the other nurses, we thought he might have Adult Attention Deficit Disorder. I had Aaron put an ad in the newspaper and it took three weeks to replace him with Tim Spalti.

Chapter 65

In early 2004, I found out that Bud Grossman had been diagnosed with Alzheimer's disease. I felt sorry for him but knew that Beverly would search high and low for the best treatments available and make sure that he had the best nursing care possible.

Around that time, I went to the state capital with my parents for a domestic violence lunch and speaking event. While eating my lunch, I was approached by a Channel 10 News reporter who asked me to give an interview. I gladly agreed.

The next morning, the woman and her camera crew came to my house to do the interview. The story featured me as a domestic violence victim and survivor. I simply answered the interviewer's questions and told my story about my first husband, and then said my second husband, John Grossman, had abused me in my wheelchair. The story aired three times the next day.

A week later, a process server came to the door. My father screamed at him, slammed the door, and yelled, "Heather!" Tim took me into the dining room and my dad said, "You won't believe this! That bastard is suing you. We don't have any money to fight him. What are we going to do?"

"Dad, calm down," I said. "Let's first read the papers and see what it's about."

John was suing me for slander and wanted me to remove my website from the Internet. I started to tear up and said, "He's never going to stop trying to hide his abusive nature. He has already taken everything from me. I wish he would just move on with his life." My father contacted friends and business associates to see if they could help in any way or had any suggestions.

After hearing this news, I went to see Dr. O'Brian the next day and told him what was going on. He couldn't believe it. Then he told me more bad news. He said, "Bud Grossman has informed the office that he will no longer pay for your visits with me."

"That's not right," I said. "They're supposed to cover all my medical care until November of 2004. I'll call my lawyers and see what they say." After calling Brian Murphy, I was told that Mr. Grossman did not consider psychological visits medical care. I started to cry and Dr. O'Brian said, "Heather, don't worry. I will cover the visits until your court case is over."

"Thank you so much," I said. "Our sessions really help me and right now I need them."

To relieve some of my stress, I watched Lauren cheer at basketball games and drove her to Mesa for gymnastics classes. I attended Joe's baseball games at Mohave, where he played pitcher or catcher. I was also busy watching Ronnie play tennis in tournaments and for his high school. On the weekends, my parents, Helen, and I were still looking for a home to purchase. At that time real estate was booming in Paradise Valley and every home was going for the asking price or higher. Some people were paying as much as $500,000 over the asking price. John sold the house we had purchased together at 1.6 million for 2.2 million. Boy, did I get screwed!

One morning my father received a call. It was a miracle. Our State Farm homeowners' insurance was going to represent me in John's lawsuit against me. A week later we met with Robert Beckett in downtown Phoenix. Mr. Beckett was six feet tall, slender, and in his thirties. My parents and I gave him the background on all the previous cases involving John.

The first thing he did was inform the opposing counsel he was representing me. Then he requested the courtroom tapes from my civil case. When we left his office I actually had hope.

One weekend, after being outbid on two homes, we met with Helen at four o'clock in the afternoon to view another house. After inspecting every room, we decided to put in a bid on it. The house was in Paradise Valley. There was a master bedroom for my mother and father, an office, another section with the children's rooms, and an area with a bathroom and a bedroom for me that was close to the laundry room and garage so the nurses would not disturb my family at night.

Helen invited us to the Wrigley mansion for a performing arts fund-raiser that evening. We had cocktails and food at the bar while we anxiously waited to hear if the owners would accept our offer on the house. Three hours later, Helen received a call from the sellers' agent saying the owners had accepted our offer. The next day, my father set up financing and hired an inspector for the house. A month later in mid-June we moved into our new home.

Everything was going fine until Denise babysat for Aaron and Stacy. When Denise came back from her three days off, she said, "There has to be something going on. When I went to Aaron and Stacey's house, parked in their garage was a brand new Nissan Maxima and a new GMC Yukon Denali. Their house is filled with top-end electronics and was completely furnished. You know when he moved here they had hardly any furniture at all."

"That's right," I said. "Aaron moved with only his bed and a few boxes. He's never said anything about buying new cars and every day he drives here in his 1990 little maroon Toyota truck with no A.C."

"Do you think John is paying him off?"

"It's possible. Why else would he have given that deposition and then stayed on with me like nothing had happened?"

"Heather, I don't know if I can look him in the face when he comes in."

"I know how you feel, Denise," I said, "but we can't let him know that we found out what he's doing."

On the day before my court case with John, I asked Aaron to change work days with Tim. I felt more comfortable talking openly to my parents around Tim. The trial lasted two days.

The first day my parents and I met Mr. Beckett outside the courtroom. I didn't want to see John. I had butterflies in my stomach and thought I would cry. When we entered the courtroom, I avoided making eye contact with John and looked straight ahead. Mr. Beckett touched my hand. "Are you okay, Heather?" he asked.

"Yes," I said. "Thank you." At that moment the judge took his place at the head of the courtroom and the case commenced.

My father and I were called to testify on the first day. Both lawyers questioned us extensively, and at the end of the day Mr. Beckett felt our case was going well. The judge paid close attention to all the testimony and did not allow John's lawyers to intimidate us as witnesses.

John testified the second day. He came off as an uncaring, pompous individual. Mr. Beckett and I were surprised that John would approach his testimony in this manner, but it made sense considering John was used to getting his way.

When we left that afternoon, I was upset the judge had not yet made his ruling. It was three weeks before Mr. Beckett called with the good news—the judge had ruled in my favor. I was so happy I called my parents and Doctor O'Brian right away. My parents were overjoyed and said, "Let's go out to dinner to celebrate."

Doctor O'Brian was happy to hear the news. "Finally," he said, "something is going your way!"

Chapter 66

A couple of months passed. We were settling into our new home, planting trees in the backyard and geraniums by the front entrance. Joe had started playing lacrosse at Mohave and Lauren was cheering and competing in gymnastics. Ronnie was meeting with his tennis coach twice a week and playing in tournaments. The autumn season was in full swing, and Mom and I were decorating for Halloween.

In October, I received a letter from Bud and Beverly Grossman's attorney. The letter stated, "Please do not have any nurses contact the Grossmans." This was the first time I had received any correspondence from them and wondered what they were talking about.

After speaking with my nurses, Trish and Denise, they informed me they both had sent letters to the Grossmans asking them to reconsider stopping payment for my medical and nursing costs. I told them both, "Thank you for being so concerned for me, but it's inevitable that Mr. Grossman will stop paying for my medical after this month. John and I will have been divorced for a year."

They were worried because, on a yearly basis, my medical costs could reach upwards of $300,000. Now my parents and I would be responsible for this exorbitant amount of money, and my settlement would be depleted quickly.

One morning, I received an unexpected call from Florida. When I answered the phone, a familiar voice said, "I've got good news, Mrs. Grossman. Ron is in custody in the US."

It was Detective Sanchez.

"Hello, Detective Sanchez," I said. "I'm so glad to hear from you!"

He said, "On October 28, Ron Samuels was brought to Louisiana to face federal passport fraud charges pertaining to the fake passports he had made for the children and himself. When he's finished, he'll be sent to Florida for the attempted murder charges."

"How long do you think it's going to take before he's in Florida?" I asked, overjoyed.

"It could take up to six months. We will inform you as soon as we book him in."

"Thank you for letting me know," I said.

When I hung up the phone, I told my parents the good news. I hadn't thought about Ron in years, but after talking to my parents I wondered how I would make it through an attempted murder trial with both John and Ron together in the courtroom.

After confiding in Tim what Aaron had done and how it hurt me, we put an ad in the newspaper to find a replacement for him. A couple of days later, I told Aaron I was firing him. This was not an easy thing to do; I had relied on him for six years of my life and thought he was a friend. But I felt like he had betrayed me, and it was causing too much anxiety in my life.

When I told him he seemed absolutely shocked. He kicked a chair and said, "I can't believe you're doing this." He had tears in his eyes. "Heather, I would do anything for you and the kids."

"You don't care about us at all, or you wouldn't have done what you did." I started to cry and told him to leave.

Unfortunately, I was so desperate to replace Aaron, I hired the first certified nursing assistant who applied, Clementine. I couldn't afford to pay nursing salaries, so I replaced two nurses with CNAs. Clementine was around three hundred pounds, and when she washed my hair her arm fat would slap me in the face. I tolerated this, but her trying to eat a foot-long sandwich while driving me around was a little dangerous. I also got tired of her swerving all over the road when she was dancing to the music playing in the car.

Three weeks later, after attending Lauren's state cheerleading competition, I fired her. She was dancing to the music in the aisle behind my wheelchair. When asked to sit down, she got into a loud argument with the usher and refused to sit. When the cheer moms around me commented on her behavior, I embarrassedly asked her to sit down. That was the final straw.

A week later I hired Lisa. She was pretty and had a bubbly personality. Even though she was slender, Lisa lifted me on my bike with ease. We quickly became friends and enjoyed each other's company.

During Thanksgiving of 2004, there was a lot to be grateful for. As we sat around our borrowed dining room table on folding chairs, we said our prayers and each of us took our turn saying what we were thankful for. I was thankful for my parents and their ability to be there for me, that my children and I were safe, and that Ron would finally be brought to justice.

One day in December, after I picked up the kids from school, we went to a local Christmas tree lot and found a twelve-foot live tree. We couldn't tie it to the top of my van so I paid a gentleman to deliver it to the house. The next day, when the kids came home from school, we had hot chocolate and decorated the tree. This was our first Christmas in our new home and I wanted everything to be perfect.

Two weeks later, my mother, the kids, and I went to Blessed Sacrament Church for Reconciliation. I felt it was time to lift the weight off of my shoulders. When it was my turn to speak to Father Pat, I said, "Forgive me, Father, for I have sinned. It has been two years since my last confession and I hold anger in my heart for my first ex-husband, Ron Samuels, who shot me and put me in my wheelchair. I am also angry with my second ex-husband, John Grossman, for abusing me in my wheelchair. I need to forgive them to find peace in myself."

Father Pat placed his hand on my shoulder and said, "Read Psalm 51 four times."

When we returned home I had dinner and Tim put me in bed. I asked Denise to get out my Bible. I read Psalm 51 numerous times and saw its relevance to my life. I could see why Father Pat had told me to read it.

Tiffany and Dale visited for the holidays, and on Christmas Eve, we all went to mass. It was wonderful to have all my children and family with me, especially my father, who had not been to church since I was shot. I never realized how difficult things had been for him until he started crying during the service. I started to tear up but felt better when I saw Tiffany and Tim put their arms around my dad to comfort him. When mass was over, we walked out together, happily singing "Joy to the World."

In January 2005, I received a call from Banner Good Samaritan Hospital. Jill Crawford asked me to mentor a newly injured quadriplegic woman. The following week, my nurse Lisa drove me to the hospital and I met Christina. I gave her a basket of products from Bath and Body Works and we sat and talked for an hour. She was still having difficulty with what had happened to her and was depressed. I helped her with finding resources around the community and told her about my life. I let her know that in time things would get better with a positive attitude and that she was fortunate to be alive for her six-year-old daughter. I did not sugarcoat things. I told her, "It sucks being in a wheelchair. Things will be harder, but you can have a great life!" When I left her that day, I felt content and soon after I started mentoring other newly injured quadriplegics at local hospitals around the valley.

Detective Sanchez called me. "On February 20, Ron Samuels was booked into West Palm Beach County Jail on two charges of attempted murder," he said.

"I can't believe he's finally in Florida," I said. "Thank you for letting me know."

"No problem, Mrs. Grossman," he replied. "I'll keep you updated on any new developments."

Two days later I received a call from Al Johnson at the Florida state attorney's office. He introduced himself and informed me that he would be handling my case.

That's when the craziness began.

I started receiving calls from Florida television stations and newspapers requesting interviews with me. The *Palm Beach Post* was sending out a featured writer and photographer to meet with me the following month.

Chapter 67

One morning, while Lisa was putting on my makeup in the bathroom, I received a call from Denise. "There's an obituary in the *Arizona Republic* for Harold Grossman," she said. "Isn't that Bud's brother?"

"Yes, it is. It's Uncle Harold. What day did he die?"

"March 3."

"I feel terrible," I said. "He was such a wonderful man. Thank you for calling me and letting me know."

When I hung up the phone, I explained to Lisa who Uncle Harold was and told my parents. After breakfast I bought a card and sent it to Gene Grossman. Even though the Grossmans had cut me off from their family, Harold and Gene were kind to me and my children.

Ten days later, at 10:30 p.m., while I was lying in bed, Joe came to my room and said, "Zach called for Ronnie and he was sleeping so I answered the phone. Mom, Zach said John died. I feel dizzy and sick to my stomach."

"Joe, are you sure?"

"Yes, Mom, I am."

"Give me Zach's number," I said, frantic. "I'm going to call him right now."

When I called, Zach answered. "Zach, Joseph just told me that John died," I said. "Is that true?"

"Yes," he answered. "He died of a massive heart attack at three thirty this morning."

"I can't believe this! He's never had any heart problems or even been sick."

"My mom and dad wanted you to know," Zach said.

Five minutes later Joe came back into my room. "Mom, I can't sleep!" he said. "I think this is a conspiracy and John is still alive and coming here to kill us all."

"Joe, why would you think that?"

"Mom, he's mad at us and I'm scared."

"Joseph, there is nothing to be scared of. John can't hurt us anymore."

"Can I sleep here with you tonight?" he asked.

"Yes, honey, you can."

Denise got his sleeping bag and put it beside my bed. We were both so upset we didn't sleep a wink that night.

The next morning, everyone was shocked. Tim and I called the coroner in San Diego and verified John's death. He died on March 13, 2005. He was only fifty-five years old. I felt sad and couldn't believe he was gone. Over the next few days, as people found out, I started to receive calls. Most of the reactions were "karma took care of him." He was evil to everyone he came in contact with.

I called Dr. O'Brian and told him about John's death. He said, "I can't believe he died."

"I've been getting calls from former employees and friends," I said. "They say it's karma. I believe in karma. What do you think?"

"It is quite fitting," he answered. "He was miserable and mean to everyone. He could have given you the divorce and been decent, but he chose not to. Husbands don't abuse their disabled wives. He had a problem."

"I didn't cry when I heard the news," I said. "I was just disappointed in the person he had become."

The following week journalists from the *Palm Beach Post* came to the house to interview me. For three days they came with me to watch Ronnie's TPA tennis match, went to one of Joe's baseball games with the family, and went out to dinner with us. They pretty much made themselves at home. On their final morning, my mom made them breakfast while they set up for their photo shoot and wrap-up interview for the paper. When the article came out, I was pleased with how well it turned out.

That summer in Arizona was scorching hot. I missed going to San Diego and feeling the cool breeze on my face and the perfect temperatures, but I would never miss the way John had treated me on our trips.

Now, with my bank accounts depleted, we were stuck in town for the summer. To stay cool the kids went to water parks and I took them to movies. In August, before school started, we shopped for school clothes for the kids. Ronnie was going into his junior year at Notre Dame Preparatory and Lauren and Joe were starting their freshman year there. Lauren received the $10,000 Catherine Harvey scholarship to the school, which really helped us out. Due to my financial situation, the Catholic Diocese and the Notre Dame scholarship fund for students in need covered Ronnie's and Joe's tuition.

In November my parents were working at a show at the Phoenix Convention Center. Knowing they would be tired when they got home, Tim and I ordered Chinese food for dinner. The kids set the table and we waited for them to come home so we could all eat together. When they arrived, my mother was carrying a white Sheba Inu puppy. The kids all screamed and ran over to look at the new puppy as my mom held it in the palm of her hand. She was a full-blooded Japanese dog. We named her Suki.

My mother, not knowing anything about this breed, looked her up on the Internet. It said, "fur ball from hell." We all laughed but soon found out she was a rambunctious little pup. She was bright, had the cutest little face, and was the princess of the house. Lucas, our cat, was excited to have a little friend. Everyone loved her, and even though Lauren still missed Raider, she grew attached to Suki.

A couple of months later, to my surprise, I started receiving calls from *48 Hours Mystery*, *Dateline NBC*, and ABC's *20/20*. They all were interested in covering my story and the murder trial. I wanted to choose the one I believed would produce the best story. I interviewed a producer from each show on the phone and decided to work with *48 Hours Mystery*. I was impressed with their professionalism and that the program would be an hour long.

In March 2006, I met with Jonathan Leach from CBS. He flew in from New York and took me and Tim to lunch. Jonathan had a great personality and we got along well. He asked me about my story and my present situation. When we were done with our meeting, I felt satisfied that *48 Hours Mystery* was the right program to portray my story.

Later that month I ran into a problem with Tim. He loved playing poker and would stay out all night long and not show up for his assigned shifts. When I called to reach him, Tim would show up three hours late, upsetting the night nurses, who had to stay until he arrived. When I spoke to him about it, he promised it wouldn't happen again, but it did. I caught him in a lie and was forced to confront him. Even though he was an excellent nurse, and my family liked him, I had to let Tim go.

I hired Mary Irvine to take his place. Mary was young and sweet, with dark hair and dimples. This was the first time I had two female nurses working the day shift, and they both did a great job.

One morning my mother received a call from Jane Grace at Senator Jon Kyl's office. She wanted to know if I would appear in a commercial with Senator Kyl, supporting his campaign and thanking him for the help I received from his office. The following week, the entire street was blocked off in preparation for his arrival with the camera crew and office staff. A hairstylist and makeup artist got me ready. Not only did I respect Senator Kyl for his achievements in office, but he was bright, funny, and my family enjoyed spending time with him. We shot the commercial outside on the back patio; it was an honor telling people about the great things he had done and the outstanding person he was.

On April 19, 2006, I turned forty years old. Terry and her husband, Mike, came into town to celebrate my birthday. Mike set up tables, chairs, and linens on the patio. As the evening started, sixty-five of my friends and family members began to arrive. It was a comfortable seventy-five degrees outside. The candle and flower arrangements looked beautiful on the tables. The caterers grilled hamburgers and served barbecued ribs, chicken, and brisket. I had a nice time and, after everything I'd been through, was grateful to have reached age forty.

Chapter 68

In July 2005 I was contacted by Peter Henderson, the producer from *48 Hours* who would be handling my story. He set up a date later in the month to meet with me and do my first interview with Troy Roberts.

A few days later I was contacted by Al Johnson from the state attorney's office in Florida. He said, "Heather, Ron's lawyers have to depose you before the criminal trial. I have arranged a day and time for the deposition. We'll be flying into Phoenix. Can you please be present on July 26? The deposition should take only one day." I said that was fine.

On the morning I met with Mr. Johnson my anxiety was high. Not only did I have to answer grueling questions about my shooting, but I also had an interview with Peter Henderson the same day.

My deposition started at ten o'clock and ended at four o'clock, with only one break for lunch. After the deposition, Mr. Johnson told me I had been precise with my answers and did an excellent job.

My nurse Mary and I met Mr. Henderson at four thirty. He was standing outside a house in Phoenix with props set up for filming. He was six feet tall, had grey hair, and was dressed casually. While they set up the lights and cameras, Mary put powder and mascara on my face and the questions began. The interview lasted an hour. Even though the questions were easy to answer, it was difficult reliving the past sixteen years, from the time I married Ron Samuels to present day. When I left Mr. Henderson, I had a good feeling about him. He helped Mary carry my things to the van and saw us off.

When I returned to the house, Al Johnson was sitting at the kitchen table with my parents and Ronnie, Lauren, and Joe. They were laughing and talking, and Mary and I joined them. Mr. Johnson stayed for an hour and declined an invitation for dinner. Before he left he said, "I have a good friend who would like to speak to you. It's Scott Richardson."

"I would love to talk to him," I said. "You can give him my number and tell him to call."

Mr. Johnson said he'd be in contact over the next couple of months to set up the tickets to Florida for me and my nurses. We all said good-bye and my father walked him to the door.

A few days later I received a call from Scott Richardson, the lawyer who'd handled the immunity deal while I was at Craig Hospital, requiring John and I to agree to give the four accomplices immunity so they would testify against Ron. After talking to him for an hour and telling him everything that had happened between me and John, he was appalled. He said, "Heather, the Grossmans totally screwed you. When I was in Colorado, John spoke abusively to his father, and just seeing that upset me."

"Over the next few years John became verbally and physically abusive to me." I said.

"I can imagine. In the hospital, he was abusive to the kids already."

"I wish things had turned out differently. It's so unfair."

"Heather," he said, "you're a strong, bright woman and I know you can overcome this."

I thanked him for his kind words and looked forward to seeing him in Florida.

Over the next few months my Mercy Care case worker had a psychologist come to the house twice a week to talk to me. I was stressed about the trial and seeing Ron for the first time since I had been shot. I was losing hair and could not sleep. It helped to vocalize my feelings during the sessions, but it didn't change the inevitable: I would still have to see Ron and go through the trial.

Four days before I left for the trial in Florida, Peter Henderson and his camera crew came to shoot some video for the program and follow me in my daily activities. On one of those days I was scheduled to speak in Casa Grande, Arizona. I was asked to be the keynote speaker for the Pinal County domestic violence conference. Mr. Henderson and his camera crew spent the afternoon following me around and filming my hour-long presentation. When the presentation was over, Mary and I drove back to the house to meet Mr. Henderson and his crew for dinner and some final filming.

The next morning, Mary was at my house at 6 a.m. Mary transferred me out of bed and put on my makeup while Ella, who had worked all night, packed last-minute medical supplies. My girlfriend Carrie and my mother loaded nine suitcases into my van and we all drove to the airport.

When we pulled up to the terminal, Mr. Henderson and his camera crew were filming our arrival. We checked our bags at the Continental Airlines counter and I kissed my mom and Carrie good-bye.

As Mary, Ella, and I walked through the airport to our gate, the cameras filmed us. People stared and wondered what was going on. While we waited to board the plane, I received a call from Al Johnson. "Please don't talk to any reporters at the airport when you arrive," he requested. "We're holding jury selection in two days."

"Don't worry," I said. "I won't talk to anyone."

When I got off the phone, Mr. Henderson bought us coffee. We drank it quickly and boarded the plane before the rest of the passengers. Mr. Henderson, Mary, and I sat in first class, and Ella and the camera crew sat in coach.

Our flight to Houston, Texas, was only two hours, but we had a four-hour layover until our connecting flight to Florida. We all waited in the Continental President's Club, and Ella was so tired she slept on the table. Mary covered me in blankets and Mr. Henderson ran back and forth with coffee, trying to keep me warm.

When we arrived in West Palm Beach, it was ten o'clock at night and we were exhausted. Mr. Henderson—or Peter, as we were now on a first-name basis—helped us gather our luggage, rode with us on the shuttle to our hotel, and made sure we were settled into our room before leaving for his hotel.

The following day I was up early. I called Donna to make plans to meet at Houston's in Boca Raton for lunch. When Mary and I arrived, Donna was waiting by the entrance of the restaurant; she gave me and big hug and kiss. I was happy to see her. When we were seated, Donna said, "Heather, everyone is staring at you."

"I know," I said. "It's creepy."

"Did you see the article about you in the *Sun Sentinel* this morning?" she asked.

"No, what did it say?"

"I brought it with me to show you," she said, pulling it out of her bag.

As I read the paper, I realized it was an interview with my father from the previous day. He was complaining about how uncomfortable my flight had been, and how I'd almost gotten hypothermia during our four-hour layover.

I looked up at Donna. "Oh, darn!" I said. "We weren't supposed to speak to the press. It never occurred to me to tell my father."

"Well, everyone knows you're in town now," she said. "After all, they've been talking about the trial on the news for days."

Donna and I had a nice lunch. We talked about our families and caught up with each other. After lunch, I followed Donna to her house so I could visit with Harvey.

When we returned to the hotel, Peter called and asked me and Mary to dinner. We met him at a restaurant in West Palm Beach. Over lobster, we discussed Ron Samuels and the thought of seeing him again after all these years. Peter was kind and concerned about my emotions.

Even though he knew the trial would be painful, he wanted the interview process to be as comfortable as possible.

The next morning I received a call from Al Johnson. He said, "If jury selection is done early, we could possibly start the trial by early afternoon." Mary and I waited patiently but the selection was not finished until three thirty that afternoon.

When I woke up the next morning, my stomach was tied in knots. As Mary drove me past the front desk of the hotel, the concierge wished me good luck in court. I thanked her and got into the van. When we arrived outside the courthouse, Peter was waiting with his camera crew to interview me. It was cool and breezy; Mary wrapped my blanket around me to keep me warm as we walked to the courthouse.

We passed through security, went up the elevators, and met Gina Leveque, Mr. Johnson's assistant, who was waiting outside the courtroom for us. "How are you feeling this morning?" she asked.

"I'm nervous and sick to my stomach," I answered, "but I'll be okay."

She said, "Judge Brown keeps the courtroom at sixty-eight degrees. I brought an electric blanket and plugged it in where you'll be sitting so that you can stay warm during the testimony." I thanked her.

When I entered the courtroom, it was freezing. Mary covered me with the electric blanket. The four bailiffs came and introduced themselves to me. I turned my head to the right and saw cameras set up in the back of the room. A man walked up to me and introduced himself as Michael Christian with Court TV. "We're going to be here filming the trial," he said. "If there is anything we can help you with, please let me know."

Donna arrived and sat down next to me. I was happy to see her. She planned to come to court every day to support me.

Soon after, two bailiffs escorted Ron Samuels into the courtroom through a side door. When he looked at me and smiled pompously, it made my skin crawl. I immediately looked the other direction.

Ron looked old and tired, and his skin had a yellow tinge to it. He was not the same man I had been accustomed to seeing in an Armani suit and gold Rolex watch.

The jury entered and everyone stood as the Honorable Judge Lucy Brown entered the courtroom. She was middle-aged with short, blonde hair. After hearing her address the jury, I could tell she was a strict, no-nonsense, straightforward judge.

The prosecutor, Al Johnson, gave his opening statement introducing his case to the jury. He portrayed Ron as a clever and greedy man who hired thugs to carry out the murder of the Grossmans. In detail he described a bitter custody battle after which Ron Samuels refused to pay child support. At the end he showed a flowchart of all the men Ron Samuels had hired to carry out the attack.

We broke for lunch and upon our return the defense gave its opening statements. Defense attorney Edward Reagan portrayed Ron as a target of the Grossmans money and influence. The defense seemed to have a weak case. After both attorneys finished their opening statements, the day came to an end. Judge Brown stated that court would reconvene on Monday, October 16, at 8 a.m.

We drove to the airport to pick up Lauren as soon as court was over. She was missing a few days of school to attend the trial and spend time with me. Lauren was excited to see her friend Ashley.

The next morning, we had breakfast at Poppy's Deli with Donna, Harvey, and Ashley. The hostess recognized me immediately. "It's nice to have you back, Mrs. Grossman," she said. "I hope your ex-husband gets what he deserves."

"Thank you," I said. "I hope he does, too."

Chapter 69

The next day my best friend, Terry Vevea, flew in. Mary, Lauren, and I picked her up from the airport. We spent the afternoon at the Breakers Hotel in West Palm Beach. I had my hair done for the evening. We then met Donna, Harvey, Ashley, and Peter for dinner at the Station House. After speaking with Donna, Peter decided to interview her for the program as well.

On Monday morning, we arrived early to the courtroom. Lauren was scared and sat in front of me between Peter and Terry, holding each of their hands. She had not seen her father since she was six years old.

When the bailiffs brought Ron into the courtroom, he could not stop staring at Lauren and started to tear up. Lauren turned and told me, "Ron looks so old and terrible. Mom, you look a hundred times better than he does."

When the trial commenced, Al Johnson called Roger Runyon to the stand. As he walked by me, my heart sank knowing he was the shooter. I did not look at him until he stepped up to the stand. He was a bald, pale, pathetic-looking man. Roger Runyon admitted shooting a high-powered rifle at me with the intention of killing me and John Grossman.

All of a sudden, during Runyon's testimony, Ron yelled out, "You despicable scum of the earth! I'll meet you in hell, you son of a bitch. I'll find you one way or another."

"You're right," Mr. Runyon responded. "I will go to hell and you'll see me there."

It was upsetting to me and I said loudly, "Lauren, are you okay?"

"Yes, Mom," she said. "I am."

Judge Brown then cleared the courtroom and threatened to remove Ron from the courtroom or gag him in front of the jury. She also admonished Mr. Runyon for responding to the outburst.

Once Judge Brown had everything under control she called the jury back into the courtroom.

As Runyon continued to talk, we all heard some enlightening testimony. He said that Eddie Stafford had enlisted him to kill me for Ron. Stafford had told him that Ron had taken out a million-dollar insurance policy on me while we were married, and he could collect if I died.

I was shocked when I heard this. I could not understand how Ron could benefit from the policy after our divorce. When Roger Runyon's testimony was over, he walked by me and tried to apologize. Mary yelled at him and said, "Get away from her."

We recessed for lunch and then returned for more testimony. Later that evening, I kissed Terry good-bye and thanked her for coming. She took a taxi to the airport.

On Tuesday, when we returned to the courtroom, the next person called to the stand was Eddie "Slim" Stafford. He was an ugly, scrawny black man whom the prosecution portrayed as a pimp and drug dealer. Lauren looked back at me and said, "Mom, this is the first drug dealer I've ever seen!"

Eddie Stafford told the jury he'd met Tony Black, Ron's alias, at two meetings and they had discussed killing me. He said he'd driven the car during the shooting and had been given immunity for his testimony.

The judge took a short recess. When I left the courtroom, Peter was waiting outside to interview me. When we reentered the courtroom, the jurors were shown pictures of the black Lincoln John had been driving when we were attacked. I had to turn my head when I saw the blood splattered all over the inside of the car.

By the time the day was over, Donna, Mary, Ashley, Lauren, and I were exhausted. We were hungry so Donna and I took everyone to an Italian restaurant for dinner. Donna and I had a glass of wine to relax as we discussed the outrageous testimony we had heard. When we returned to the hotel, Lauren stayed with me for a couple of hours while Ella did my night care. As usual we watched the news and relived the day's events.

The last day Lauren was there for court, the prosecutor brought back Eddie Stafford to testify again. He clarified the testimony regarding the life insurance policy. It looked obvious that Ron had intended to cash in on the million-dollar policy after the shooting was completed.

After lunch we went back to the courthouse to hear more testimony from Eddie Stafford. Lauren didn't want to leave. She gave me a big kiss and hug, and I told her I loved her. Peter was nice enough to drive her to the airport so I could stay and listen to more testimony.

The next morning, Mary and I were at the courthouse by seven thirty. Peter met us with two hot coffees and we rode the elevator together. As we walked toward the courtroom, there were many people standing around. I noticed a man pacing back and forth, but I didn't know who he was.

We walked into the courtroom and the judge commenced the trial for the morning. The prosecution called their first witness, Hugh Estes. He was the man I had seen outside.

The guy looked like a scumbag. An old man with a wrinkled, drawn-out face, he was an old friend of Ron's and an insurance agent Ron had known since the '70s. He testified that Ron had hired him to find somebody to kill me. "He wanted his wife whacked," Hugh Estes told the jurors. "He was obsessed with this." Estes had been addicted to crack cocaine and owned the car used in the shooting.

Judge Brown recessed for lunch at that point. Peter, Donna, Mary, and I went across the street and had a bowl of hot soup. With the time we had left, we sat in the sun to warm up before reentering the freezing courtroom.

When we returned to the courtroom, Mary and I saw Ron laughing with his defense lawyers. As we waited for the judge, all of a sudden Mary said, "Oh my God, Heather! Ron just winked at me!"

"He's such a disgusting person," I said. "I'm sorry, Mary."

She laughed. "He doesn't bother me, but it is a little creepy."

The prosecution called Hugh Estes back to the stand. We listened to his testimony describing himself as "toxic" during his period of drug use. He explained that Ron would call him between three and four times a day asking when the hit was going to happen, because I needed to be eliminated before the custody hearing. In the end, Estes tried to portray himself as remorseful and seeking guidance from God and Alcoholics Anonymous.

When his testimony was over, I was disgusted that somebody could care so little for human life. After sitting and listening to all the witnesses that past week, I wanted nothing more than to leave the courtroom. What these men had done was inexcusable. To make matters worse, they would all walk away and not spend a single day in jail for their crimes.

Leaving the courtroom was like a breath of fresh air. As Mary loaded me into our van, Peter asked us to meet him for drinks and dinner. Mary and I went back to the hotel to freshen up. I called the kids to find out how they were doing. Ronnie and Lauren told me that after school they had been watching the court case live on Court TV. We met Peter and his friends at Legal Seafood for another evening of interesting conversation over dinner.

Mary and I left early for court on Friday. The moment we stepped off the elevator, I started to cough and choke. Mary had to take me into the bathroom and suction me to clear my lungs. When I felt better, Mary and I sat outside the courtroom and waited for Peter and Donna to arrive. Peter arrived first with a hot cup of coffee and Donna came a few minutes later and gave me a big kiss and hug.

We entered the courtroom and sat in our usual spots. The jurors came in and Judge Brown commenced the trial. Al Johnson called

Geoffrey Pollock to the stand. When I heard that name, I remembered the call I had received before Ron picked up the kids one Thanksgiving. It had been him on the phone, trying to scare me into not letting the children go.

Another one of Ron's degenerate friends, Geoffrey Pollock was thirty-five years old, was uneducated, and had never amounted to anything. He was Ron's workhorse and tagalong.

Pollock testified that Ron had wanted to send me a message, meaning he wanted me beaten up. Two weeks before the shooting, he had met with Ron, Estes, and Stafford at a Denny's restaurant. Ron said he wanted his ex-wife taken care of and made a motion of a gun with his hand. Pollock went on to testify that Ron had pressured him to escort Estes and Stafford around Boca Raton, recording my daily routine. The men cased my home, John's workplace, and the children's school.

Pollock said he knew he had been "duped" when he spent the morning of the shooting with Ron having breakfast and visiting a car dealership. Around midday Ron received a phone call that elated him. Pollock suspected someone had been hurt when Ron headed straight to an attorney's office in Miami and handed him $5,000 in cash. When Pollock stepped down from the stand, I felt immense anger toward him because of his stupidity. I only had one way to describe him: a low-life, disgusting scum of the earth. Following Pollock's testimony, Judge Brown called for a one-hour recess for lunch.

Peter, Donna, Mary, and I walked to a Middle Eastern café. Peter asked, "Did you have any idea they were following you?"

"No, I didn't," I said, "but after hearing that I feel violated and disgusted."

"I'm sure they were following us, Heather," Donna said.

"It's so unfair that all these men got immunity," Peter said.

"I know," I replied. "It makes me sick to my stomach. They all contributed to what happened to me."

We rushed back to the courtroom and standing outside the door was my handsome plastic surgeon, Dr. Raphael Cabrera, who saved my life. He gave me a kiss on the cheek and said, "Hello, Heather! You look great."

"It's so nice to see you again," I said.

"How are your beautiful children?"

"They're growing like crazy and doing well. Thank you for asking."

Court was about to begin, so we said we'd talk afterward. Before Mary and I entered the courtroom, Al Johnson came walking toward us. "Heather," he warned, "I don't know if you want to watch the testimony from your doctor; it's going to be graphic. He's going to show pictures of the gunshot wound to your neck."

"I want to be there," I said. "If it bothers me I can always leave."

When we entered, Dr. Cabrera was already testifying to the jury. He described my massive wounds and how he communicated with me by having me blink my eyes once for yes and twice for no. He described the wound size by saying he could take his fist and put it through the right side of my neck and out the left. When the jurors heard this, they made sounds of empathy.

When Dr. Cabrera finished testifying, I followed him into the hallway to talk to him some more. We talked and laughed a little and he leaned toward my ear and said, "Do you remember what happened before I took you into surgery?"

"No, I don't remember anything."

"You were telling me you didn't want to live. Look how everything turned out. You've been able to see your children grow up and be a part of their lives."

"Thank you for not listening to me," I said. "It's true; I love my children more than anything."

We said good-bye to each other and I thanked him again for saving my life. Court was adjourned for the weekend. Thank God it was Friday.

Chapter 70

Over the weekend, Mary was off and the state attorney's office hired a nursing agency to cover her shift. When the nurse arrived Saturday morning, he introduced himself as Al Roberts, but I called him "Big Al." He was six-foot-five, in his forties, and had a great personality. On our first day together we drove to Boca to watch Ashley's soccer game with Donna and Harvey.

Around seven we went to dinner at Henry's, a neighborhood restaurant that Donna and Harvey ate at often. When we sat down at the table, Donna introduced me to the waiter, who was a friend of theirs. You would have thought I was a celebrity! I was surprised he was so excited to meet me. I said hello and we proceeded to order dinner.

At the end of our meal, while Harvey was paying the check, a gentleman walked up to our table and said, "I know you don't know me, Mrs. Grossman, but I live in The Seasons and was a neighbor of yours when you and your husband were shot. I just want to say I'm so glad you lived that day and are able to come back here and get justice after all of these years."

"Thank you," I said. "It was kind of you to say that."

"Seeing you here reminds me exactly what I was doing on the day you were shot."

"Oh, really?"

"It's not every day that somebody gets shot in Boca," he said. He then touched my hand and added, "Good luck in court. I'm rooting for you."

Big Al and I said good night to Donna and Harvey. When we returned to the hotel it was ten o'clock at night. Al transferred me into bed, and Ella started my night care while I fell fast asleep.

On Sunday morning I spoke with Susan Spencer, a reporter from the *Palm Beach Post*. She interviewed me over the phone for a short article that would be appearing in the paper. The rest of the afternoon Al and I watched a movie in the room, and at dinnertime Ella and Mary joined us for some pizza and wings.

On Monday morning, I felt relaxed from the weekend and was ready to sit in court and listen to Detective Sanchez testify about my case. When the prosecution called him to the stand, he gave a detailed summary of each individual's involvement in the murder plot. He continued his testimony by describing evidence he'd found in Ron's home in Boca Raton, such as a pink Post-it note with the name, birth date, and Social Security number of Thomas Jordan, one of Ron's aliases. He also described several bank statements belonging to Ron's company, Brooklyn Inc., which held $1.1 million in one of the Cayman Island accounts.

The second witness to testify that day was a woman from the telephone company who showed detailed cell phone records that gave a history of continued communication between Roger Runyon, Hugh Estes, Eddie Stafford, and Ron Samuels. Al Johnson pointed out that once I was shot, the phone calls between these individuals ceased. Following her testimony, the judge adjourned for the day and instructed us to return the next morning by 8 a.m.

Ella had me ready by six o'clock Tuesday morning. Peter and his camera crew were filming Mary styling my hair and putting on my makeup before we left for court. Mary and I were walking toward the courthouse and were two blocks away when we heard the screeching of tires. When we looked over, we saw a tall man with dark hair jump out of his car and start walking straight toward us.

"That man just left his door open and his car running in the middle of the street," Mary said. "Do you know who that is?"

When he got closer, I answered in a shocked voice, "It's Mark Samuels, Ron's brother!"

Mark kissed me on the cheek. Wiping tears from his eyes, he said, "Heather, how are you?"

"I'm fine, Mark. It's nice to see you."

"I'm so sorry you're in a wheelchair like this," he said.

I started to tear up. "Mark," I said, "why don't you park your car and get it out of the street. I'll see you in the courthouse."

When Mark left, I told Mary, "I haven't seen him in fourteen years. I can't believe he's here."

Mark met us in front of the metal detectors; we went through them and rode the elevator to the courtroom together. It was awkward standing next to him and I could tell he didn't know what to say.

When we entered the courtroom, Mark sat two rows in front of me. When the bailiffs brought Ron in, Mark went over and spoke to his brother.

Al Johnson had one of his key witnesses testifying. It was Debbie Love, the woman Ron had married after our divorce. When Debbie took the stand, she gave an account of how lavish her life with Ron had been at first. She then went on to describe the defendant as "controlling and domineering." She said she had done exactly what Ron wanted because she "feared him."

Then came the testimony that solidified the prosecution's case. Al Johnson asked Debbie, "How did Ron Samuels talk about his first wife, Heather Grossman?"

She said, "He wished her dead and told me multiple times that 'the bitch should be dead' and 'someone needs to kill that bitch.'"

When I looked around in the courtroom, everyone was on the edge of their seat, listening closely to Debbie's testimony. Debbie then went on to corroborate what Detective Sanchez had said, even adding that Ron would send her to the Cayman Islands to get cash for him. Debbie's testimony concluded around four thirty, at which time Judge Brown adjourned for the day.

    Mary and I left the courtroom in a hurry because we were on our way to pick up Ronnie at the airport. We drove back to the hotel and checked Ronnie into his room. An hour later Al Johnson and a female prosecutor met us in the lobby of the hotel to discuss Ronnie's testimony for the next day. Ronnie was nervous and I appreciated them coming by to put his mind at ease and tell him in advance what questions they would be asking him.

    When they were finished meeting with Ronnie, we all met Peter for dinner. Peter and Ronnie talked and got to know each other better. Everybody had a nice evening.

    When we woke up the next day, Ronnie was anxious. He ran into my room and said, "Mom, I forgot my belt!"

    While Mary and I drove to the courthouse, Peter picked up Ronnie and quickly took him to buy a belt. When we arrived at the courthouse, I was worried for Ronnie. I knew he was afraid to see Ron and I knew it would be difficult for him.

    When I saw Peter and Ronnie, I gave Ronnie a big kiss. "Honey, you're going to do a great job," I said.

    Mary and I entered the courtroom and sat in our usual spots. Judge Brown entered and started the proceedings. The female prosecutor called Ronnie to the stand; he was seventeen years old at the time. When Ronnie entered the courtroom, four bailiffs walked to the right of him so he wouldn't have to look at Ron. Despite his earlier anxiety, Ronnie testified confidently. I looked over at Ron and he was holding back tears.

    Ronnie told the jurors that Ron had emotionally abused and intimidated him. He continued by saying, "I was scared of Ron. He was a large man with a deep voice and he wanted me to lie about the abuse so he could take me away from mom and John."

    When the defense cross-examined Ronnie, Edward Reagan asked him, "Are you changing your story because your mom is disabled?"

Ronnie said, "No, that's not true. I'm angry every day that my mom has to wake up in a wheelchair and go through what she does. And that anger goes toward whoever is the cause of this."

When Ronnie stepped off the stand, I was proud of him. Judge Brown recessed for lunch and told us to return in an hour. Donna, Peter, and I brought Ronnie to our usual lunch spot. When we returned to the courthouse, Ronnie was interviewed by a local TV station.

Before we reentered the courtroom, we saw that Mark was standing outside. I introduced Ronnie to the uncle he hadn't seen since he was four years old. They exchanged a few words and we all reentered the courtroom.

Chapter 71

It was my turn to testify. I had butterflies in my stomach, and there was not an empty seat in the courtroom. When Al Johnson called me to the stand, Mary pushed my wheelchair to the front of the room and faced me toward the jury. I wore my brown Vertigo suit, and was wrapped in my blue electric blanket to keep warm. Al Johnson started by asking, "What was your relationship with Ron Samuels following your divorce?"

I told the jury that Ron refused to pay his child support, and when I got involved with John Grossman, he falsely accused my mother and John of child abuse. I said, "Things became way worse when John and I married. We started receiving death threats in the middle of the night."

"Do you remember being shot?"

"When the bullet ripped through my spinal cord, my body felt like a machine shutting down. I tried to yell out for help but the word wouldn't come out. I don't remember anything after that, but I died at the scene of the crime."

"Could you describe your recovery process?"

"I was in ICU for five and a half weeks and spent six months in rehab at Craig Hospital in Colorado," I said. "I had to relearn how to swallow, eat, drink, and speak during my time there. I have absolutely no diaphragm, so I had to learn how to speak through a trach and use a ventilator for my breathing."

When I was done testifying, Mary drove my wheelchair back to my spot in the courtroom. Al Johnson gave his closing statement and the state rested.

Outside the courthouse, Mark Samuels came over to talk to me. "What do you think of the testimony so far?" I asked.

"Debbie Love is a liar!" he said. "Heather, do you think Ron did this?"

"Mark, of course he did!" I said. "I know it's hard to believe your brother could be so evil, but I know you and Ron have never gotten along."

I could tell Mark was not happy with my response and that he was in denial about the whole situation. Upset, I told him good-bye and left.

On Thursday morning, Ronnie, Mary, and I were up early and had breakfast at the hotel. Now that the prosecution had finished, we did not know what action the defense team would take. As Ronnie and I walked through the metal detectors at the courthouse, a gentleman next to us said, "Good luck in court. Give them hell, Mrs. Grossman."

I smiled and said, "Thank you."

Peter was waiting outside the courtroom with two cups of hot coffee for Mary and me. He said good morning to Ronnie and we all sat in our usual places.

To everyone's surprise, the defense called Ron to the stand. Even though his lawyers had advised him against testifying, Ron was determined to tell his side of the story.

I sat back and listened to him spew his lies. Ron denied having anything to do with the shooting, saying, "I wouldn't want anything like that to happen to her." He then went on to admit that he'd misrepresented his finances to avoid paying child support.

He explained just how far he'd been willing to go to gain custody of his children, even obtaining the credit report and other personal information of his old friend Thomas Jordan, in case he ever needed a new identity. Ron said, "I was eventually going to become him and take my kids if necessary."

Ron denied any and all involvement in the murder plot. He said he'd never met Eddie Stafford or paid anyone to kill his wife. He went on to say that the only relationship he had with Hugh Estes was a business one, established when he bought car insurance from him.

When Ron was done testifying, the defense gave its closing statement and rested. Jury deliberation started Friday. I had the long weekend ahead to await the verdict.

On Friday, Mary and I met Susan Spencer in the lobby of the hotel for a photo shoot and interview for the *Palm Beach Post*. Afterward, Mary drove Ronnie and I to Donna and Harvey's. Donna and I sat on the patio and had iced tea while Ronnie and Harvey played table tennis. That evening we all went to Henry's again for dinner.

Ronnie, Al, and I were in Boca Raton by noon the next day. I went to Donna's hairstylist to get my hair done for the evening. Peter was taking everyone to Morton's Steakhouse in West Palm Beach for dinner.

When we arrived, the hostess took us to a private room where Peter and the camera crew were waiting for us. I had also invited Donna and Harvey and my nurses, Mary and Ella, to join us because Al was working that shift.

As the waiter took our orders, I looked around and felt sorrow in my heart, remembering when John and I had celebrated our rehearsal dinner with family and friends in the same room. I had always thought John and I would be together forever. It was hard to believe he was gone.

The following day, Al and I took Ronnie to the airport. Ronnie wanted to stay and hear the verdict, but he had to be back at school. Trying to pass the time, Al and I went to the movies. We were back at the hotel by five o'clock and ordered Chinese food to the room for dinner.

I woke up tired on Monday morning. The anticipation of the jury coming back with its verdict made it hard to sleep well. Mary and I split a sandwich for lunch and waited to hear something from Al Johnson.

By three o'clock I became worried and called his office. His assistant, Gina, answered. "Has Al heard anything?" I asked.

"The jury came back this morning and asked a few more questions," she said. "Al doesn't think he'll hear anything until tomorrow."

Peter asked me and Mary to meet him for dinner. The three of us sat anxiously wondering why the jury was still deliberating. After all, the prosecution's case was strong. I had thought they would come back with the verdict on Friday.

Finally, I received a call from Al Johnson on Tuesday morning telling me I had to be in court that afternoon to hear the verdict. I quickly got ready, called Peter and Donna, and told them to meet Mary and me at the courthouse.

As I walked up to the courthouse, Troy Roberts interviewed me and asked how I was feeling. "I have anxiety but I'm also excited," I said. "I have waited nine years to get justice, and today might be that day."

When I entered the courtroom, I sat in my usual spot. Gina stood on one side of my wheelchair and Donna stood on the other. When Judge Brown entered the courtroom, she asked if the jury had reached a verdict. The jury answered yes and the clerk showed the verdict to the judge. The judge then asked the clerk to read the verdict aloud.

As the clerk read the verdict, Ron stared straight ahead with a frown on his face. The jury had found Ron guilty on seven charges. Each time they read "guilty," I smiled from ear to ear and said, "Yes, yes, yes!" Donna jumped up and down with her hands in the air. I hadn't felt that joyful in a long time.

Judge Brown excused the jurors and recessed for an hour. Donna, Peter, Mary and I went outside the courtroom, where *48 Hours Mystery* interviewed me on how I felt about Ron's charges while we waited to return.

Once we returned to the courtroom, I waited patiently to give my final remarks on Ron's sentencing to Judge Brown. When they brought Ron back to the courtroom, he was dressed in jail clothes; his arms were handcuffed and his feet were chained. The bailiff came up to me and said,

"He wanted to keep his suit on and cried like a little baby when we demanded that he change."

"It's gratifying to know he'll be wearing those clothes for a long time," I said.

Judge Brown commenced the sentencing and Mary brought me in front of the judge. I told Judge Brown, "Ron Samuels has made my life a nightmare for the past sixteen years. He abused me when I was married to him, he stalked me after our divorce, he legally harassed me through the court system, and when he couldn't get his way, he filed phony child abuse charges against John Grossman, my parents, and myself. Finally, he had me shot and I am confined to a ventilator and a wheelchair for the rest of my life."

I went on to tell her how difficult my life was, and that in a moment if I was not suctioned by a nurse to clear my lungs I could die. I explained, "When you're a quadriplegic, a bed sore or pneumonia can take your life." I broke down and said, "All my money has been spent paying for twenty-four-hour nursing care, and now the responsibility has fallen on my parents, who are older. They work every day without a break to try to keep me out of a nursing home. The guilt I feel is overwhelming and at times makes me physically sick. He's a monster and he deserves life in prison."

When I was done speaking to the judge, Mary took me back to my seat. Ron was given the chance to speak before his sentencing. He said, "Heather, I am not guilty. I wouldn't harm the mother of my children." Then he proceeded to address in Spanish his Mexican wife, whom he married while in prison. "What an idiot," I thought to myself. "She's not even here."

Ron Samuels was sentenced to life in prison without parole, plus 120 consecutive years. Judge Brown stated, "Ron Samuels was the mastermind and deserves to be punished for the shooting of Mrs. Grossman." She ordered Ron to pay $300,000 restitution to me; however, I never received a cent and the money in the Grand Caymans was never found.

The bailiffs handcuffed Ron, and his head hung low as they took him from the courtroom. Al Johnson came up to me and said, "Congratulations."

"Thank you for all your help," I said. "I am so happy with the verdict."

After a few interviews outside the courtroom, I called my parents and children and told them the good news. Mary and I drove back to the hotel. Mary touched up my makeup and Peter took my friends and nurses to a lobster dinner to celebrate. I felt funny letting Peter pay for dinner once again, but, after all, I had let *48 Hours* into my life for the past month and was not paid anything for my story.

As I enjoyed the celebration, the image of Ron being led away in handcuffs stayed on my mind. "It's over," I thought. "There is no more torture; there is no more fear. I can sleep at night knowing this man will never harm us again."

Chapter 72

Over the next two days, I finished up interviews with Peter Henderson and the *48 Hours Mystery* crew in Florida. Everywhere I went in Boca Raton, people reached out and told me how happy they were about the verdict. Donna and Harvey were kind enough to allow Troy Roberts and me into their home for my final interview after hearing the sentencing.

On my last day in Florida, I met Peter and Troy at Yamato Road and Federal Highway, the intersection where I'd been shot. As Troy Roberts interviewed me about that day, I became overwhelmed and started to cry. Troy put his hand on my shoulder and said, "Are you going to be okay? If this is too hard on you, we can stop right now."

"Troy, just give me a minute and I'll be fine," I said.

Just then a postman driving by saw me on the sidewalk and yelled out, "God bless you, Heather Grossman!" I immediately felt better and was able to finish the interview.

The following day Peter met us in the lobby while we were loading our suitcases into the van to go the airport. He kissed Mary and me good-bye and said, "I'll see you in Arizona in a few months."

On my first day back in Arizona, all I wanted to do was stay home and relax. When the kids arrived home from school, they had many questions about the trial. I tried to answer them the best I could. We sat down as a family to have dinner. After four weeks of eating out, I could not wait to have one of my mother's home-cooked meals.

As we sat down Lauren asked me, "Mom, would you be upset if I went to Florida to see Ron in jail?"

"Why would you want to do that?" I asked.

"I'd like to get Ron's hopes up to see me, and then walk in there and say, 'I hate you and I wish you would die,' and then walk right out."

I thought for a moment and said, "Honey, if that would give you closure and you would feel better, then I guess I wouldn't mind." After that day Lauren never mentioned it again. I believe it was just her way of expressing her anger. Ronnie said he "felt relieved" and that "Ron was exactly where he belonged." Joe said he felt safe.

"Justice has prevailed," he concluded.

Chapter 73

In January 2007, I hired Helen Dike to work the day shift with Mary. Helen was from Nigeria, well dressed, and had a bubbly personality.

Over the next few months I was busy mentoring newly injured quadriplegics for the Arizona Spinal Cord Association. I also continued speaking out against domestic violence. I spoke to a group of Arizona judges and also to the Phoenix Police Department. I was asked to speak to the students at Arizona State University's Sandra Day O'Connor law school in their criminal law classes. I enjoyed educating people about domestic violence and giving back to the community. Soon I was doing at least four speaking engagements a month.

Peter and his camera crew came to Arizona to finish up their program for *48 Hours Mystery*. We went through old tapes and pictures of my family and my marriages to both Ron and John. I gave him some to take back to New York to use in the editing process.

One afternoon in March, I was shopping at Saks Fifth Avenue when a woman approached me. "Hi! My name is Denise Icard," she said. "You are very pretty. Have you thought about becoming a contestant in the Ms. Wheelchair Arizona Pageant?"

We talked for a while. I asked her for her card and told her I would get back to her. On the way home I said, "Mary, can you believe there is a beauty pageant for people in wheelchairs?"

"No, I can't," she said. "But I think you should consider doing it."

At dinner I spoke to my family about the pageant. They all thought it was a great idea and wanted me to participate. Over the next month, I prepared my speech and Mary and Helen helped me practice it. In April, my parents and kids watched as I competed in the Ms. Wheelchair Arizona Pageant. There were five contestants. That evening I was crowned Ms. Wheelchair Arizona 2007.

The month of May was a time to celebrate and it flew by fast. On May 11, Ronnie graduated from high school at Notre Dame Preparatory Academy. He would be attending Arizona State University's W. P. Carey School of Business in the fall. The rest of the month was dedicated to putting the finishing touches on Tiffany's wedding plans. On May 19, my sister married Dale Timmer in our backyard. It was a small, beautiful ceremony with thirty-five friends and family members in attendance. After the ceremony, my parents hosted a dinner reception at the Chart House. I had never seen two people more happy and in love.

I spent the following month raising funds so that my nurses and I could travel to Maryland for the Ms. Wheelchair America pageant. I was able to raise $25,000. Before I knew it, the nurses and I were packing and on a flight to Bethesda, Maryland.

We spent eleven grueling days in Maryland. Every participant was expected to attend every interview with the judges and every scheduled pageant function. I was the only high-level quadriplegic on a ventilator out of thirty-two contestants. It was challenging but I was up to the task. As the week progressed, I enjoyed getting to know all the contestants. I was impressed with all the things these women had accomplished, even with their disabilities.

On July 28, 2007, the final night of judging, Ms. Chicago took the title and I won first runner-up. I also received the Nicki Ard Achievement Award for my disability and domestic violence advocacy work. By the time my nurses and I returned home, everyone was exhausted.

In August, I spoke in front of three thousand adults who were attending Nouveau Riche Real Estate Investment College. The owner, Jim Piccolo, asked me to give an inspirational speech. I was a little nervous, because this would be the largest group of people I had ever spoken in front of. The evening went well, and at the end of my lecture Mr. Piccolo presented me with a bronze eagle statue.

Two days later I received a call from Ellen Sherman, a producer for *Dateline NBC*. They were interested in telling my story. *48 Hours* had aired my story in April, so I was surprised that *Dateline* was interested also. A week later, Ellen Sherman, Keith Morrison, and a camera crew spent the day at my home interviewing me. The interview lasted a few hours and when they finished, they went on their way to Boca Raton, Florida, to interview Detective Sanchez, Al Johnson, and Debbie Love.

Joseph and Lauren were going into their junior year of high school, and Ronnie had started college at Arizona State University. My parents were working and traveling out of state for their shoe company. Every month they had to work hard to cover the burden of my medical care and the household expenses. My time was spent taking care of my kids and doing public speaking events. Everything seemed to be moving along smoothly until Mary hit a light pole and totaled her truck. She was thrown in jail for a DUI. Mary was great nurse, but I had to find somebody quickly to replace her.

At the end of October I received a call from Senator Jon Kyl's office. Jane Grace said, "Heather, because of your accomplishments, you have been chosen by President George W. Bush to fly to Washington, DC, and meet him and go on a private tour of the White House."

"You have to be kidding!" I said. "I'm so surprised."

We agreed I'd arrive in Washington on November 6. I hung up the phone, told my parents, and eagerly started to plan my trip. Even though my whole family was invited, the boys stayed home. There was a large group of us going: my parents, Lauren, two of my nurses—Ella and Helen— and myself.

Our flight from Arizona to DC was long and tiresome. I wasn't prepared for the weather, and on the drive to our hotel my dad blasted the heater. When we arrived at the hotel, we checked into our rooms and went out to have a quick dinner. I was up at six o'clock the next morning wearing a suit with my hair styled and my makeup on. I had only slept five hours the prior night, but I was excited for the day's events to start.

When we arrived at the White House, I gave them my name and the guard let us through the gate. A woman met us and escorted us in. She gave us a tour of several well-known rooms in the White House. The historical art that hung throughout the hallways was magnificent. We also went to the press room. I was surprised it looked so small in person compared to on TV.

Our guide brought us back to the Cabinet Room. When it was time to meet the president, we followed a gentleman through the hallway where two Secret Service men stood. We entered the Oval Office and President Bush came toward me, bent down, and put his hands on my hands. "It's a pleasure to meet you, Heather," he said. "I'm so glad you could come."

"Thank you for inviting me," I said. "It's a pleasure to meet you, too!"

I then introduced him to my mother and father. They both shook his hand and my father said, "I have a great deal of respect for you and for your father."

He said, "Thank you very much."

I then introduced him to Lauren and my nurses, Ella and Helen. While Helen was shaking his hand she dropped some papers on the ground. President Bush proceeded to pick them up. I was a little embarrassed and said, "Helen, help him!"

"Oh, that's okay. I've got it," he said. He was friendly and spoke to each of us. President Bush and I talked about his daughter Jenna's upcoming wedding, about his wonderful wife, Laura, and about my accomplishments since the shooting. We joked about the Ms. Wheelchair America Pageant. When I told him I was first runner-up, he said, "If I'd been judging, you'd have taken the title! They really messed up."

He asked Lauren questions about her school and activities. He put his arm around her and said, "It must be hard on you to have your mother in a wheelchair, knowing your father did this to her." They talked about it for a while and Lauren told him, "At first it was, but my mother is an amazing woman and she lives her life to the fullest."

After we were done talking, the White House photographer took individual photos of all of us with the president. President Bush was down to earth, genuine, and friendly. We spent an hour in the Oval Office, and it was one of the most fulfilling experiences of my life.

Afterward my father took us for a late lunch near the White House. I then met with two journalists for interviews regarding my visit with the president. One was from the *Arizona Republic* and the other from the *Palm Beach Post*.

Our next stop was the Russell Senate Office Building, where we met with Senator Kyl. We talked about our visit with the president and took pictures with him. He told us about his upcoming schedule of events. After our meeting, we grabbed a quick bite and returned to the hotel, exhausted and ready for bed.

On the final day of the trip it was cold and windy. My nurses bundled me up and we drove to the National Mall to see some of the famous monuments. We visited the Lincoln Memorial, and took pictures in front of the Washington Monument. Our last stop was the Arlington National Cemetery.

We went to dinner and then drove to the hotel to start packing. The next morning we were up early to catch the long flight back to Arizona. Our trip was short but meaningful. I will never forget the time we spent there.

At the White House 2007.

With President Bush 2007.

With Elizabeth Dole, Sen Jon Kyle, Ellen Chow, and Susan Collins2008/

Chapter 74

The day after we got back to Arizona, my mother put an ad in the paper for a day nurse. I interviewed Kurt Funfsinn and hired him on the spot. He had just moved from Chicago with his wife and little boy, Noah. He was six-foot-one, and slender with short, black hair. He was easygoing, funny, and always came to work with a smile on his face. He picked up on my care quickly and everyone liked him.

In January 2008, my 501(c)(3) foundation was approved. I named it Heather's Haven of Hope. Our mission was to provide medical, dental, and psychological care for children and women in domestic violence shelters around the valley. Over the next few months, I approached several doctors, dentists, and other medical professionals to become the foundation's providers. Their hard work and dedication to helping the victims of domestic violence would have a life-changing impact for many women and children.

In the springtime my board had its first meeting to plan our inaugural fund-raiser. I had no idea what a large task I had undertaken. Every month thereafter we had a meeting and luncheon at my home to prepare for the event.

The committee members, volunteers, and my personal friends looked at different venues and dates that would accommodate our fund-raiser. We had to have invitations printed and look for sponsorships. We found a keynote speaker, booked the entertainment, chose a menu for the evening, and hired two announcers to help the event go smoothly. My girlfriend Margie Traylor took professional photos of all the doctors and prepared a visual presentation to be played during the dinner. Once all of this was in place, everyone reached out to the community for silent and live auction items.

In July, after Helen Dike had worked for me for a year, she went back to school to take a refresher course for her RN nursing license. She trained Kyle Funfsinn, Kurt's brother, for the other day position. Kyle was twenty-four years old and single. He moved in with Kurt and his wife, Paige, to take the job. Kurt and Kyle were both a big help during the planning of the fund-raiser.

Everything was coming together perfectly until a week before the fundraiser, when Kurt brought me to urgent care. I had hives up and down my back and on the sides of my hips. The stress from all the planning was finally taking a toll on me. My doctor advised me to take it easy.

On December 7, our inaugural fundraiser was held at the Phoenician Hotel. One hundred thirty guests mingled and enjoyed cocktails and hors d'oeuvres while they bid on silent auction items. A professional pianist played Christmas music on a baby grand piano. When it was time to eat, everyone sat down to dinner and enjoyed a fantastic meal of prime rib and grilled salmon.

Our emcees, Eddie Johnson and Tim Kempton, introduced Senator Jon Kyl as our main speaker for the evening. He talked about victims' rights and domestic violence, and the effects it had on the nation. His talk was powerful and everyone clapped as he left the podium.

Next Eddie and Tim introduced the different groups of doctors involved with Heather's Haven of Hope. Each group spoke about their specialty and specific involvement with the foundation. Eddie and Tim then started the slide show and live auction, and the guests had fun bidding against each other. Following the live auction I went up and thanked all the guests for coming and sponsoring Heather's Haven of Hope. I then thanked everyone involved who assisted in making the event possible.

Our first fund-raiser was a huge success. We raised $56,000 for Heather's Haven of Hope. The next day I received calls from guests who attended, complimenting me on a wonderful evening and thanking me for the good time they'd had.

In January 2009 I spoke at the Barton House in Scottsdale. The Barton House is a specialized facility dedicated to the care of Alzheimer's patients. I took a tour of the facility and then educated the staff on elder abuse, which refers to any knowing, intentional, or negligent act by a caregiver or any other person that causes harm or serious risk of harm to a vulnerable adult. This was my specialty because I could talk firsthand about the abuse I had received from John. The staff was bright and inquisitive, and I was impressed with their willingness to learn about the issue.

When I was done talking, the director donated furniture and a piano to Heather's Haven of Hope. I immediately had the furniture delivered to the Sojourner Center, a domestic violence shelter in the valley. This furniture would eventually be given to a woman and her children to set up their home once they left the shelter.

Our foundation also donated children's clothing, women's business attire, sheets, pillows and bare necessities such as diapers, shampoo, toothpaste, and soap to the shelter. So many women leaving a domestic violence situation leave with nothing but the clothes on their backs and their children. Even the simplest of donations can mean a lot to the victims of domestic violence. I received great satisfaction in helping these women, because at one time I had been in the same situation.

Chapter 75

In February 2009 I was out of commission. After many years, my Ford Econoline van, which I had named Bessie, finally gave out and could not be fixed. I couldn't afford to buy a disability van, so most of the time I was stuck at home. When I had a scheduled speaking event or something important to attend, my parents would have to rent a disability van. The rental company would charge us $130 a day, and that was money my parents could not afford. It was difficult to be without transportation but I managed the best I could.

Over the next three months, I worked hard on my foundation and spoke at several events on domestic violence. Before I knew it, it was May, and Lauren and Joe were both graduating from Notre Dame Preparatory Academy High School. I couldn't believe how quickly time had flown by. On the day they graduated I was delighted to see them receive their diplomas. I was proud of both of them for all their accomplishments and good grades. Lauren was accepted into eight colleges, and she choose to attend Pepperdine University on scholarships and grants. Joe applied only to Arizona State University's criminal justice program and was accepted with a full scholarship.

On May 10, my parents and I threw Lauren and Joe a graduation party. One hundred thirty friends and family members came to the house to celebrate their accomplishments. I felt fortunate to be alive to celebrate with my twins.

A week later I received a letter from Florida. When I opened it I told my mom, "The state attorney's office is informing me that Ron's second appeal has been denied."

"That's great, Heather," she said. "I'm surprised he tried to appeal it again. He just won't give up, will he?"

"I hate to say this, but I just wish he would die."

"The evil ones live forever," she said.

Even though I never thought about Ron anymore, he refused to leave us alone. Six months prior, he had mailed a letter to Ronnie. Thank God I caught it before Ronnie could read it. It said, "If you come see me in jail I will buy you a car. I am innocent. I would never hurt your mother. I love you, son." The children wanted nothing to do with him.

By the Fourth of July, Kurt, Kyle, and I were going stir crazy in the house. I was an active quadriplegic and had been used to leaving the house every day in the van. To pass the time Kurt and I would walk to The Gainey Shops and walk around the boutiques. I also enjoyed morning walks around the neighborhood with my mom and Suki.

The summer was coming to an end and my teenagers were going to college. Ronnie was entering his junior year at business school. We helped Joe move into his dorm at the downtown campus of Arizona State University. It was 115 degrees that day. To make it more comfortable the school passed out water bottles to the students and their families as they unloaded their belongings.

The moment I dreaded more than anything was kissing Lauren and telling her good-bye. As I watched my parents and Lauren leave for their drive to Malibu, California, I knew I would miss her the most because she was going to school so far away. My parents had volunteered to go to orientation with Lauren at Pepperdine University. I really wanted to go, but the campus was hilly and not exactly handicap accessible.

My mom and dad were troopers. In four days time they helped Lauren move into her dorm, went to all the scheduled events, tirelessly walking up and down hills, and stocked Lauren's room with all the supplies she would need for school. Over the next few weeks I talked to the twins every day. I wanted to make sure they were settling into their classes and everything was going fine. I missed the noisy chatter at dinnertime, but whenever they had a problem I was the first one they called.

Over the fall months I continued to rent a van whenever I had a speaking engagement. I was praying for a miracle. I really needed a new van but God hadn't answered yet.

A week before Thanksgiving, Kurt told me he was moving back to Chicago. His wife, Paige, was homesick and wanted to be near her family. Kurt had worked for me for two years and was one of the best nurses I had worked with so far. I was sad because I knew he would be hard to replace. Kurt and I interviewed many people but were unable to find the right person. Three days before Christmas, Kurt worked his last day and then left for Chicago to spend the holidays with his family.

Everyone was looking forward to the holidays this year. Lauren was coming home for two weeks over winter break and my sister and Dale would be here for Christmas. I rented a van on the weekends and did all the Christmas shopping I could while I was mobile.

We had Christmas dinner with my Nigerian friends, the Omatseye family. I had met Sonny, Ebiyemi, and their five children two years before through my nurse, Helen Dike. When we arrived at their home, Sonny invited everyone in. He introduced us to his sister Esighemi Osoba, who had flown in from England with her two boys.

Ebiyemi and Esigbemi prepared a Christmas feast for twenty people. We enjoyed an assortment of traditional British and Nigerian food. For dessert we all had Christmas pudding. As we were leaving we thanked them for the lovely meal. We were thrilled to spend the holiday with our friends.

After the New Year, I looked frantically for a day nurse. After one nurse who didn't work out, the agency sent Cynthia Champion. Cynthia was five-foot-eight with short blonde hair. She was a skilled RN who took her nursing seriously. Cynthia was a couple of years older than me and we quickly became friends.

The next couple of months were uneventful. My nurses and I were stuck at home watching movies, and we'd occasionally rent a van for a speaking engagement. One day I received a call.

"Is this Heather Grossman?" asked a cheery voice.

"Yes, it is."

"My name is Michelle and I work at Vantage Mobility International," she said. "On behalf of our company and Phoenix International Raceway, we are donating a disability van to you."

I couldn't believe what I was hearing. I wanted to shout, "Hallelujah, hallelujah!"

"Oh my gosh," I said, "thank you so much! I've been without my van for over a year. This will help me out tremendously!"

"I'll call you with the arrangements. Both companies would like to do an article and take pictures with you."

"Absolutely!" I said. "I'll wait for your call. Thank you again! You've made my day."

When I hung up the phone I told my parents and Cynthia the good news. Then I called Lauren, Ronnie, and Joe to let them know, too. Everyone was happy for me and could not wait to see the van.

A week later, I met Michelle at Vantage Mobility International. She drove up the van they were donating to me. The van was a 2008 silver Dodge Caravan. It was two years old but I didn't care. I finally had a way to get around.

On the morning of April 12, 2010, Pat Bonser from Vantage Mobility International brought my van to the house. My family and I followed Pat and his wife to the Phoenix International Raceway. I was invited to watch the NASCAR race and take pictures in the winner's area with the president of the racetrack and the owner of VMI.

At a scheduled time, we met with Jenniffer Wentzel, the executive representative for the racetrack, by the winner's area. Tiffany, Kyle, and

Joe were all invited to drive around the track in a racecar with a professional driver. We shot publicity photos and spoke to the press.

Senator Kyl, a huge NASCAR fan, was watching the race that day. When I saw him I gave him a kiss. He asked me, "Heather, how are you handling the heat?"

"It's warm," I said, "but I'm managing."

"I want you to be comfortable. Let me see if I can get a suite for you and your friends to wait in until the race starts," he said.

The senator made a call and, before we knew it, we were on our way to a suite. When we opened the suite door, a woman greeted us and brought us drinks. I don't know if it was the heat off the pavement, or the sun beating down on me all day, but I was glad to feel the cool air. Everyone relaxed and had lunch.

When the race started, everyone got up to go to their seats, but when we opened the door the heat and noise were overwhelming. We decided to enjoy the race indoors. I wanted Jeff Gordon to win but unfortunately he got second place; Ryan Newman won.

Best of all, I was back in business with a "new" van, thanks to the generosity and support of so many wonderful people.

Chapter 76

As the twins' school year drew to a close, I was excited for Lauren to come home. She was going to be home for three months before leaving to study abroad in Buenos Aires, Argentina. She would be there the entire following year.

She worked for Ed Marshall Jewelers six days a week to save money for her trip. Ronnie worked at All About Tennis, stringing rackets and selling tennis merchandise, and Joe interned for Senator Kyl in his Phoenix office. I was proud of my children for maintaining excellent grades while participating in extracurricular activities and working part-time jobs.

My nurse Kyle was involved in a car accident that totaled his car. He rode his bike in the hot Arizona summer for two months, and I could tell it was getting to him. One afternoon, after taking Lauren shopping, I asked Kyle to pull into the drive-through at McDonald's. Lauren couldn't decide what she wanted. Kyle began screaming at her to hurry up and make up her mind. I said, "Kyle do not talk to her that way."

He yelled at me and then Lauren yelled at him. It turned into a huge argument.

After we left, there was silence the rest of the way home. When we came into the house, Kyle started complaining about Lauren again.

"I don't want to hear it," I said. "I don't want you ever swearing and yelling at my daughter like that again." That night I decided it was time for Kyle and I to part ways. Shortly after, I let Kyle go and hired his replacement, Mike Hoffman.

The summer flew by and soon my mom, Cynthia, and I were helping Lauren pack. The first week of September, I drove Lauren to the airport. With tears in our eyes, we said good-bye to each other. I was going to miss her, but we planned to Skype every other day so we could talk.

After she was there a week, Lauren contacted me through Skype. She told me her Argentinean family was nice, but they spoke no English and the mother was a chain smoker. She also told me she liked all of her teachers, but transportation to and from school was difficult. Taking a taxi was too expensive so she took the local bus. She had gotten on the wrong bus twice and ended up late for school. I was glad to hear she was doing fine and adjusting to their culture.

Even though Lauren couldn't be with us for Thanksgiving, she had a month off for Christmas. The two of us went shopping, saw movies, and ate lunch out with friends. Tiffany and Dale flew in for the holidays, and we attended mass and celebrated Christmas Eve in our traditional way.

We spent Christmas Day with the Omatseye family once again. My nurse Kevin was a trooper; not only did he work Christmas Day, but after we returned home from dinner, my night nurse Mylani called and said she could not come in. Kevin stayed and worked a twenty-four-hour shift so that I would be taken care of during the night.

Before I knew it Tiffany and Dale were on their way back to Minnesota, and Kevin and I were helping Lauren pack to return to Argentina. As a farewell to Lauren, the family went to Fez restaurant in Phoenix for dinner. My good friend Tom Smith was the general manager, and after we finished our meal, he gave us five different desserts to try and share. I dreaded saying good-bye to Lauren, and the two of us cried again. I loved having my family around.

Chapter 77

The Sunday before the Super Bowl, my night nurse, Raquel, and I were watching TV and having coffee while we waited for the day nurse to arrive. At 9:15 a.m., with no sign of Kevin, I began calling his cell phone. There was no answer. I called the agency and told them that Kevin had not shown up and asked if they could call Cynthia to come in. When Cynthia arrived, we made a few more calls to Kevin, but again there was no answer.

A week later, Cynthia was driving me to pick up a scarf from the seamstress when she saw a friend of Kevin's and slammed on the brakes. She got out of the van and asked, "Do you know where Kevin is? He never showed up to work a week ago."

His friend said, "He's in jail for violating his parole."

Cynthia got back in the van and the two of us laughed the whole way home. As soon as she drove me into the house, I put in another ad for a day nurse.

I hired Najla Coates. She was smart and cute, with long dark-black hair. Her father was born in Iran and her mother was a citizen of the United States. She had moved back to the US with her mother a few years prior. Najla was a great cook, besides being a skilled nurse, and loved to make me eggplant parmesan and chicken curry.

On one of our first outings, Najla put me in my van and buckled me in. As she walked by, she closed the ramp door. When she got to the driver's side, she realized she had locked me in and the keys were sitting on her seat. She panicked and said, "Heather, what do I do?"

I was terrified. I had never been locked in the van before. I said to her, "Go inside and get help."

She looked at me with a blank look and I realized she couldn't hear me. I tried mouthing "go get help."

I kept thinking to myself, "Please don't spasm! Please don't choke!"

She ran in the house and found Ronnie. The two of them searched for the extra key and, fifteen minutes later, Najla unlocked the door. "Oh Heather," she said, "I'm so sorry! That will never happen again." She brought me a glass of water and we left to run our errands.

In April, Mom and I received a call from Helen Pugh's daughter. "Could you please help take care of my mom when she gets out of the rehabilitation center?" she asked. "I'm going back to California. She just had another treatment of chemotherapy and is going to be weak."

When my mother hung up the phone, the two of us felt sick. The last time we'd seen Helen was at our party on New Year's Eve. She had been happy, vibrant, and having a great time. We had no idea she had cancer and wondered why she hadn't said anything to us. When we talked to Helen on the phone, she said, "I didn't want to bother you. You have enough to worry about."

Helen never left the rehabilitation center. On April 15, she passed away. My parents were out of town working. Cynthia drove me to Scottsdale Bible Church on Shea Boulevard to attend the service. My heart sank as I heard her children and grandchildren talk about her. She was a kind soul who would go out of her way to help anyone. I did not attend the reception; it was too emotional for me.

On Easter morning, my parents, the two boys, and I left early for Easter mass at Blessed Sacrament. We always attended the outside service, so it was important to get seats in the shade. The weather was a pleasant eighty degrees as we listened to Father Pat say mass.

As we were leaving, I wished Father Pat a happy Easter. I left feeling serene and closer to God. Lauren could not be with us and everyone missed her. I asked Cynthia and her fiancé, James, to celebrate with us. James and Cynthia had become engaged over Christmas. The two of them planned to get married a year later, in April 2012. It was nice having them join us.

    Lauren came back from Buenos Aires at the end of April. Boy, was I excited to see her! She was going to summer school that year at Pepperdine, so we only had a month before she had to leave again. This time when she went back, she would be staying in a dorm during the summertime, so we didn't have to worry about moving her until August.

Chapter 78

On June 1, I received a call from Nick Baker at Make Believe Media, Incorporated. The company was based in Vancouver, Canada, and affiliated with Oprah's OWN network. Mr. Baker, in his Canadian accent, said, "Mrs. Grossman, we would love to produce a documentary on your story."

"That's wonderful," I said, "but *48 Hours Mystery* and *Dateline NBC* have already done one."

"Ours would be different. It would be shown not only in the United States but also in Canada and worldwide. We want to call it 'The Devil You Know' and we would like to interview not only you, but Debbie Samuels as well. Do you have any way of getting in touch with her?"

"Yes, I do," I said. "But I would like to speak to her first, to see if she's willing to do the documentary. Let me contact her and I'll get back to you."

I had kept in contact with Debbie Samuels, who now went by Debbie Love. We spoke every so often about the kids and about our lives.

When I called the law office she worked at in Boca Raton, Debbie answered the phone. "Hello, Heather," she said. "How are you doing and how are the kids?"

"I'm doing fine and the kids are great!" I said. "A producer called me from Canada and would like to do a documentary with both of us. Would you mind talking to him?"

"I'd do anything for you, Heather." she said.

"Thanks, Debbie," I replied. "Hopefully our story can raise awareness about domestic violence." We caught up with each other and I gave her Nick Baker's number.

Soon after I had a contract with Make Believe Studios. Nick Baker spent hours upon hours thoroughly interviewing me on the phone. He also interviewed Debbie, Detective Sanchez, Susan Spencer, and Al Johnson. After Nick had obtained all the background information, he contacted me again and we made a timeline of my life for the production team. It was difficult reliving these painful events from the past once again, but I believed my story could help others, and I was proud to be a part of this new project.

Chapter 79

I could hardly believe that my twins were entering their third year of college and Ronnie was in his final year at ASU. Lauren and I spent two weeks together before my parents helped her move into her first apartment in Malibu. She was rooming with two friends, and their apartment was close to Pepperdine. Joe had been elected student body president. My parents also helped him move into his apartment, two blocks from his classes at the downtown campus.

After my kids were settled back in school, I received a call from Gus, a rehab coordinator at St. Joseph's Hospital, asking me to mentor two female patients. The first patient he introduced me to was Mary. After talking to her for an hour, I could tell she was nervous about leaving the hospital and was in need of a disability van. I gave her numbers of people who could possibly help her out with an adaptive computer and funding for a minivan.

When I was finished speaking to Mary, Gus introduced me to Sheila. She was married and had a daughter in high school. She was a little more upbeat and her husband did an excellent job finding local resources for them to use. After sharing some words of encouragement, I met Gus by the rehabilitation area. He thanked me for coming. "No problem," I told him. "Anytime you have somebody you'd like me to see, just let me know."

On our drive home, Najla, texted me and asked me to call her. When we spoke, she said, "I'm giving you a heads up. I'm moving to London in a month."

Surprised, I asked, "When did you make this decision?"

"My mother works for Tiffany's as a general manager, and they're promoting her to the London office. It's an amazing opportunity and she's asked me to go along."

"I'm very happy for you, but I'm going to miss you."

"Thank you," she said. "I am so excited to go."

When I hung up the phone, I told Cynthia about Najla leaving for London and we started the process of hiring a new day nurse. Two weeks later I hired Rachel Keeling.

Rachel had just moved here from California with her two kids and lived five minutes from my house. She had an upbeat personality and always came to work with a smile on her face. She was a more caring nurse and ended up doing a better job than her predecessor. Sometimes things happen for a reason.

Chapter 80

In November, Lauren flew in from California to celebrate Thanksgiving with the family. My mother prepared her traditional Thanksgiving dinner. The next morning, Mom woke everyone up at 8 a.m. to take down the fall decorations and decorate for Christmas. We had only three days to get the house in order before Make Believe Studios arrived on Monday morning. By Sunday evening we were finished with all the Christmas decorations, just in time for my dad to drive Lauren to the airport.

I was up early the next morning having my coffee when the doorbell rang. It was the production team from Canada. The director walked over and introduced herself as Bonny Lou Wagner. Bonny interviewed my mother first. Two and a half hours later my mother had completed her interview and the crew was taking a break. When I looked at my mom, I could tell she was tired. "Are you okay?" I asked her.

"I'm fine," she said. "There were so many questions and talking about Ron upsets me."

"Well, I'm glad it's over," I said. "I'm sure you did a good job."

When the break was over it was my turn to be interviewed. Most of the questions were in chronological order of my life, starting with my childhood. When we finished at eight o'clock that night, we had only gotten up to my marriage to Ron. As Bonny and the camera crew were leaving for the night, Bonny told me I was doing an outstanding job.

The second day was a repeat of the first. Bonny and the camera guys showed up early and we started from where we had left off. The questions became more difficult to answer as the afternoon wore on, and at one point I found myself crying. Bonny said, "Let's take a break."

Everyone had a late lunch. When we were done eating, the cameramen took a family picture of Mom, Dad, Ronnie, Joe, and myself out by the pool. They also filmed my mother and I sitting out on the patio. When we came back inside the house, Bonny brought me in front of the camera for three more hours of interviewing.

When Bonny was finally satisfied with all the information she had, she said, "That's a wrap." She leaned over, touched my knee, and said, "Your story is very compelling. Thank you for sharing it with us." That evening, while my night nurse was doing my care, I was so tired I could hardly keep my eyes open.

Chapter 81

Over the next few months, I helped Cynthia plan her wedding. The date was set for April 21, 2012. While Tiffany was in town, she and Cynthia went shopping for invitations, ribbons, and fans for guests to use during the wedding.

In February, the attorney general's office contacted me and asked if I would be the keynote speaker for Victims' Rights Week at the Arizona State Capitol. Jan Brewer, our governor; Tom Horne, our attorney general; and Bill Montgomery, our county attorney, were honoring police officers and government officials for their contributions to those who were victimized by crime. I told them I would be happy to do it. In addition to helping Cynthia with her wedding, I took time out to write my speech.

Over the next few weeks, Cynthia and I enjoyed tasting cupcakes from various shops and bakeries around the Scottsdale area. She finally chose a shop called 21 Cakes. We met with the owner so Cynthia could pay the deposit, choose the flavors, and set up the delivery date.

When we arrived back at the house, Cynthia put down the ramp of my van and proceeded to drive me down it. All of a sudden I yelled, "Cynthia, help! I'm falling!" My head was coming out of my scarf and my body was falling out of the wheelchair. Before I hit the ground, Cynthia somehow threw her body underneath me and I landed on top of her. As we lay there in the hot sun I said, "Thank God you caught me. Are you okay?"

"I'm fine," she replied. "Are you okay?"

"I don't think I broke anything, but what are we going to do now?"

"Let's yell," she suggested. "Maybe somebody in the house will hear us!" We screamed as loudly as we could until Tiffany came running outside. When she saw the two of us lying in the driveway, she panicked and started shaking in fear. She yelled out, "Oh my God! Heather, are you okay?"

"Don't worry, Tiffany," I said. "I'm fine. You just have to figure out how to get me off the ground and back in my chair."

Cynthia told Tiffany to call 911. About ten minutes later, the Paradise Valley Fire Department was in my driveway and I was looking up at five buff and cute firemen. The chief introduced himself and one of the firemen asked Cynthia, "What's the best way for us to help you?"

Cynthia instructed them on what to do, and before I knew it, I was back in my wheelchair, thanking them for all their help. The chief wanted me to go to the emergency room, but I said I felt fine and would go later if there were any complications.

In April I held a bridal shower for Cynthia and her girlfriends at a restaurant in Mesa. I wanted to do something special for her because she had become such a close friend. My girlfriend Cami, my mother, Tiffany, and I arrived early to decorate our section with balloons and table toppers. I also picked up a white chocolate raspberry cake for dessert. After everyone arrived, we drank margaritas, had dinner, and played shower games. At the end of the evening, Cynthia thanked everyone for coming.

On April 19, 2012, my parents, the boys, Tiffany, Dale, and I celebrated my forty-seventh birthday at the Grand Lux Café in Scottsdale. After dinner I opened my gifts and cards. Joe had written me a beautiful letter for my birthday:

"Happy Birthday Mom,

> We have honestly come a very long way and I wouldn't be who I am today if it weren't for all the amazing things you have done for this family. Often people don't realize how much we have gone through but to be a product of such an environment has truly been a blessing. You continually exemplify the miracle that we have and are the strongest, most inspirational person I know.

When I say I wouldn't be who I am today, that is not to be taken lightly. We are not perfect but we are blessed. With every day that comes and year that passes I am more thankful for the wonderful life you and Grandma and Grandpa have given us. It is often in one's darkest times that you truly see the light, and of that light comes an experience, growth, and development that forever alters an individual. You have been my light, guiding me through life and exemplifying what purpose, love, strength, family, dedication, service, and passion truly mean. For this we are ahead in life, and I love you more than words can describe and am so thankful for everything you do, everything you are, and for being the best mother anyone could ask for. Today is just another birthday with many more to come, but it is the perfect opportunity to thank you for being as incredible as you are. With every day you make the world a better place as well as this family. You will always be my number one supporter, a driving force behind every impact I will make, and forever be my light as we continue to experience all the many beauties, hardships, lessons, and wisdom life has to offer. I see God in you and always have, and forever you know I will always be there to help. I see the hard days you go through at times and wish I could take away the pain and hardships; if only I could. You are my advocate and have instilled in me what most people will often never obtain: a heart devoted to others, a heart that cares, a heart that loves, a heart that is selfless, and a heart that will change the world. It is my heart that makes me who I am and it is my heart that directs my life—not my mind, but my heart, the thing you have given me. I couldn't ask for a better life and am honored, proud, and blessed to have you as my mother and a part of my life. I love you, Mom, and thank you for being the most incredible person on this planet. Your strength moves mountains, your heart moves others, and your will is of God. I continue to learn every day from you and even as I age and become successful, it is all because of you. Thank you for your continual support, guidance, belief, and inspiration. Thank you for being my mother and for being my light.

I love you more than words can describe. Happy birthday, Mom! To the most incredible woman I know, you deserve everything plus more.

Your son, your #1 advocate, and your forever mentee,

I love you, Mom!

Joseph"

Two days later, Tiffany, Dale, Rachel, and I attended Cynthia and James's wedding. The ceremony was held at a country church at the Superstition Mountain Museum. You could tell it was a country wedding when the outlaws came in shooting their guns and tried to steal Cynthia away from James. After they exchanged their vows, the wedding party took pictures while the guests drove to the reception at the Mining Camp.

When the bride and groom arrived, everyone stood up and clapped. We listened to a comedy skit and a bluegrass performance by the Amazing McNasty Brothers. Before we left, I kissed Cynthia and James on the cheek and said, "Congratulations again. Have a wonderful time in Germany."

The next morning, Rachel drove me to the Arizona state capitol for my speech. There were four hundred people in attendance, sitting under a tent on a beautiful spring afternoon. When it was my turn to speak, I was introduced by Sean McLaughlin from Channel 5 News. I gave the audience a brief overview of my story and talked about victims' rights and how the shooting had affected my family. I ended by talking about legislation that should be changed to allow victims more rights. When I finished, my family and I stayed and talked with friends and other individuals.

On May 2, Rachel and I went to the Department of Economic Security. I was participating in a symposium as an expert speaker on domestic violence. I was asked questions not only from those in attendance but also via satellite from Tucson, Georgia, Texas, and New Mexico. I was there for three hours. I enjoyed the opportunity but was tired by the time we left.

Lauren was back in town and had finished her junior year at Pepperdine. Both Ronnie and Joe came over for a family dinner that night. It was wonderful seeing my children together, laughing and talking.

The following morning Cynthia was back at work after her honeymoon. She arrived at 6 a.m. to get me ready. We had to be at the Wells Fargo arena in Tempe at 8 a.m. for Ronnie's college graduation.

I was so proud when Ronnie received his diploma. We took pictures outside and then all went to breakfast. Later that evening, we celebrated Lauren and Joe's twenty-first birthdays and Ronnie's graduation at the Grand Lux Café. We ate outside on the patio and the kids opened their gifts. It was a memorable night.

The following week, after turmoil with my healthcare provider, I met with Pat Lundberg from Nursing Solutions to discuss switching to their agency. After I spoke with her, I decided to make the switch to their company. When Cynthia came into work the next day she talked with Pat on the phone. She negotiated her pay, which ended up giving her a raise. Cynthia said, "Heather, Pat is sending me a packet to fill out so I can sign up with them. It should be an easy move."

"That's good," I said, "because I told Pat how important you are to me and you would have to be happy with the pay to agree to change agencies."

The next afternoon I met with Pat Lundberg at our house to go over the nursing schedule. Rachel, Pat, and I sat at the kitchen table having sodas and waiting for Cynthia to arrive. After waiting an hour, I called Cynthia to find out what was taking her so long. I couldn't reach her so I left a message asking her to call me. I then said good-bye to Pat and told her Cynthia and I would be in touch with her the next day.

The next day, I still hadn't heard anything from Cynthia, so I again tried to call her cell phone, but there was no answer. I left another message and waited for her to call me back. When my mother and Lauren came home from grocery shopping, I told them I couldn't reach Cynthia and was worried.

At the end of the day, I called Pat and told her I still hadn't heard from Cynthia. "Have you heard anything from her?" I asked. Pat said she hadn't

When I hung up with her, I began to worry. Rachel said, "Calm down, Heather. Don't be upset."

"I always hear from Cynthia on her three days off," I said. "Something is wrong."

The next day went by without any word from Cynthia. Twenty-four hours later Cynthia did not show up for work. I was stunned. Cynthia was my nurse and friend and had worked for me for two and half years. Yet she didn't have the decency to call and tell me what was going on.

I called Pat and told her the news about Cynthia. Pat said, "Heather, I'm sorry to say this, but we'll have to put an ad in for her position."

I'd had a lot of nurses come and go. I'd had nurses who were careless, dangerous, and even stolen money and medication from me. Aaron had destroyed me; Cynthia hurt me badly. But the good nurses, the ones I cared about and considered family, were priceless.

Over the next couple of weeks, Pat and I were busy interviewing nurses. At the end of May, Lauren went back to California for a summer marketing internship. I was sad to see her go.

At the end of the summer, Rachel came to me and told me she was pregnant. Shocked I said, "How did that happen? I thought you didn't want any more children."

"Yesterday I went to my doctor's appointment to get my tubes tied, and he told me I was pregnant. Trust me, I'm as shocked as you are," she said.

"Oh, Rachel, I'm happy for you, but I love you and don't want you to go."

I was a little worried at this point, because not only did I not have a good day nurse, but now I was losing Rachel. I put in an ad immediately to replace her.

A couple of days later, I received a call from Peter Baker at Make Believe Studios. He excitedly told me, "Your hour-long documentary is playing in Canada now and we are getting a huge response from the viewers."

"You are? That's great! When is it going to show in the United States?"

"That's why I'm calling you," he said. "It's going to air on Oprah's OWN channel on October 17."

On October 17, 2012, my family and friends gathered in our family room and we watched the program together. Within a day, I was receiving emails from viewers in Canada, the US, Latin America, and Africa. I had received emails when my *48 Hours* and *Dateline NBC* programs aired. This time it seemed like I was getting a great deal more.

After reading the emails, I realized how much of an impact my story had on others. I decided to write a book, to help other people who may be in a similar situation as the one I was in.

In October 2012 I finally hired a good nurse. Her name was Carrie Leiman. She had an athletic build and shoulder-length blonde hair. Everyone in the family liked her and the two of us got along well.

Ronnie started his first job at Grand Canyon University. He was working in their business department and pursing his master's degree in business, finance, and marketing. He chose that job because the university was willing to pay for his degree.

My parents helped Lauren move into a new apartment in Malibu. She was in her senior year at Pepperdine University. Joe had been re-elected student body president at ASU and was living in his same off-campus apartment.

At this time I hired Dustin Rhodes to fill the other day-shift position. Dustin looked like a lumberjack. He was six-foot-one with dark hair and had a kind disposition.

Chapter 82

Fall arrived and I received a call from Joe's teacher, Ms. Robin Brooks. "Hello, Mrs. Grossman," she said. "I wanted to know if you could speak to my criminal justice class on Thursday next week?"

"Yes," I said, "I would be glad to."

"I'd like you to give a background of your story and how the criminal justice system helped or failed you," she said.

"Thank you for asking me," I said. "I will see you on Thursday."

The following week, my nurse, Carrie, and I drove to Phoenix. I introduced myself to Joe's teacher and she put my video into their DVD projector. Carrie and I sat at the front of the room as we waited for the students to arrive. When every seat was filled, Mrs. Brooks introduced me. I spoke for an hour and answered questions afterward.

I wished Joe would have been in class that day, but he was in Washington, DC, attending a conference for the university. After he returned, he told me his classmates and friends said I did a great job. Two weeks later I spoke again at ASU. This time Joe was in the classroom.

The holidays came and I was grateful to spend another year with my family. Lauren came home for Christmas break. On Christmas Eve, after mass, my parents, children, and I celebrated a quiet night opening presents by the Christmas tree. A few days later we celebrated New Year's and toasted in 2013. Another year had passed, and my parents at the ages of seventy and seventy-one were still working every day to pay their bills and my medical expenses. The burden weighed heavily on me, but we were still strong as a family despite all the challenges.

In January 2013, Dustin, my day nurse, went back to school to earn his RN license. Pat Lundberg, the director of Nursing Solutions, came to my house to introduce me to a nurse who was interested in the position. "This is Crystal Perlmutter," she said. "I'm going to let the two of you talk so you can become better acquainted."

Crystal was five-foot-four, skinny, and pretty. I really liked her but I said, "Do you think you can transfer me from the bed to the bike?"

"I may look small but I'm strong," she said.

Pat and I looked at each other skeptically. Pat said, "Well, let's go to Heather's bedroom and you can try lifting Brenda, the housekeeper, from the bed to the bike."

While Pat and I watched, Crystal lifted Brenda to the bike with ease. The two of us laughed, because we could hardly believe it. Crystal said, "I told you I could do it." Of course I hired her.

We walked back to the kitchen and Pat and Crystal decided when she would start training. Crystal caught on quickly and soon the two of us were running errands and doing e-stim on my shoulders.

Crystal always came with a positive attitude, coffee in one hand, and Paradise Bakery's cookies in the other. After getting to know her better, I learned the two of us shared something in common. Her ex-husband had been abusive during their marriage and refused to pay child support for their fourteen-year-old son. I felt sorry for her and tried to encourage her by saying, "Life is too short. You are happy and healthy; just let it go." I don't know if she took my advice to heart, but I really hope she did.

Chapter 83

On the morning of February 8, 2013, I was awakened by a telephone call. It was Carrie saying she was sick and would not be able to make it in to work. She said she had called Crystal, who had agreed to come in and cover her shift. This was the day I was expecting the Australian production crew to do their interview.

Shortly after Crystal arrived, the doorbell rang. She answered the door and said, "It's the production crew from Australia. They're looking for a place in the house to do the interview."

The production manager walked up to me and introduced herself as Cathy Napoli. She was excited to meet me and talked quickly in her Australian accent. Cathy interviewed me for five hours with two fifteen-minute breaks. After the interview was done, she had the cameramen shoot some footage of various pictures for their program. The crew cleaned up and Cathy said, "Thank you for giving us this interview. It was very nice to meet you. I will be in touch if we need any additional photos or information."

That night, when Crystal laid me down in bed, I was so tired I could hardly keep my eyes open. I think I said goodnight to her, and when I woke up Raquel was already there, finishing my night care.

Chapter 84

Over the next few months, Carrie and Crystal helped me plan my trip to Malibu for Lauren's college graduation. My parents couldn't make it to the graduation because they were doing a show. Lauren was disappointed, but at least I'd be there with her brothers. Lauren also invited my best friend, Terry, and her husband, Mike, along with her best friend from high school, Analise, and her parents, Cathy and Steve Grosvenor.

I booked all the reservations and scheduled the nurses' shifts; I was taking Carrie to work the days and Raquel to work the nights. Five days before we were supposed to leave, Carrie called me and said, "I don't think I can go to Malibu."

"What do you mean?" I asked. "We've been planning this for months."

"I just don't think I can," she said.

Panicked, I began calling my old nurses to see if any of them could go on such short notice. Two days before our trip, I received a call from Rachel, my old day nurse who had just had a baby. "I really want to help you out," she said. "My daughter, Emma, is a month old now. Let me see if my mother will babysit her for me so I can take you."

An hour later Rachel called back. She was able to go, and I thanked her profusely.

The morning of the trip we packed our things in the car and Rachel, Raquel, and I left on time. The drive took us eight hours. Every two hours we stopped at a rest stop so Rachel could pump her breast milk and everyone could use the restroom. While we were driving, Ronnie and

Joe flew into the Los Angeles airport, got a rental car, and planned to meet us at the hotel at Thousand Oaks.

When we arrived at the Hyatt, the bellhop unloaded our bags while we checked in at the front desk. The hotel staff was friendly and made sure we had everything we needed. I told them that my daughter, Lauren, and my sons, Joe and Ronnie, would be arriving shortly and would check in soon.

Lauren and her friend Laura arrived first, happy and excited to be done with their finals. Half an hour later Ronnie and Joe showed up and checked into their room. The first thing out their mouths was, "What's for dinner?"

After taking fifteen minutes to decide, we went across the street to Fins Seafood Grill for dinner. When we sat down at the table the kids were in an energetic mood, laughing and talking. Afterward, we returned to the hotel and Ronnie, Lauren, and Joe came to my room. They talked and goofed around until eleven thirty, at which point everyone decided to go to bed.

On Friday morning everyone got ready and met for breakfast downstairs. When we finished with breakfast, the boys relaxed by the pool while Lauren went to pick up Mr. Grosvenor from the airport. Rachel and I drove across the street, where I had my hair washed and styled for that evening.

When we got back to the hotel, we were just in time to see Terry and Mike checking in at the front desk. We all hugged and made plans to meet at the pool when they were checked into their room. Terry, Mike, the boys, and I spent an hour talking by the pool, and then everyone went up to their rooms to relax and get ready for dinner.

When we arrived at Nobu for dinner, they sat us at a large, round table that looked out onto their patio and the ocean. The waiter took our drink order and then explained the menu. We decided to order fifteen different dishes and share them around the table. When they took away the empty plates, they replaced them with a platter featuring five of their best desserts. We all agreed it was one of the best meals we'd ever had.

On Saturday morning everyone was up early for the graduation. The graduation was held outside on Pepperdine's Alumni Field, overlooking the ocean. It was a cool seventy-five degrees but sunny. President Andrew Benton had prepared a spot right up front by the stage with an umbrella and chairs for Terry, Rachel, and me. I could see everything perfectly. We had coffee and waited for the ceremony to begin.

All of a sudden my vent battery started alarming loudly. Rachel looked at it and said, "Heather, it says 'low battery.' I don't think it was charged last night."

"Rachel," I said, "we're in big trouble. I only have forty-five minutes before the vent shuts off and I'm not breathing."

Panicked, Terry called Ronnie and Joe and told them what was going on. Two minutes later, Steve and Cathy Grosvenor and the boys came over and asked, "What can we do to help?"

"I'm screwed," I said. "I'm on top of a hill and in the middle of the canyon in Malibu. My batteries are back at the hotel."

While Rachel informed President Benton that I wouldn't be able to breathe in forty minutes, the students started walking in and taking their seats. When Rachel came back I said, "Call the Hyatt and let me talk to the front desk."

After Rachel got them on the line she held my cell phone to my ear. "It's an emergency," I said. "This is Heather Grossman, the woman in the wheelchair. I need you to find my night nurse Raquel and have her get in a taxi and drive my battery charger to my daughter's graduation at Pepperdine University."

The man on the phone said, "Stay on the line. I'm going to send someone to her room to find her."

Ten minutes later Raquel was on the phone and I told her what I needed her to do. The taxi driver and Raquel had only twenty-five minutes to get my battery to me. Meanwhile, President Benton had extension cords run to where I was sitting and covered so nobody would trip on them. They also called the paramedics and had them on standby in case Raquel didn't make it.

While we waited, the commencement started and I prayed that they would make it on time. The last thing I wanted was to make a scene and miss Lauren's graduation. With a couple minutes of air left on my ventilator, I saw Raquel and felt a big sigh of relief. She said, "Heather, I can't believe this happened. Are you okay?"

"I'm fine now that you are here," I said.

Rachel and Raquel hooked up the batteries and we watched the rest of the graduation. I ended up paying the taxi driver one hundred dollars, but it was the best money I'd ever spent.

After the ceremony we all took pictures together. When it was time to go I was cold and told Rachel to get the van. She loaded me in and we started to leave and the van died. As if things could get any worse the van had run out of gas. I wanted to cry but I composed myself and called Ronnie, Lauren, and Joe to see if someone could help us.

Thirty minutes later a man in a Pepperdine golf cart stopped outside my van and put a container of gas in the tank. I thanked him and Rachel and I drove back to the hotel to meet everyone else. Rachel teared up and said, "Heather, I am so sorry all this happened today."

"Don't be upset!" I said. "Crazy things always happen to me. You should know that by now."

The next morning everyone went down for breakfast. After we ate, we checked out of the hotel and Rachel, Raquel, and I started our long drive back. Lauren was sad to see us go. She had been chosen to fly to New York and shadow the CEO of Sapient Nitro for a week. When she returned to California, she would be starting her first job with Shift Marketing Group.

The drive back seemed much shorter to us. We arrived at the house around seven o'clock in the evening. I thanked Rachel, who could not wait to get back to her daughter. After I had a grilled tuna and cheese sandwich for dinner Raquel got me ready for bed.

Chapter 85

The next day Pat Lundberg called me from Nursing Solutions and asked if I wanted Carrie to come back. I said, "No, Carrie was sick way too many times and turned out to be unreliable. Let's put an ad in and hire another nurse."

Pat said, "That sounds good. Let's get to work on it right away."

I hired Christina Gutierrez. Crystal trained her in three days. Christina had long, light-brown hair and was a Latin diva. Her favorite singer was Mariah Carey.

My parents left for a show in Wichita, Kansas, two days before Joe's college graduation. They were upset they had to miss it but they had to work. On May 9, 2013, Crystal and I attended two graduations for Joe. The first was at ten in the morning, at the Phoenix Convention Center, where he graduated with a degree in criminal justice from Arizona State University. I was so proud to see him get his diploma.

At six o'clock, I met Joe at the Frank Kush Field and we went up to a suite for appetizers with President Crow and the deans and teachers from the University. We found our seats and watched Joe graduate with his entire university. Being the student body president, Joe gave the commencement speech to his class. After the ceremony, Crystal and I took Joe and his good friend Dave out for an Italian dinner to celebrate.

I was so delighted about the twins' graduations that I wanted to throw them a party. Lauren and Joe decided on the Chart House restaurant. Aunt Donna flew in from Minnesota to spend the week with us, along with my cousin Beverly. Saturday morning our house was filled with family talking and having breakfast. There were a few last-minute details to finish before the party, so I delegated duties to all the kids to help out.

The immediate family arrived at the restaurant fifteen minutes early to make sure everything was ready and to greet the guests. When my nurse, Christina, brought me into the room we had reserved, the staff had done a great job decorating and setting up the flower arrangements. The room had floor-to-ceiling glass windows with a view of the lake. We were expecting forty-five to fifty of Lauren and Joe's friends.

As the guests arrived, they drank and mingled. My parents introduced Aunt Donna and Beverly to our friends. I enjoyed seeing and talking to my friends, some of whom were past nurses. When they served dessert and coffee, Christina took me around in my wheelchair so I could say hello to some of Lauren and Joe's friends.

When the party was over we said good-bye to the guests as they began to leave. Afterward, close friends and family went to the house to talk and reminisce about Lauren and Joe when they were younger.

As a graduation gift, Joe's girlfriend, Kulsum, made him a memory book filled with pictures and letters from family, professors, and friends. Everyone sat around the table and Joe shared the letters with all who were there. After hearing just a few of them, several of us started to tear up with emotion; they were happy tears. They did nothing but praise the man Joe had become.

Epilogue

Looking back, I could not have imagined I would be at the point of seeing my children graduate from college. The doctors gave me seven years to live, and I am going on twenty-one years since the shooting. My children were just six and eight years old when my injury occurred, and now here they are, fully grown and independent adults.

Domestic violence can destroy you and your family. Twice I made the decision to raise my children in a home without domestic violence. I encourage anyone in an abusive situation to find help and get out before it's too late. I know from personal experience it's easy for people to say this, but when you're scared it's hard to find the courage to leave. When a woman leaves, it's a dangerous time. However, you and your children should not have to live in fear. Your decision to leave will have a positive impact on your family's future.

If you or someone you know is in an abusive situation, investigate the local services that are available. Many communities have shelters where you can go and be safe. You can call the national hotline 1-800-799-SAFE (7233) (TTY 1-800-787-9224) for assistance.

Today, I live a full and happy life, appreciating every day I am alive. I do not let grass grow under my wheels or my condition run my life. I get dressed, do my hair and makeup, and almost every day we are off somewhere. Most importantly, I actively mentor spinal cord injury patients and speak out on domestic violence whenever and wherever I can to create awareness. I give speeches across the country to law enforcement agencies, law students, civic groups, and domestic violence fund-raisers.

I believe that my faith in God and the love I have for my children has given me the strength to keep going. I never chose to become a quadriplegic, and although my life has not been easy, I have achieved and experienced things that I possibly never would have if I wasn't in my situation. It has been a true blessing to help others and I will continue to be a source of encouragement to any person in need.

♦ ♦ ♦

Visit Heather's website:
www.FriendsOfHeatherGrossman.com

to learn more about Heather, find information and links to resources for domestic violence, or to make a donation to help cover Heather's medical expenses.

With Celine Dion.

With Arizona Governor Ducey.

Heather and her family: Her parents, Ralph and Florence, and her three children, Lauren, Joe and Ronnie.

Heather and Denise Brown, sister of Nicole Brown Simpson.

Heather at one of her speaking engagements at the Sandra Day O'Connor College of Law at Arizona State University.

Made in United States
Orlando, FL
20 June 2024